# Computerized Accounting System

# Computerized Accounting System

**Rohit Khar**

RANDOM

RANDOM PUBLICATIONS

NEW DELHI (INDIA)

**Computerized Accounting System**

---

ISBN 978-93-5111-229-7


Published in 2014 in India by

**RANDOM PUBLICATIONS**

4376-A/4B, Gali Murari Lal, Ansari Road
New Delhi-110 002
Phone : +91-11-43580356, +91-11-23289044
e-mail: randomexports@gmail.com, sales@randompublications.com, info@randompublications.com

Reprinted 2026

*Type Setting by* : Keystoneprintads, Delhi-110051

# Preface

A computerized accounting system has great potential to increase productivity, streamline workflow, reduce data redundancy and error reconciliation, and help with financial management for large and small businesses. There are many different accounting options to choose from, including Microsoft Money, Microsoft Dynamics, Oracle, QuickBooks, Sage, and Xero.

Choose between downloadable or installable software that lives on your desktop computer and web-based software that you access remotely. Neither option is better than the other. They both have advantages. With a web-based offering, you receive maintenance and upgrades automatically, as the software provider performs them for you. You can also purchase only the accounting modules that you need, then upgrade your plan to incorporate new functions at the moment of need.

Because you access your data via the web, you can view your financial data any time. However, you'll also pay more as you use more server space and functionalities, and this can add up fast. With software, you have to perform maintenance and troubleshooting, but you retain the ability to maintain sensitive data storage in-house.

A good computerized accounting system or CAS will have a clean, easy-to-use interface. From this interface, you should be able to enter data, export data into other formats, and perform data validation operations. On the back end, databases will drive your CAS, responding to queries about the information stored therein. Your consultant should be able to install the CAS. While you don't need a large IT staff to install your computerized accounting system and get started, it helps if you need to troubleshoot operations or need help performing a specific function.

Switching to a CAS can feel overwhelming. To get started on the right foot, review your finances before the migration and reconcile any errors. You may wish to hire an accountant or financial manager to review your documents for you. Once you have everything in order, install your chosen CAS or purchase a web-based system. Upload your existing data, or enter data by hand if you need to. As you add the data, reconcile it with the existing accounting to make sure that you don't introduce mistakes into the work. Transition to the new system, but continue to use the old system for a while until you feel comfortable with the new system.

I thank all members of my team who have helped in the preparation of the book. My special thanks go to "Random Publications" who have published the book.

***– Rohit Khar***

# Contents

# 1

# Accounting: An Introduction

In all activities (whether business activities or non-business activities) and in all organizations (whether business organizations like a manufacturing entity or trading entity or non-business organizations like schools, colleges, hospitals, libraries, clubs, temples, political parties) which require money and other economic resources, accounting is required to account for these resources. In other words, wherever money is involved, accounting is required to account for it. Accounting is often called the language of business. The basic function of any language is to serve as a means of communication. Accounting also serves this function.

## MEANING AND DEFINITION OF BOOK- KEEPING

### MEANING

Book- keeping includes recording of journal, posting in ledgers and balancing of accounts. All the records before the preparation of trail balance is the whole subject matter of book- keeping. Thus, book- keeping many be defined as the science and art of recording transactions in money or money's worth so accurately and systematically, in a certain set of books, regularly that the true state of businessman's affairs can be correctly ascertained. Here it is important to note that only those transactions related to business are recorded which can be expressed in terms of money.

### DEFINITION

- "Book- keeping is the art of recording business transactions in a systematic manner". A.H. Rosenkamph.
- "Book- keeping is the science and art of correctly recording in books of account all those business transactions that result in the transfer of money or money's worth". R.N.Carter

### OBJECTIVES OF BOOK- KEEPING

- Book- keeping provides a permanent record of each transactions.
- Soundness of a firm can be assessed from the records of assets and abilities on a particular date.

- Entries related to incomes and expenditures of a concern facilitate to know the profit and loss for a given period.
- It enables to prepare a list of customers and suppliers to ascertain the amount to be received or paid.
- It is a method gives opportunities to review the business policies in the light of the past records.
- Amendment of business laws, provision of licenses, assessment of taxes etc., are based on records.

## ACCOUNTING

### MEANING OF ACCOUNTING

Accounting, as an information system is the process of identifying, measuring and communicating the economic information of an organization to its users who need the information for decision making. It identifies transactions and events of a specific entity. A transaction is an exchange in which each participant receives or sacrifices value (*e.g.* purchase of raw material). An event (whether internal or external) is a happening of consequence to an entity (*e.g.* use of raw material for production). An entity means an economic unit that performs economic activities.

### DEFINITION OF ACCOUNTING

American Institute of Certified Public Accountants (AICPA) which defines accounting as "the art of recording, classifying and summarizing in a significant manner and in terms of money, transactions and events, which are, in part at least, of a financial character and interpreting the results thereof".

### OBJECTIVE OF ACCOUNTING

Objective of accounting may differ from business to business depending upon their specific requirements.

*However, the following are the general objectives of accounting*:

- *To keeping systematic record*: It is very difficult to remember all the business transactions that take place. Accounting serves this purpose of record keeping by promptly recording all the business transactions in the books of account.
- *To ascertain the results of the operation*: Accounting helps in ascertaining result *i.e.,* profit earned or loss suffered in business during a particular period. For this purpose, a business entity prepares either a Trading and Profit and Loss account or an Income and Expenditure account which shows the profit or loss of the business by matching the items of revenue and expenditure of the some period.
- *To ascertain the financial position of the business*: In addition to profit, a businessman must know his financial position *i.e.,* availability of

cash, position of assets and liabilities etc. This helps the businessman to know his financial strength. Financial statements are barometers of health of a business entity.

- *To portray the liquidity position*: Financial reporting should provide information about how an enterprise obtains and spends cash, about its borrowing and repayment of borrowing, about its capital transactions, cash dividends and other distributions of resources by the enterprise to owners and about other factors that may affect an enterprise's liquidity and solvency.
- *To protect business properties*: Accounting provides upto date information about the various assets that the firm possesses and the liabilities the firm owes, so that nobody can claim a payment which is not due to him.
- *To facilitate rational decision–making*: Accounting records and financial statements provide financial information which help the business in making rational decisions about the steps to be taken in respect of various aspects of business.
- *To satisfy the requirements of law*: Entities such as companies, societies, public trusts are compulsorily required to maintain accounts as per the law governing their operations such as the Companies Act, Societies Act, and Public Trust Act etc. Maintenance of accounts is also compulsory under the Sales Tax Act and Income Tax Act.

## IMPORTANCE OF ACCOUNTING

- *Owners*: The owners provide funds or capital for the organization. They possess curiosity in knowing whether the business is being conducted on sound lines or not and whether the capital is being employed properly or not. Owners, being businessmen, always keep an eye on the returns from the investment. Comparing the accounts of various years helps in getting good pieces of information.
- *Management*: The management of the business is greatly interested in knowing the position of the firm. The accounts are the basis, the management can study the merits and demerits of the business activity. Thus, the management is interested in financial accounting to find whether the business carried on is profitable or not. The financial accounting is the "eyes and ears of management and facilitates in drawing future course of action, further expansion etc."
- *Creditors*: Creditors are the persons who supply goods on credit, or bankers or lenders of money. It is usual that these groups are interested to know the financial soundness before granting credit. The progress and prosperity of the firm, two which credits are extended, are largely watched by creditors from the point of view of security and further credit. Profit and Loss Account and Balance Sheet are nerve centres to know the soundness of the firm.

- *Employees*: Payment of bonus depends upon the size of profit earned by the firm. The more important point is that the workers expect regular income for the bread. The demand for wage rise, bonus, better working conditions etc. depend upon the profitability of the firm and in turn depends upon financial position. For these reasons, this group is interested in accounting.
- *Investors*: The prospective investors, who want to invest their money in a firm, of course wish to see the progress and prosperity of the firm, before investing their amount, by going through the financial statements of the firm. This is to safeguard the investment. For this, this group is eager to go through the accounting which enables them to know the safety of investment.
- *Government*: Government keeps a close watch on the firms which yield good amount of profits. The state and central Governments are interested in the financial statements to know the earnings for the purpose of taxation. To compile national accounting is essential.
- *Consumers*: These groups are interested in getting the goods at reduced price. Therefore, they wish to know the establishment of a proper accounting control, which in turn will reduce to cost of production, in turn less price to be paid by the consumers. Researchers are also interested in accounting for interpretation.
- *Research Scholars*: Accounting information, being a mirror of the financial performance of a business organization, is of immense value to the research scholar who wants to make a study into the financial operations of a particular firm. To make a study into the financial operations of a particular firm, the research scholar needs detailed accounting information relating to purchases, sales, expenses, cost of materials used, current assets, current liabilities, fixed assets, long-term liabilities and share-holders funds which is available in the accounting record maintained by the firm.

## FUNCTIONS OF ACCOUNTING

- *Record Keeping Function*: The primary function of accounting relates to recording, classification and summary of financial transactions-journalisation, posting, and preparation of final statements. These facilitate to know operating results and financial positions. The purpose of this function is to report regularly to the interested parties by means of financial statements. Thus accounting performs historical function *i.e.,* attention on the past performance of a business; and this facilitates decision making programme for future activities.
- *Managerial Function*: Decision making programme is greatly assisted by accounting. The managerial function and decision making

programmes, without accounting, may mislead. The day-to-day operations are compared with some predetermined standard. The variations of actual operations with pre-determined standards and their analysis is possible only with the help of accounting.

- *Legal Requirement function*: Auditing is compulsory in case of registered firms. Auditing is not possible without accounting. Thus accounting becomes compulsory to comply with legal requirements. Accounting is a base and with its help various returns, documents, statements etc., are prepared.
- *Language of Business*: Accounting is the language of business. Various transactions are communicated through accounting. There are many parties-owners, creditors, government, employees etc., who are interested in knowing the results of the firm and this can be communicated only through accounting. The accounting shows a real and true position of the firm or the business.

## ADVANTAGES OF ACCOUNTING

*The following are the advantages of accounting to a business*:

- It helps in having complete record of business transactions.
- It gives information about the profit or loss made by the business at the close of a year and its financial conditions. The basic function of accounting is to supply meaningful information about the financial activities of the business to the owners and the managers.
- It provides useful information form making economic decisions,
- It facilitates comparative study of current year's profit, sales, expenses etc., with those of the previous years.
- It supplies information useful in judging the management's ability to utilise enterprise resources effectively in achieving primary enterprise goals.
- It provides users with factual and interpretive information about transactions and other events which are useful for predicting, comparing and evaluation the enterprise's earning power.
- It helps in complying with certain legal formalities like filing of income tax and sales-tax returns. If the accounts are properly maintained, the assessment of taxes is greatly facilitated.

## LIMITATIONS OF ACCOUNTING

- *Accounting is historical in nature*: It does not reflect the current financial position or worth of a business.
- Transactions of non-monetary mature do not find place in accounting. Accounting is limited to monetary transactions only. It excludes qualitative elements like management, reputation, employee morale, labour strike etc.

- Facts recorded in financial statements are greatly influenced by accounting conventions and personal judgements of the Accountant or Management. Valuation of inventory, provision for doubtful debts and assumption about useful life of an asset may, therefore, differ from one business house to another.
- Accounting principles are not static or unchanging-alternative accounting procedures are often equally acceptable. Therefore, accounting statements do not always present comparable data
- Cost concept is found in accounting. Price changes are not considered. Money value is bound to change often from time to time. This is a strong limitation of accounting.
- Accounting statements do not show the impact of inflation.
- The accounting statements do not reflect those increase in net asset values that are not considered realised.

## METHODS OF ACCOUNTING

*Business transactions are recorded in two different ways.*

- *Single Entry:* It is incomplete system of recording business transactions. The business organization maintains only cash book and personal accounts of debtors and creditors. So the complete recording of transactions cannot be made and trail balance cannot be prepared.
- *Double Entry*: It this system every business transaction is having a two fold effect of benefits giving and benefit receiving aspects. The recording is made on the basis of both these aspects. Double Entry is an accounting system that records the effects of transactions and other events in atleast two accounts with equal debits and credits.

## STEPS INVOLVED IN DOUBLE ENTRY SYSTEM

- *Preparation of Journal*: Journal is called the book of original entry. It records the effect of all transactions for the first time. Here the job of recording takes place.
- *Preparation of Ledger*: Ledger is the collection of all accounts used by a business. Here the grouping of accounts is performed. Journal is posted to ledger.
- *Trial Balance preparation*: Summarizing. It is a summary of ledge balances prepared in the form of a list.
- *Preparation of Final Account*: At the end of the accounting period to know the achievements of the organization and its financial state of affairs, the final accounts are prepared.

## ADVANTAGES OF DOUBLE ENTRY SYSTEM

- *Scientific system*: This system is the only scientific system of recording business transactions in a set of accounting records. It helps to attain the objectives of accounting.

- *Complete record of transactions*: This system maintains a complete record of all business transactions.
- *A check on the accuracy of accounts*: By use of this system the accuracy of accounting book can be established through the device called a Trail balance.
- *Ascertainment of profit or loss*: The profit earned or loss suffered during a period can be ascertained together with details by the preparation of Profit and Loss Account.
- *Knowledge of the financial position of the business*: The financial position of the firm can be ascertained at the end of each period, through the preparation of balance sheet.
- *Full details for purposes of control*: This system permits accounts to be prepared or kept in as much detail as necessary and, therefore, affords significant information for purposes of control etc.
- *Comparative study is possible*: Results of one year may be compared with those of the precious year and reasons for the change may be ascertained.
- *Helps management in decision making*: The management may be also to obtain good information for its work, specially for making decisions.
- *No scope for fraud*: The firm is saved from frauds and misappropriations since full information about all assets and liabilities will be available.

## MEANING OF DEBIT AND CREDIT

The term 'debit' is supposed to have derived from 'debit' and the term 'credit' from 'creditable'. For convenience 'Dr' is used for debit and 'Cr' is used for credit. Recording of transactions require a thorough understanding of the rules of debit and credit relating to accounts. Both debit and credit may represent either increase or decrease, depending upon the nature of account.

## TYPES OF ACCOUNTING

### TYPES OF ACCOUNTS

The object of book-keeping is to keep a complete record of all the transactions that place in the business. To achieve this object, business transactions have been classified into three categories:

1. Transactions relating to persons.
2. Transactions relating to properties and assets
3. Transactions relating to incomes and expenses.

The accounts falling under the first heading are known as 'personal Accounts'. The accounts falling under the second heading are known as 'Real Accounts', The accounts falling under the third heading are called 'Nominal Accounts'. The accounts can also be classified as personal and impersonal.

*The following chart will show the various types of accounts*:

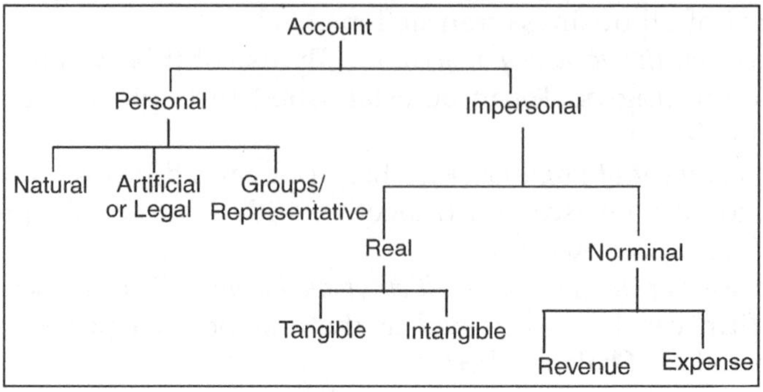


## PERSONAL ACCOUNTS

Accounts recording transactions with a person or group of persons are known as personal accounts. These accounts are necessary, in particular, to record credit transactions.

*Personal accounts are of the following types*:

- *Natural persons*: An account recording transactions with an individual human being is termed as a natural persons' personal account. eg., Kamal's account, Mala's account, Sharma's accounts. Both males and females are included in it
- *Artificial or legal persons*: An account recording financial transactions with an artificial person created by law or otherwise is termed as an artificial person, personal account, *e.g.* Firms' accounts, limited companies' accounts, educational institutions' accounts, Co-operative society account.
- *Groups/Representative personal Accounts*: An account indirectly representing a person or persons is known as representative personal account. When accounts are of a similar nature and their number is large, it is better tot group them under one head and open a representative personal accounts. *e.g.*, prepaid insurance, outstanding salaries, rent, wages etc.

When a person starts a business, he is known as proprietor. This proprietor is represented by capital account for all that he invests in business and by drawings accounts for all that which he withdraws from business. So, capital accounts and drawings account are also personal accounts.

The rule for personal accounts is : Debit the receiver

Credit the giver

## REAL ACCOUNTS

Accounts relating to properties or assets are known as 'Real Accounts', A separate account is maintained for each asset *e.g.*, Cash Machinery, Building, etc.,

*Real accounts can be further classified into tangible and intangible*:

- *Tangible Real Accounts*: These accounts represent assets and properties which can be seen, touched, felt, measured, purchased and sold. *e.g.* Machinery account Cash account, Furniture account, stock account etc.
- *Intangible Real Accounts*: These accounts represent assets and properties which cannot be seen, touched or felt but they can be measured in terms of money. *e.g.*, Goodwill accounts, patents account, Trademarks account, Copyrights account, etc.

The rule for Real accounts is : Debit what come in

Credit what goes out

## NOMINAL ACCOUNTS

Accounts relating to income, revenue, gain expenses and losses are termed as nominal accounts. These accounts are also known as fictitious accounts as they do not represent any tangible asset. A separate account is maintained for each head or expense or loss and gain or income. Wages account, Rent account Commission account, Interest received account are some examples of nominal account

The rule for Nominal accounts is : Debit all expense and losses

Credit all income and gains

## DISTINCTION BETWEEN BOOK-KEEPING AND ACCOUNTING

**Table. The Difference Between book-keeping and Accounting can be Summarized in a Tabular from as Under**

| Basis of | Book-keeping | Accounting |
|---|---|---|
| Difference Transactions | Recording of transactions in books of original entry. | To examine these recorded transactions in order to find out their accuracy. |
| Posting | To make posting in ledger | To examine this posting in order to ascertain its accuracy. |
| Total and Balance | To make total of the amount in journal and accounts of ledger. To ascertain balance in all the accounts. | To prepare trial balance with the help of balances of ledger accounts. |
| Income Statement and | Preparation of trading, Profit and loss account | Preparation of trading, profits and |

| | | |
|---|---|---|
| Balance Sheet | and balance sheet is not book keeping | loss account and balance sheet is included in it. |
| Rectification of errors | These are not included in book-keeping | These are included in accounting. |
| Special skill and knowledge | It does not require any special skill and knowledge as in advanced countries this work is done by machines. | It requires special skill and knowledge. |
| Liability | A book-keeper is not liable for accountancy work. | An accountant is liable for the work of bookkeeper. |

## BRANCHES OF ACCOUNTING

The changing business scenario over the centuries gave rise to specialized branches of accounting which could cater to the changing requirements.

*The branches of accounting are*:

- Financial accounting;
- Cost accounting; and
- Management accounting.
- Now, let us understand these terms.

### FINANCIAL ACCOUNTING

The accounting system concerned only with the financial state of affairs and financial results of operations is known as Financial Accounting. It is the original from of accounting. It is mainly concerned with the preparation of financial statements for the use of outsiders like creditors, debenture holders, investors and financial institutions.

The financial statements *i.e.*, the profit and loss account and the balance sheet, show them the manner in which operations of the business have been conducted during a specified period.

### COST ACCOUNTING

In view of the limitations of financial accounting in respect of information relating to the cost of individual products, cost accounting was developed. It is that branch of accounting which is concerned with the accumulation and assignment of historical costs to units of product and department, primarily for the purpose of valuation of stock and measurement of profits.

Cost accounting seeks to ascertain the cost of unit produced and sold or the services rendered by the business unit with a view to exercising control over these costs to assess profitability and efficiency of the enterprise. It generally relates to the future and involves an estimation of future costs to be incurred. The process of cost accounting based on the data provided by the financial accounting.

## MANAGEMENT ACCOUNTING

It is an accounting for the management *i.e.*, accounting which provides necessary information to the management for discharging its functions. he Anglo-American Council on productivity, "Management accounting is the presentation of accounting information is such a way as to assist management in the creation of policy and the day-to-day operation of an undertaking."

It covers all arrangements and combinations or adjustments of the orthodox information to provide the Chief Executive with the information from which he can control the business *e.g.* Information about funds, costs, profits etc. Management accounting is not only confined to the area of cost accounting but also covers other areas (such as capital expenditure decisions, capital structure decisions, and dividend decisions) as well.

## PRINCIPLES OF ACCOUNTING

The word 'Principle' has been differently viewed by different schools of thought. The American Institute of Certified Public Accountants (AICPA) has viewed the word 'principle' as a general law of rule adopted or professed as a guide to action; a settled ground or basis of conduct of practice" Accounting principles refer, to certain rules, procedures and conventions which represent a consensus view by those indulging in good accounting practices and procedures.

Canadian Institute of Chartered Accountants defined accounting principle as "the body of doctrines commonly associated with the theory and procedure of accounting, serving as an explanation of current practices as a guide for the selection of conventions or procedures where alternatives exist.

Rules governing the formation of accounting axioms and the principles derived from them have arisen from common experiences, historical precedent, statements by individuals and professional bodies and regulations of Governmental agencies".

To be more reliable, accounting statements are prepared in conformity with these principles. If not, chaotic conditions would result. But in reality as all the businesses are not alike, each one has its own method of accounting. However, to be more acceptable, the accounting principles should satisfy the following three basic qualities, *viz.*, relevance, objectivity and feasibility. The accounting principle is considered to be relevant and useful to the extent that it increases the utility of the records to its readers.

It is said to be objective to the extent that it is supported by the facts and free from personal bias. It is considered to be feasible to the extent that it is practicable with the least complication or cost. Though accounting principles are denoted by various terms such as concepts, conventions, doctrines, tenets, assumptions, axioms, postulates, etc., it can be classified into two groups, *viz.*, accounting concepts and accounting conventions.

## ACCOUNTING CONCEPTS AND CONVENTIONS

### *Accounting Concepts*

The term 'concept' is used to denote accounting postulates, *i.e.*, basic assumptions or conditions upon the edifice of which the accounting superstructure is based.

*The following are the common accounting concepts adopted by many business concerns*:

- Business Entity Concept
- Money Measurement Concept
- Going Concern Concept
- Dual Aspect Concept
- Periodicity Concept
- Historical Cost Concept
- Matching Concept
- Realisation Concept
- Accrual Concept
- Objective Evidence Concept

### *Business Entity Concept*

A business unit is an organization of persons established to accomplish an economic goal. Business entity concept implies that the business unit is separate and distinct from the persons who provide the required capital to it. This concept can be expressed through an accounting equation, *viz.*, Assets = Liabilities + Capital. The equation clearly shows that the business itself owns the assets and in turn owes to various claimants. The business entity concept as applied in accounting for sole trading units is different from the legal concept. The expenses, income, assets and liabilities not related to the sole proprietorship business are excluded from accounting. However, a sole proprietor is personally liable and required to utilize non-business assets or private assets also to settle the business creditors as per law.

Thus, in the case of sole proprietorship, business and non-business assets and liabilities are treated alike in the eyes of law. In the case of a partnership, firm, for paying the business liabilities the business assets are used first and it any surplus remains thereafter, it can be used for paying off the private liabilities of each partner. Similarly, the private assets are first used to pay off the private liabilities of partners and if any surplus remains, it is treated as part of the firm's property and is used for paying the firm's liabilities. In the case of a company, its existence does not depend on the life span of any shareholder.

### *Money Measurement Concept*

In accounting all events and transactions are recode in terms of money. Money is considered as a common denominator, by means of which various facts, events and transactions about a business can be expressed in terms of numbers. In other words, facts, events and transactions which cannot be expressed in monetary terms are not recorded in accounting. Hence, the accounting does not give a complete picture of all the transactions of a business unit. This concept does not also take care of the effects of inflation because it assumes a stable value for measuring.

### *Going Concern Concept*

Under this concept, the transactions are recorded assuming that the business will exist for a longer period of time, *i.e.*, a business unit is considered to be a going concern and not a liquidated one. Keeping this in view, the suppliers and other companies enter into business transactions with the business unit. This assumption supports the concept of valuing the assets at historical cost or replacement cost. This concept also supports the treatment of prepaid expenses as assets, although they may be practically unsaleable.

### *Dual Aspect Concept*

This basic concept of accounting, every transaction has a two-fold aspect, *Viz.*, 1.giving certain benefits and 2. Receiving certain benefits. The basic principle of double entry system is that every debit has a corresponding and equal amount of credit. This is the underlying assumption of this concept. The accounting equation *viz.*, Assets = Capital + Liabilities or Capital = Assets–Liabilities, will further clarify this concept, *i.e.*, at any point of time the total assets of the business unit are equal to its total liabilities. Liabilities here relate both to the outsiders and the owners. Liabilities to the owners are considered as capital.

### *Periodicity Concept*

Under this concept, the life of the business is segmented into different periods and accordingly the result of each period is ascertained. Though the business is assumed to be continuing in future (as per going concern concept), the measurement of income and studying the financial position of the business for a shorter and definite period will help in taking corrective steps at the appropriate time. Each segmented period is called "accounting period" and the same is normally a year. The businessman has to analyse and evaluate the results ascertained periodically. At the end of an accounting period, an Income Statement is prepared to ascertain the profit or loss made during that accounting period and Balance Sheet is prepared which depicts the financial position of the business as on the last day of that period. During the course of preparation of these statements capital revenue items are to be necessarily distinguished.

### *Historical Cost Concept*

The transactions are recorded in the books of account with the respective amounts involved. For example, if an asset is purchases, it is entered in the accounting record at the price paid to acquire the same and that cost is considered to be the base for all future accounting. It means that the asset is recorded at cost at the time of purchase but it may be methodically reduced in its value by way of charging depreciation. However, in the light of inflationary conditions, the application of this concept is considered highly irrelevant for judging the financial position of the business.

### *Matching Concept*

The essence of the matching concept lies in the view that all costs which are associated to a particular period should be compared with the revenues associated to the same period to obtain the net income of the business. Under this concept, the accounting period concept is relevant and it is this concept (matching concept) which necessitated the provisions of different adjustments for recording outstanding expenses, prepaid expenses, outstanding incomes, incomes received in advance, etc., during the course of preparing the financial statements at the end of the accounting period.

### *Realisation Concept*

This concept assumes or recognizes revenue when a sale is made. Sale is considered to be complete when the ownership and property are transferred from the seller to the buyer and the consideration is paid in full.

*However, there are two exceptions to this concept, viz.,:*

1. Hire purchase system where the ownership is transferred to the buyer when the last instalment is paid and
2. Contract accounts, in which the contractor is liable to pay only when the whole contract is completed, the profit is calculated on the basis of work certified each year.

### *Accrual Concept*

The revenue is recognized on its realization and not on its actual receipt. Similarly the costs are recognized when they are incurred and not when payment is made. This assumption makes it necessary to give certain adjustments in the preparation of income statement regarding revenues and costs. But under cash accounting system, the revenues and costs are recognized only when they are actually received or paid. Hence, the combination of both cash and accrual system is preferable to get rid of the limitations of each system.

### *Objective Evidence Concept*

This concept ensures that all accounting must be based on objective evidence, *i.e.*, every transaction recorded in the books of account must have a verifiable document in support of its, existence. Only then, the transactions can be verified by the auditors and declared as true or otherwise. The verifiable evidence for the transactions should be free from the personal bias, *i.e.*, it should be objective in nature and not subjective. However, in reality the subjectivity cannot be avoided in the aspects like provision for bad and doubtful debts, provision for depreciation, valuation of inventory, etc., and the accountants are required to disclose the regulations followed.

### *Accounting Conventions*

*The following conventions are to be followed to have a clear and meaningful information and data in accounting*:

- *Consistency*: The convention of consistency refers to the state of accounting rules, concepts, principles, practices and conventions being observed and applied constantly, *i.e.*, from one year to another there should not be any change. If consistency is there, the results and performance of one period can he compared easily and meaningfully with the other. It also prevents personal bias as the persons involved have to follow the consistent rules, principles, concepts and conventions. This convention, however, does not completely ignore changes. It admits changes wherever indispensable and adds to the improved and modern techniques of accounting.
- *Disclosure*: The convention of disclosure stresses the importance of providing accurate, full and reliable information and data in the financial statements which is of material interest to the users and readers of such statements. This convention is given due legal emphasis by the Companies Act, 1956 by prescribing formats for the preparation of financial statements. However, the term disclosure does not mean all information that one desires to get should be included in accounting statements. It is enough if sufficient information, which is of material interest to the users, is included.
- *Conservatism*: In the prevailing present day uncertainties, the convention of conservatism has its own importance. This convention follows the policy of caution or playing safe. It takes into account all possible losses but not the possible profits or gains. A view opposed to this convention is that there is the possibility of creation of secret reserves when conservatism is excessively applied, which is directly opposed to the convention of full disclosure. Thus, the convention of conservatism should be applied very cautiously.

## BASES OF ACCOUNTING

There are three bases of accounting in common usage. Any one of the following bases may be used to finalise accounts:

1. Cash basis
2. Accrual or Mercantile basis
3. Mixed or Hybrid basis.

### *Accounting on 'Cash Basis*

Under cash basis accounting, entries are recorded only when cash is received or paid. No entry is passed when a payment or receipt becomes due. Income under cash basis of accounting, therefore, represents excess of receipts over payments during an accounting period.

Government system of accounting is mostly on cash basis. Certain professional people record their income on cash basis, but while recording expenses they take into account the outstanding expenses also. In such a case, the financial statements prepared by them for determination of their income is termed as Receipts and Expenditure Account.

### *Accrual Basis of Accounting or Mercantile System*

Under accrual basis of accounting, accounting entries are made on the basis of amounts having become due for payment or receipt. Incomes are credited to the period in which they are earned whether cash is received or not.

Similarly, expenses and losses ere detailed to the period in which, they arc incurred, whether cash is paid or not. The profit or loss of any accounting period is the difference between incomes earned and expenses incurred, irrespective of cash payment or receipt. All outstanding expenses and prepaid expenses, accrued incomes and incomes received in advance are adjusted while finalising the accounts. Under the Companies Act 1956, all companies are required to maintain the books of accounts just as to accrual basis of accounting.

### *Mixed or Hybrid Basis of Accounting*

When certain items of revenue or expenditure are recorded in the books of account on cash basis and certain items on mercantile basis, the basis of accounting so employed is called 'hybrid basis of accounting'. For example, a company may follow mercantile system of accounting in respect of its export business.

However, government subsidies and duty drawbacks on exports to be received from government are recorded only when they are actually received *i.e.,* on cash basis.

Such a method could be adopted because of uncertainty with respect of quantum, amount and time of receipt of such incentives and drawbacks. Such a method of accounting followed by the company is called the hybrid basis of accounting. In practice, the profit or loss shown under this basis will not be realistic. Conservative people who prefer recognising income when received but cautious to provide for all expenses, whether paid or not prefer this system. It is not widely practised due to the inconsistency.

## ACCOUNTING TERMINOLOGY

It is necessary to understand some basic accounting terms which are daily in business world.

*These terms are called accounting terminology*:

- *Transaction*: "An event the recognition of which gives rise to an entry in accounting records. It is an event which results in change in the balance sheet equation. That is, which changes the value of assets and equity. In a simple statement, transaction means the exchange of money or moneys worth from one account to another account Events like purchase and sale of goods, receipt and payment of cash for services or on personal accounts, loss or profit in dealings etc., are the transactions".Cash transaction is one where cash receipt or payment is involved in the exchange. Credit transaction, on the other hand, will not have 'cash' either received or paid, for something given or received respectively, but gives rise to debtor and creditor relationship. Non-cash transaction is one where the question of receipt or payment of cash does not at all arise, *e.g.* Depreciation, return of goods etc.,
- *Debtor*: A person who owes money to the firm mostly on account of credit sales of goods is called a debtor. For example, when goods are sold to a person on credit that person pays the price in future, he is called a debtor because he owes the amount to the firm.
- *Creditor*: A person to whom money is owing by the firm is called creditor. For example, Madan is a creditor of the firm when goods are purchased on credit from him
- *Capital*: It means the amount (in terms of money or assets having money value) which the proprietor has invested in the firm or can claim from the firm. It is also known as owner's equity or net worth. Owner's equity means owner's claim against the assets. It will always be equal to assets less liabilities, say:
- Capital = Assets - Liabilities.
- *Liability*: It means the amount which the firm owes to outsiders that is, excepting the proprietors. In the words of Finny and Miller, "Liabilities are debts; they are amounts owed to creditors; thus the claims of those who ate not owners are called liabilities". In simple terms, debts repayable to outsiders by the business are known as liabilities.
- *Asset*: Any physical thing or right owned that has a money value is an asset. In other words, an asset is that expenditure which results in acquiring of some property or benefits of a lasting nature.

- *Goods*: It is a general term used for the articles in which the business deals; that is, only those articles which are bought for resale for profit are known as Goods.
- *Revenue*: It means the amount which, as a result of operations, is added to the capital. It is defined as the inflow of assets which result in an increase in the owner's equity. It includes all incomes like sales receipts, interest, commission, brokerage etc., However, receipts of capital nature like additional capital, sale of assets etc., are not a pant of revenue.
- *Expense*: The terms 'expense' refers to the amount incurred in the process of earning revenue. If the benefit of an expenditure is limited to one year, it is treated as an expense (also know is as revenue expenditure) such as payment of salaries and rent.
- *Expenditure*: Expenditure takes place when an asset or service is acquired. The purchase of goods is expenditure, where as cost of goods sold is an expense. Similarly, if an asset is acquired during the year, it is expenditure, if it is consumed during the same year, it is also an expense of the year.
- *Purchases*: Buying of goods by the trader for selling them to his customers is known as purchases. As the trade is buying and selling of commodities purchase is the main function of a trade. Here, the trader gets possession of the goods which are not for own use but for resale. Purchases can be of two types. viz, cash purchases and credit purchases. If cash is paid immediately for the purchase, it is cash purchases, If the payment is postponed, it is credit purchases.
- *Sales*: When the goods purchased are sold out, it is known as sales. Here, the possession and the ownership right over the goods are transferred to the buyer. It is known as. 'Business Turnover' or sales proceeds. It can be of two types, *viz.,,* cash sales and credit sales. If the sale is for immediate cash payment, it is cash sales. If payment for sales is postponed, it is credit sales.
- *Stock*: The goods purchased are for selling, if the goods are not sold out fully, a part of the total goods purchased is kept with the trader unlit it is sold out, it is said to be a stock. If there is stock at the end of the accounting year, it is said to be a closing stock. This closing stock at the year end will be the opening stock for the subsequent year.
- *Drawings*: It is the amount of money or the value of goods which the proprietor takes for his domestic or personal use. It is usually subtracted from capital.
- *Losses*: Loss really means something against which the firm receives no benefit. It represents money given up without any return. It may

be noted that expense leads to revenue but losses do not. (*e.g.*) loss due to fire, theft and damages payable to others,

- *Account*: It is a statement of the various dealings which occur between a customer and the firm. It can also be expressed as a clear and concise record of the transaction relating to a person or a firm or a property (or assets) or a liability or an expense or an income.
- *Invoice*: While making a sale, the seller prepares a statement giving the particulars such as the quantity, price per unit, the total amount payable, any deductions made and shows the net amount payable by the buyer. Such a statement is called an invoice.
- *Voucher*: A voucher is a written document in support of a transaction. It is a proof that a particular transaction has taken place for the value stated in the voucher. Voucher is necessary to audit the accounts.
- *Proprietor*: The person who makes the investment and bears all the risks connected with the business is known as proprietor.
- *Discount*: When customers are allowed any type of deduction in the prices of goods by the businessman that is called discount. When some discount is allowed in prices of goods on the basis of sales of the items, that is termed as trade discount, but when debtors are allowed some discount in prices of the goods for quick payment, that is termed as cash discount.
- *Solvent*: A person who has assets with realizable values which exceeds his liabilities is nsolvent.
- *Insolvent*: A person whose liabilities are more than the realizable values of his assets is called an insolvent.

## ACCOUNTING EQUATION

As indicated earlier, every business transaction has two aspects. One aspect is debited other aspect is credited. Both the aspects have to be recorded in accounts appropriately. American Accountants have derived the rules of debit and credit through a 'novel' medium, *i.e.*, accounting equation.

*The equation is as follows*:

- Assets = Equities

The equation is based on the principle that accounting deals with property and rights to property and the sum of the properties owned is equal to the sum of the rights to the properties. The properties owned by a business are called assets and the rights to properties are known as liabilities or equities of the business. Equities can be subdivided into equity of the owners which is known as capital and equity of creditors who represent the debts of the business know as liabilities. These equities may also be called internal equity and external equity. Internal equity represents the owner's equity in the assets and external represents he outsider's interest in the asset.

*Based on the bifurcation of equity, the accounting equation can be restated as follows*:

Assets = Liabilities + Capital

(Or)

Capital = Assets–Liabilities

(Or)

Liabilities = Assets–Capital.

The equation is fundamental in the sense that it gives a foundation to the double entry book-keeping system. This equation holds good for all transaction and events and at all periods of time since every transaction and events has two aspects.

# 2

# Accounting Standard

## INTRODUCTION

Accounting Standards are the defined accounting policies issued by Government or expert institute. These standards are issued to bring harmonization in follow up of accounting policies.

*Accounting Standards as listed below*:

- AS 01. Disclosure of Accounting Policies
- AS 02. Valuation of Inventories
- AS 03. Cash Flow Statements
- AS 04. Contingencies and Events Occurring After the Balance Sheet Date
- AS 05. Net Profit or Loss for the Period, Prior Period Items and Changes in Accounting Policies
- AS 06. Depreciation Accounting
- AS 07. Construction Contracts
- AS 08. Accounting for Research and Development (Not Applicable now)
- AS 09. Revenue Recognition
- AS 10. Accounting for Fixed Assets
- AS 11. Accounting for the Effects of Changes in Foreign Exchange Rates
- AS 12. Accounting for Government Grants
- AS 13. Accounting for Investments
- AS 14. Accounting for Amalgamation
- AS 15. Accounting for Retirement Benefits in the financial Statements of Employers
- AS 16. Borrowing Costs
- AS 17. Segment Reporting
- AS 18. Related Party Disclosure
- AS 19. Leases
- AS 20. Earning Per Share
- AS 21. Consolidated Financial Statements

- AS 22. Accounting for Taxes on Income
- AS 23. Accounting for Investments in Associates in Consolidated Financial Statements
- AS 24. Discontinuing Operations
- AS 25. Interim Financial Reporting
- AS 26. Intangible Assets
- AS 27. Financial Reporting of Interests in Joint Ventures
- AS 28. Impairment of Assets
- AS 29. Provisions, Contingent Liabilities and Contingent Assets

## PROCEDURE FOR ISSUING ACCOUNTING STANDARDS

- Accounting Standard Board (ASB) determines the broad areas in which Accounting Standards need to be formulated.
- In the preparation of AS, ASB is assisted by Study Groups.
- ASB also holds discussions with representative of Government, Public Sector Undertakings, Industry and other organizations (ICSI/ ICWAI) for ascertaining their views.
- An exposure draft of the proposed standard is prepared and issued for comments by members of ICAI and the public at large.
- After taking into consideration the comments received, the draft of the proposed standard will be finalized by ASB and submitted to the council of the Institute.
- The council of the Institute will consider the final draft of the proposed Standard and If found necessary, modify the same in consultation with ASB. The AS on the relevant subject will then be issued under the authority of the council.

## DISCLOSURE OF ACCOUNTING POLICY

Accounting policies are the specific accounting principles and the methods of applying those principles adopted by an enterprise in the preparation and presentation of financial statements.

- All significant accounting policies should be disclosed.
- Such disclosure form part of financial statements.
- All disclosures should be made at one place.
- Specific disclosure for the adoption of fundamental accounting assumptions is not required.
- Disclosure of accounting policies cannot remedy a wrong or inappropriate treatment of the item in the accounts.

Any change in accounting policies which has a material effect in the current period or which is reasonably expected to have material effect in later periods should be disclosed. In the case of a change in accounting policies, which has a material effect in the current period, the amount by which any item in the financial statements is affected by such change should also be disclosed to the extent ascertainable. Where such amount is not ascertainable, the fact should be indicated.

*Fundamental Accounting Assumption*: (GCA):

- Going Concern
- Consistency
- Accrual

*The following are examples of the areas in which different accounting policies may be adopted by different enterprises*:

- Methods of depreciation
- Methods of translation of foreign currency
- Valuation of inventories
- Valuation of investments
- Treatment of retirement benefits
- Treatment of contingent liabilities etc.

## VALUATION OF INVENTORY

*Inventories are assets*:

- Held for sale in ordinary course of business;
- In the process of production fro such sale (WIP);
- In the form of materials or supplies to be consumed in the production process or in the rendering of services.

*However, this standard does not apply to the valuation of following inventories*:

- WIP arising under construction contract;
- WIP arising in the ordinary course of business of service providers;
- Shares, debentures and other financial instruments held as stock in trade; and
- Producers' inventories of livestock, agricultural and forest products, and mineral oils, ores and gases to the extent that they are measured at net realizable value in accordance with well established practices in those industries.

Inventories should be valued at the lower of cost and net realizable value.

*The cost of inventories should comprise*:

- All costs of purchase
- Costs of conversion
- Other costs incurred in bringing the inventories to their present location and condition.

*The costs of purchase consist of*:

- The purchase price
- Duties and taxes (other than those subsequently recoverable by the enterprise from the taxing authorities like CENVAT credit)
- Freight inwards and other expenditure directly attributable to the acquisition.

Trade discounts (but not cash discounts), rebates, duty drawbacks and other similar items are deducted in determining the costs of purchase. The costs of conversion include direct costs and systematic allocation of fixed and variable production overhead. Allocation of fixed overheads is based on the normal capacity of the production facilities. Normal capacity is the production, expected to be achieved on an average over a number of periods or seasons under normal circumstances, taking into account the loss of capacity resulting from planned maintenance.

## UNDER RECOVERY

Unallocated overheads are recognized as an expense in the period in which they are incurred.

*Example*:

| | |
|---|---|
| Normal capacity | = 20000 units |
| Production | = 18000 units |
| Sales | = 16000 units |
| Closing Stock | = 2000 units |
| Fixed Overheads | = ₹60000/- |
| Then, Recovery rate | = ₹60000/20000 = ₹3 per unit |
| **Fixed Overheads will be bifurcated into three parts** | |
| Cost of Sales | : 16000 × 3 = 48000 |
| Closing Stock | : 2000 × 3 = 6000 |
| Under Recovery | : ₹6000 (to be charged to P/L) |

(Apparently it seems that fixed cost element in closing stock should be 60000/18000 × 2000 =₹ 6666.67. but this is wrong as per AS-2)

## OVER RECOVERY

In period of high production, the amount of fixed production overheads is allocated to each unit of production is decreased so that inventories.

*Example*:

| | |
|---|---|
| Normal capacity | = 20000 units |
| Production | = 25000 units |
| Sales | = 23000 units |
| Closing Stock | = 2000 units |
| Fixed Overheads | = ₹60000/- |
| Than, Recovery Rate | = ₹60000/20000 = ₹3 per unit |
| But, Revised Recovery Rate | = ₹ 60000/25000 = ₹ 2.40 per unit |
| Cost of Sales | : 23000 × 2.4 = ₹55200 |
| Closing Stock | : 2000 × 2.4 = ₹ 4800 |

## JOINT OR BY PRODUCTS

In case of joint or by products, the costs incurred up to the stage of split off should be allocated on a rational and consistent basis. The basis of allocation may be sale value at split off point or sale value at the completion of production. In case of the by products of negligible value or wastes, valuation may be taken at net realizable value. The cost of main product is then joint cost minus net realizable value of by product or waste. The other costs are also included in the cost of inventory to the extent they contribute in bringing the inventory to its present location and condition. Interest and other borrowing costs are usually not included in cost of inventory. However, AS-16 recommends the areas where borrowing costs are taken as cost of inventory.

*Certain costs are strictly not taken as cost of inventory*:

- Abnormal amounts of wasted materials, labour, or other production costs;
- Storage costs, unless those costs are necessary in the production process prior to a further production stage;
- Administrative overheads that do not contribute to bringing the inventories to their present location and condition; and
- Selling and Distribution costs.

## COST FORMULA

- Specific identification method for determining cost of inventories
- Specific identification method means directly linking the cost with specific item of inventories. This method has application in following conditions:
- In case of purchase of item specifically segregated for specific project and is not ordinarily interchangeable.
- In case of goods of services produced and segregated for specific project.
- Where Specific Identification method is not applicable
- The cost of inventories is valued by the following methods;
- FIFO (First In First Out) Method
- Weighted Average Cost

## COST OF INVENTORIES IN CERTAIN CONDITIONS

*The following methods may be used for convenience if the results approximate actual cost*:

- *Standard Cost*: It takes into account normal level of consumption of material and supplies, labour, efficiency and capacity utilization. It must be regularly reviewed taking into consideration the current condition.
- *Retail Method*: Normally applicable for retail trade. Cost of inventory is determined by reducing the gross margin from the sale value of inventory.
- *Net Realisable Value*: NRV means the estimated selling price in ordinary course of business, at the time of valuation, less estimated cost of completion and estimated cost necessary to make the sale.

## COMPARISON BETWEEN NET REALIZABLE VALUE AND COST OF INVENTORY

The comparison between cost and net realizable value should be made on item-by-item basis. (In some cases, group of items-by-group of item basis)

*For Example*:

| | Cost | NRV | Inventory Value as per AS-2 |
|---|---|---|---|
| Item A | 100 | 90 | 90 |
| Item B | 100 | 115 | 100 |
| Total | 200 | 205 | ~~200~~ 190 |

## RAW MATERIAL VALUATION

If the finished goods, to which raw material is applied, is sold at profit, RAW MATERIAL is valued at cost irrespective of its NRV level being lower to its costs.

# CASH FLOW STATEMENT

- *Definitions*: Cash comprises cash on hand and cash at bank. (Demand Deposits with bank) Cash Equivalents are:
  - Short Term
  - Highly Liquid Investments (Maturity around 3 months)
  - Subject to insignificant risk of changes in value.
  - Cash Flows are inflows and outflows of cash and cash equivalents.
  - Cash Flow Statement represents the cash flows during the specified period by operating, investing and financing activities.
  - Operating Activities are the principal revenue-producing activities of the enterprise and other activities that are not investing activities and financing activities.
- *Example*:
  - Cash receipts from sales of goods/services
  - Cash receipts from royalties, fees and other revenue items
  - Cash payments for salaries, wages and rent
  - Cash payment to suppliers for goods
  - Cash payments or refunds of Income Tax unless they can be specifically identified with financing or investing activities
  - Cash receipts and payments to future contracts, forward contracts when the contracts are held for trading purposes.
  - Investing Activities are the acquisition and disposal of long-term assets and other investments not included in cash equivalents.
  - Cash payments/receipts to acquire/sale of fixed assets including intangible assets
  - Cash payments to acquire shares or interest in joint ventures (other than the cases where instruments are considered as cash equivalents)

- Cash advances and loans made to third parties (Loan sanctioned by a financial enterprise is operating activity)
- Dividends and Interest received
- Cash flows from acquisitions and disposal of subsidiaries
- Financing Activities are activities that result in changes in the size and composition of the owners' capital (including preference share capital in the case of a company) and borrowing of the enterprise.
- Cash proceeds from issue of shares and debentures
- Buy back of shares
- Redemption of Preference shares or debentures
- Cash repayments of amount borrowed.
- Dividend and Interest paid

An enterprise should report separately major classes of gross cash receipts and gross cash payments arising from investing and financing activities.

*However, cash flows from following activities may be reported on a net basis*:

- Cash receipts and payments on behalf of customers
- Cash collected on behalf of, and paid over to, the owners of properties.
- Cash flows from items in which turnover is quick, the amounts are large and the maturities are short.
- Purchase and sale of investments
- *For Financial Enterprise*:
  - Cash receipts and payments for the acceptance and repayment of deposits with a fixed maturity date.
  - Deposits placed/withdrawn from other financial enterprises
  - Cash advances and loans made to customers and the repayment of those advances and loans.

## FOREIGN CURRENCY CASH FLOWS

Cash flows arising in foreign currency should be recorded in enterprise' reporting currency applying the exchange conversion rate existing on the date of cash flow. The effect of changes in exchange rates of cash and cash equivalents held in foreign currency should be reported as separate part of the reconciliation of the changes in cash and cash equivalents during the period.

## EXTRAORDINARY ITEMS

These items should be separately shown under respective heads of cash from operating, investing and financing activities. Investing and financing transactions that do not require the use of cash and cash equivalents should be excluded from a cash flow statement.

*For Example*:

- The conversion of debt to equity
- Acquisition of an enterprise by means of issue of shares

## OTHER DISCLOSURE

- Components of cash and cash equivalents.
- Reconciliation of closing cash and cash equivalents with items of balance sheet.
- The amount of significant cash and cash equivalent balances held by the enterprise, which are not available for use by it.

## CONTINGENCIES AND EVENTS OCCURRING AFTER THE BALANCE SHEET DATE

- *Contingency*: A contingency is a condition or situation, the ultimate outcome of which, gain or loss, will be known or determined only on the occurrence, or non-occurrence, of one or more uncertain future events.

## ACCOUNTING TREATMENT

*If it is likely that a contingency will result in*:

- *Loss*: It is prudent to provide for that loss in the financial statements.
- *Profit*: Not recognized as revenue (However, when the realization of a gain is virtually certain, then such gain is not a contingency and accounting for the gain is appropriate.)

*The estimates of the outcome and of the financial effect of contingencies are determined*:

- By the judgment of the management by review of events occurring after the balance sheet date.
- By experience of the enterprise in similar transaction
- By reviewing reports from independent experts

If estimation cannot be made, disclosure is made of the existence and nature of the contingency. Provisions for contingencies are not made in respect of general or unspecified risks. The existence and amount of guarantees and obligations arising from discounted bills of exchange are generally disclosed by way of note even though the possibility of loss is remote.

*The amount of a contingent loss should be provided for by a charge in the statement of profit and loss if*:

- It is probable that future events will confirm that, after taking into account any related probable recovery, an asset has been impaired or a liability has been incurred as at the balance sheet date, and
- A reasonable estimate of the amount of the resulting loss can be made.

If either of aforesaid two conditions is not met, *e.g.* where a reasonable estimate of the loss is not practicable, the existence of the contingency should be disclosed by way of note unless the possibility of loss is remote.

*Such disclosure should provide following information*:

- The nature of the contingency;

- The uncertainties which may affect the future outcome;
- An estimate of the financial effect or a statement that such an estimate cannot be made.

## EVENTS OCCURRING AFTER THE BALANCE SHEET DATE

Events occurring after the balance sheet date are those significant events, both favourable and unfavourable, that occur between the balance sheet date and the date on which the financial statements are approved by the Board of Directors in case of a company, and, by the corresponding approving authority in the case of any other entity.

### *Adjusting Event*

Those, which provide further evidence of conditions that, existed at the balance sheet date. Actual adjustments in financial statements are required for adjusting event.

*Exceptions*:

- Although, not adjusting event, Proposed dividend are adjusted in books of account.
- Adjustments are required for the events, which occur after balance sheet date that indicates that fundamental accounting assumption of going concern is no longer, appropriate.

### *Non-Adjusting Events*

Those, hitch are indicative of conditions that arose subsequent to the balance sheet date. No adjustments are required to be made for such events. But, disclosures should be made in the report of the approving authority of those events occurring after the balance sheet date that represent material changes and commitments affecting the financial position of the enterprise.

*Such disclosure should provide following information*:

- The nature of the events
- An estimate of the financial effect, or a statement that such an estimate cannot be made.

## NET PROFIT OR LOSS FOR THE PERIOD, PRIOR PERIOD ITEMS AND CHANGES IN ACCOUNTING POLICY

All items of income and expense, which are recognized in a period, should be included in the determination of net profit or loss for the period unless an Accounting Standard requires or permits otherwise. The net profit or loss for the period comprises the following components, each of which should be disclosed on the face of the statement of profit and loss:

- Profit or loss from ordinary activities; and
- Extraordinary items.

Ordinary Activities are any activities, which are undertaken by an enterprise as part of its business, and such related activities in which the enterprise engages in furtherance of, incidental to, or arising from, these activities.

When items of income and expenses within profit or loss from ordinary activities are of such size, nature that their disclosure is relevant to explain the performance of the enterprise for the period, the nature and amount of such items should be disclosed properly.

*Examples of such circumstances are*:

- Disposal of items of fixed assets
- Litigation settlements
- Legislative changes having retrospective application
- Disposal of long term investments
- Reversal of provisions

Extraordinary items are income or expense that arises from events or transactions that are clearly distinct from the ordinary activities of the enterprise and, therefore, are not expected to recur frequently or regularly.

*Examples of events or transactions that generally give rise to extraordinary items for most enterprises are*:

- Attachment of property of the enterprise;
- An earthquake

However, claims from policyholders arising from an earthquake do not qualify as an extraordinary item for an insurance enterprise that insures against such risks. Extraordinary items should be disclosed in the statement of profit and loss as a part of net profit or loss for the period. The nature and the amount of each extraordinary item should be separately disclosed in the statement of profit and loss in a manner that its impact on current profit or loss can be perceived.

## PRIOR PERIOD ITEMS

Prior period items are income or expenses that arise in the current period as a result of ERROR or OMMISSIONS in the preparation of the financial statements of one or more prior periods. The nature and amount of prior period items should be separately disclosed in the statement of profit and loss in a manner that their impact on the current profit or loss can be perceived.

## CHANGES IN ACCOUNTING POLICY

Accounting policies are the specific accounting principles and the methods of applying those principles adopted by an enterprise in the preparation and presentation of financial statements.

*A change in an accounting policy should be made only if the adoption of a different accounting policy is required*:

- By statute
- For compliance with an accounting standard

- If it is considered that the change would result in a more appropriate presentation of the financial statements of the enterprise.

Any change in accounting policy which has a material effect, should be disclosed. Such changes should be disclosed in the statement of profit and loss in a manner that their impact on profit or loss can be perceived. Where the effect of such change is not ascertainable, the fact should be indicated.

If a change is made in the accounting policies which has no material effect on the financial statements for the current period but which is reasonably expected to have material effect in later periods, the fact of such change should be appropriately disclosed in the period in which the change is adopted.

*The following are not changes in accounting policies*:

- The adoption of an accounting policy for events which differ in substance from previously occurring events *e.g.* introduction of a formal retirement gratuity scheme by an employer in place of ad hoc ex-gratia payments to employees on retirement; and
- The adoption of a new accounting policy for events or transactions which did not occur previously or that were immaterial.

## CHANGE IN ACCOUNTING ESTIMATE

The nature and amount of a change in an accounting estimate which has a material effect in the current period, or which is expected to have a material effect in subsequent periods, should be disclosed. If it is impracticable to quantify the amount, this fact should be disclosed.

The effect of a change in an accounting estimate should be classified using the same classification in the statement of profit and loss as was previously for the estimate. For example, the effect of a change in an accounting estimate that was previously included as an extraordinary item is reported as an extraordinary item.

## CLARIFICATIONS

- Change in accounting estimate does not bring the adjustment within the definitions of an extraordinary item or a prior period item.
- Sometimes, it is difficult to distinguish between a change in an accounting policy and a change in accounting estimate. In such cases, the change is treated as a change in an accounting estimate, with appropriate disclosures.

# DEPRECIATION ACCOUNTING

Depreciation is a measure of the wearing out, consumption or other loss of value of a depreciable asset arising from use, passage of time or obsolescence through technology and market changes.

Depreciation is allocated so as to charge a fair proportion of the depreciable amount in each accounting period during the expected useful life of the asset. Depreciation includes amortisation of assets whose useful life is predetermined. The depreciable amount of a depreciable asset should be allocated on a systematic basis to each accounting period during the useful life of the asset.

*Depreciable assets are assets which*:

- Are expected to be used during more than one accounting period; and
- Have a limited useful life; and
- Are held by an enterprise for use in the production or supply or for administrative purposes

Depreciable amount of a depreciable asset is its historical cost, or other amount substituted for historical cost less the estimated residual value. Useful life is the period over which a depreciable asset is expected to be used by the enterprise. The useful life of a depreciable asset is shorter than its physical life.

*There are two method of depreciation*:

1. Straight Line Method (SLM)
2. Written Down Value Method (WDVM)

The depreciation method selected should be applied consistently from period to period. The change in method of depreciation should be made only if; The adoption of the new method is required by statute; OR For compliance with an accounting standard; OR If it is considered that change would result in a more appropriate preparation of financial statement; or When there is change in method of depreciation, depreciation should be recalculated in accordance with the new method from the date of the assets coming into use. (*i.e.* retrospectively) The deficiency or surplus arising from such recomputation should be adjusted in the year of change through profit and loss account.

Such change should be treated as a change in accounting policy and its effect should be quantified and disclosed. The useful lives of major depreciable assets may be reviewed periodically.

Where there is a revision of the estimated useful life, the unamortised depreciable amount should be charged over the revised remaining useful life. (*i.e.* PROSPECTIVELY) Any addition or extension which becomes an integral part of the existing asset should be depreciated over the remaining useful life of that asset.

The depreciation on such addition may also be applied at the rate applied to the existing asset. Where an addition or extension retains a separate identity and is capable of being used after the existing asset is disposed of, depreciation should be provided independently on the basis of estimate of its own useful life.

Where the historical cost of a depreciable asset has undergone a change due to increase or decrease in the long term liability on account of exchange fluctuations, price adjustments, changes in duties or similar factors, the depreciation on the revised unamortised depreciable amount should be provided prospectively over the residual useful life of the asset.

*This accounting standard is not applied on the following items:*

- Forests and plantations
- Wasting assets
- Research and development expenditure
- Goodwill
- Live stock

*Disclosure Requirements*:

- The historical cost
- Total depreciation for each class charged during the period
- The related accumulated depreciation
- Depreciation method used (Accounting policy)
- Depreciation rates if they are different from those prescribed by the statute governing the enterprise

## CONSTRUCTION CONTRACT

A Construction contract is a contract specifically negotiated for the construction of an asset or a combination of assets that are closely interrelated or interdependent in terms of their design, technology and function or their ultimate purpose or use.

### RECOGNITION OF CONTRACT REVENUE AND CONTRACT COST

When the outcome of a construction contract can be estimated reliably, contract revenue and contract cost should be recognized as revenue and expenses by reference to the stage of construction.

This accounting standard recommends the use of percentage of completion method). When the outcome of a construction contract cannot be estimated reliably,

- Revenue should be recognized only to the extent of contract costs incurred of which recovery is probable. (*i.e.* Revenue recognized = Costs Incurred)
- Contract costs should be recognized as an expense in the period in which they are incurred.

*The outcome of a construction contract can be estimated reliably when all the following conditions are satisfied*:

- Total contract revenue can be measured reliably;
- The receipt of revenue is probable;
- The contract costs to complete the contract can be measured reliably;
- The stage of completion at the reporting date can be measured reliably;
- The contract costs attributable to the contract can be clearly identified.

*Contract Revenue should comprise the initial amount of revenue agreed in the contract; and variations in amount to be received*:

- To the extent that it is probable that they will result in revenue; and
- They are capable of being reliably measured. (Contract can of two kinds: Fixed Price contract and Cost Plus contract)

*Contract Costs should comprise*:

- Costs that relate directly to the specific contract;
- Costs that are attributable to contract activity in general and can be allocated to the contract.
- At any stage of contract, when it is probable that total contract costs will exceed total contract revenue, the expected loss should be recognized as an expense immediately. The amount of such loss is determined irrespective of:
  - Whether or not work has commenced on the contract;
  - The stage of completion of contract activity; or
  - Whether outcome of contract is estimated or not
- When an uncertainty arises about the collectability of an amount already included in contract revenue, and already recognized in the statement of profit and loss, the uncollectable amount or the amount in respect of which recovery has ceased to be probable is recognized as an expense rather than an adjustment of the amount of contract revenue.
- Contract costs that relate to future activity, are recognized as an asset provided it is probable that they will be recovered. Such asset is classified as Contract WIP.
- The stage of completion of a contract may be determined by following ways;
  - Surveys of work done
  - Completion of physical proportion of the contract work
  - The proportion that contract costs incurred for work performed upto
  - The reporting date bear to the estimated total contract costs
- When a contract covers a number of assets, the construction of each asset should be treated as a separate construction of each asset should be treated as separate construction contract when
  - Separate proposals have been submitted for each asset;
  - Each asset has been subject to separate negotiation
  - The costs and revenues of each asset can be identified
- A group of contracts, whether with a single customer or with several customers, should be treated as a single construction contract when
  - The group of contracts is negotiated as a single ackage;
  - The contracts are very closely interrelated
  - The contracts are performed concurrently or in a continuous sequence.

- The recognition of revenue and expenses in construction contract is based on reliable estimate. This estimate may vary from one accounting year to another accounting year. The effect of change in estimate should be treated as per AS-5. *i.e.* It should not be treated as prior period item or extraordinary item.
- *Disclosure*:
  - Contract Revenue recognized as revenue
  - Method used to determine the contract revenue
  - Method used to determine the stage of completion
  - Contract costs incurred + Recognised Profit–Recognised Loss
  - Amount of advances received
  - Amount due from customers
  - Amount due to customers

## REVENUE RECOGNITION

Revenue is the gross inflow of cash, receivables or other consideration arising in the course of the ordinary activities of an enterprise from the sale of goods, from the rendering of services, and from the use by others of enterprise resources yielding interest, royalties and dividends.

- *Revenue Includes*:
  - Proceeds from sale of goods
  - Proceeds from rendering of services
  - Interest, royalty and dividends.
- *Sale of goods*:
  - Revenue from sales should be recognized when
  - All significant risks and rewards of ownership have been transferred to the buyer from the seller.
  - Ultimate reliability of receipt is reasonably certain.
- *Rendering of Services*: Revenue from service transactions is usually recognized as the service is performed, either by proportionate completion method or by the completed service contract method.
- *Proportionate Completion Method*: This is a method of accounting, which recognises revenue in the statement of profit and loss proportionately with degree of completion of services under a contract. Revenue is recognised by reference to the performance of each act. The revenue recognised under this method would be determined on the basis of contract value, associated costs, number of acts or other suitable basis.
- *Completed Service Contract Method*: This is a method of accounting, which recognises revenue in the statement of profit and loss only when the rendering of services under a contract is completed or substantially completed. Revenue under this method is recognised on completion or substantial completion of the job.

- *Revenue from Interest*: Recognised on time proportion basis
- *Revenue from Royalties*: Recognised on accrual basis in accordance with the terms of the relevant agreement.
- *Revenue from Dividends*: Recognised when right to receive is established
- *Subsequent Uncertainty In Collection*: When the uncertainty relating to collectability arises subsequent to the time of sale or the rendering of services, it is more appropriate to make a separate provision to reflect the uncertainty rather than to adjust the amount of revenue originally recorded.
- *Disclosure*: An enterprise should disclose the circumstances in which revenue recognition has been postponed pending the resolution of significant uncertainties.

## EXAMPLES

- *On sale, buyer takes title and accepts billing but delivery is delayed at buyer's request*: Revenue should be recognised notwithstanding that physical delivery has not been completed.
- *Delivery subject to installations and inspections*: Revenue should not be recognised until the customer accepts delivery and installation and inspection are complete. However, when installation process is very simple, revenue should be recognised. For example, Television sale subject to installation.
- *Sale on approval*: Revenue should not be recognised until the goods have been formally accepted or time for rejection has elapsed or where no time has been fixed, a reasonable time has elapsed.
- *Sales with the condition of 'money back if not completely satisfied'*: It may be appropriate to recognize the sale but to make suitable provision for returns based on previous experience.
- *Consignment sales*: Revenue should not be recognised until the goods are sold to a third party.
- *Installment sales*: Revenue of sale price excluding interest should be recognised on the date of sale.
- *Special order and shipments*: Revenue from such sales should be recognized when the goods are identified and ready for delivery.
- *Where seller concurrently agrees to repurchase the same goods at a later date*: The sale should not be recognised, as this is a financial arrangement.
- *Subscriptions received for publications*: Revenue received or billed should be deferred and recognised either on a straight-line basis over time or where the items delivered vary in value from period to period, revenue should be based on the sales value of the item delivered.

- *Advertisement commission received*: It is recognised when the advertisement appears before public.
- *Tuition fees received*: Should be recognised over the period of instruction.
- Entrance and membership fees Entrance fee is generally capitalized If the membership fee permits only membership and all other services or products are paid for separately, the fee should be recognised when received. If the membership fee entitles the member to services or publications to be provided during the year, it should be recognised on a systematic and rational basis having regard to the timing and nature of all services.
- *Sale of show tickets*: Revenue should be recognised when the event takes place.
- *Guaranteed sales of agricultural crops*: When sale is assured under forward contract or government guarantee, the crops can be recognised at net realizable value although it does not satisfy the criteria of revenue recognition.

*The accounting standard is not applicable for*:

- Revenue arising from construction contracts
- Revenue arising from hire purchase, lease agreements
- Revenue arising from Government grants and subsidies
- Revenue of Insurance companies arising from insurance contracts
- Profit or loss on sale of fixed assets
- Realised or unrealized gains resulting from changes in foreign exchange rates

## ACCOUNTING FOR FIXED ASSETS

This Accounting Standard includes paragraphs set in bold italic type and plain type, which have equal authority. Paragraphs in bold italic type indicate the main principles.

### INTRODUCTION

Financial statements disclose certain information relating to fixed assets. In many enterprises these assets are grouped into various categories, such as land, buildings, plant and machinery, vehicles, furniture and fittings, goodwill, patents, trade marks and designs.

This standard does not deal with the specialised aspects of accounting for fixed assets that arise under a comprehensive system reflecting the effects of changing prices but applies to financial statements prepared on historical cost basis.

*This standard does not deal with accounting for the following items to which special considerations apply*:

- Forests, plantations and similar regenerative natural resources;

- Wasting assets including mineral rights, expenditure on the exploration for and extraction of minerals, oil, natural gas and similar non-regenerative resources;
- Expenditure on real estate development; and
- Livestock.

Expenditure on individual items of fixed assets used to develop or maintain the activities covered in (i) to (iv) above, but separable from those activities, are to be accounted for in accordance with this Standard. This standard does not cover the allocation of the depreciable amount of fixed assets to future periods since this subject is dealt with in Accounting Standard 6 on 'Depreciation Accounting'. This standard does not deal with the treatment of government grants and subsidies, and assets under leasing rights. It makes only a brief reference to the capitalisation of borrowing costs and to assets acquired in an amalgamation or merger. These subjects require more extensive consideration than can be given within this Standard.

***Definitions***

*The following terms are used in this Standard with the meanings specified*:

- Fixed asset is an asset held with the intention of being used for the purpose of producing or providing goods or services and is not held for sale in the normal course of business.
- Fair market value is the price that would be agreed to in an open and unrestricted market between knowledgeable and willing parties dealing at arm's length who are fully informed and are not under any compulsion to transact.
- Gross book value of a fixed asset is its historical cost or other amount substituted for historical cost in the books of account or financial statements. When this amount is shown net of accumulated depreciation, it is termed as net book value.

## EXPLANATION

Fixed assets often comprise a significant portion of the total assets of an enterprise, and therefore are important in the presentation of financial position. Furthermore, the determination of whether an expenditure represents an asset or an expense can have a material effect on an enterprise's reported results of operations.

## IDENTIFICATION OF FIXED ASSETS

The definition in paragraph 6.1 gives criteria for determining whether items are to be classified as fixed assets. Judgement is required in applying the criteria to specific circumstances or specific types of enterprises. It may be appropriate to aggregate individually insignificant items, and to apply the criteria to the aggregate value. An enterprise may decide to expense an item which could otherwise have been included as fixed asset, because the amount of the expenditure is not material. Stand-by equipment and servicing equipment are normally capitalised.

Machinery spares are usually charged to the profit and loss statement as and when consumed. However, if such spares can be used only in connection with an item of fixed asset and their use is expected to be irregular, it may be appropriate to allocate the total cost on a systematic basis over a period not exceeding the useful life of the principal item.

In certain circumstances, the accounting for an item of fixed asset may be improved if the total expenditure thereon is allocated to its component parts, provided they are in practice separable, and estimates are made of the useful lives of these components.

For example, rather than treat an aircraft and its engines as one unit, it may be better to treat the engines as a separate unit if it is likely that their useful life is shorter than that of the aircraft as a whole.

## COMPONENTS OF COST

The cost of an item of fixed asset comprises its purchase price, including import duties and other non-refundable taxes or levies and any directly attributable cost of bringing the asset to its working condition for its intended use; any trade discounts and rebates are deducted in arriving at the purchase price.

*Examples of directly attributable costs are*:

- Site preparation;
- Initial delivery and handling costs;
- Installation cost, such as special foundations for plant; and
- Professional fees, for example fees of architects and engineers.

The cost of a fixed asset may undergo changes subsequent to its acquisition or construction on account of exchange fluctuations, price adjustments, changes in duties or similar factors.

Administration and other general overhead expenses are usually excluded from the cost of fixed assets because they do not relate to a specific fixed asset. However, in some circumstances, such expenses as are specifically attributable to construction of a project or to the acquisition of a fixed asset or bringing it to its working condition, may be included as part of the cost of the construction project or as a part of the cost of the fixed asset.

The expenditure incurred on start-up and commissioning of the project, including the expenditure incurred on test runs and experimental production, is usually capitalised as an indirect element of the construction cost. However, the expenditure incurred after the plant has begun commercial production, *i.e.*, production intended for sale or captive consumption, is not capitalised and is treated as revenue expenditure even though the contract may stipulate that the plant will not be finally taken over until after the satisfactory completion If the interval between the date a project is ready to commence commercial production and the date at which commercial production actually begins is prolonged, all expenses incurred during this period are charged to the profit and loss statement. However, the expenditure incurred during this period is also sometimes treated as deferred revenue expenditure to be amortised over a period not exceeding 3 to 5 years after the commencement

## SELF-CONSTRUCTED FIXED ASSETS

In arriving at the gross book value of self-constructed fixed assets, the same principles apply as those described in paragraphs 9.1 to 9.5. Included in the gross book value are costs of construction that relate directly to the specific asset and costs that are attributable to the construction activity in general and can be allocated to the specific asset. Any internal profits are eliminated in arriving at such costs.

## NON-MONETARY CONSIDERATION

When a fixed asset is acquired in exchange for another asset, its cost is usually determined by reference to the fair market value of the consideration given. It may be appropriate to consider also the fair market value of the asset acquired if this is more clearly evident. An alternative accounting treatment that is sometimes used for an exchange of assets, particularly when the assets exchanged are similar, is to record the asset acquired at the net book value of the asset given up; in each case an adjustment is made for any balancing receipt or payment of cash or other consideration. When a fixed asset is acquired in exchange for shares or other securities in the enterprise, it is usually recorded at its fair market value, or the fair market value of the securities issued, whichever is more clearly evident.

## IMPROVEMENTS AND REPAIRS

Frequently, it is difficult to determine whether subsequent expenditure related to fixed asset represents improvements that ought to be added to the gross book value or repairs that ought to be charged to the profit and loss statement. Only expenditure that increases the future benefits from the existing asset beyond its previously assessed standard of performance is included in the gross book value, *e.g.,* an increase in capacity. The cost of an addition or extension to an existing asset which is of a capital nature and which becomes an integral part of the existing asset is usually added to its gross book value. Any addition or extension, which has a separate identity and is capable of being used after the existing asset is disposed of, is accounted for separately.

## AMOUNT SUBSTITUTED FOR HISTORICAL COST

Sometimes financial statements that are otherwise prepared on a historical cost basis include part or all of fixed assets at a valuation in substitution for historical costs and depreciation is calculated accordingly. A commonly accepted and preferred method of restating fixed assets is by appraisal, normally undertaken by competent valuers. Other methods sometimes used are indexation and reference to current prices which when applied are cross checked periodically by appraisal method.

The revalued amounts of fixed assets are presented in financial statements either by restating both the gross book value and accumulated depreciation so as to give a net book value equal to the net revalued amount or by restating the net book value by adding therein the net increase on account of revaluation. An upward revaluation does not provide a basis for crediting to the profit and loss statement the accumulated depreciation existing at the date of revaluation. Different bases of valuation are sometimes used in the same financial statements to determine the book value of the separate items within each of the categories of fixed assets or for the different categories of fixed assets.

In such cases, it is necessary to disclose the gross book value included on each basis. Selective revaluation of assets can lead to unrepresentative amounts being reported in financial statements. When revaluations do not cover all the assets of a given class, it is appropriate that the selection of assets to be revalued be made on a systematic basis. For example, an enterprise may revalue a whole class of assets within a unit. It is not appropriate for the revaluation of a class of assets to result in the net book value of that class being greater than the recoverable amount of the assets of that class. An increase in net book value arising on revaluation of fixed assets is normally credited directly to owner's interests under the heading of revaluation reserves and is regarded as not available for distribution.

A decrease in net book value arising on revaluation of fixed assets is charged to profit and loss statement except that, to the extent that such a decrease is considered to be related to a previous increase on revaluation that is included in revaluation reserve, it is sometimes charged against that earlier increase. It sometimes happens that an increase to be recorded is a reversal of a previous decrease arising on revaluation which has been charged to profit and loss statement in which case the increase is credited to profit and loss statement to the extent that it offsets the previously recorded decrease.

## RETIREMENTS AND DISPOSALS

An item of fixed asset is eliminated from the financial statements on disposal. Items of fixed assets that have been retired from active use and are held for disposal are stated at the lower of their net book value and net realisable value and are shown separately in the financial statements. Any expected loss is recognised immediately in the profit and loss statement. In historical cost financial statements, gains or losses arising on disposal are generally recognised in the profit and loss statement.

On disposal of a previously revalued itemof fixed asset, the difference between net disposal proceeds and the net book value is normally charged or credited to the profit and loss statement except that, to the extent such a loss is related to an increase which was previously recorded as a credit to revaluation reserve and which has not been subsequently reversed or utilised, it is charged directly to that account. The amount standing in revaluation reserve following the retirement or disposal of an asset which relates to that asset may be transferred to general reserve.

## VALUATION OF FIXED ASSETS IN SPECIAL CASES

In the case of fixed assets acquired on hire purchase terms, although legal ownership does not vest in the enterprise, such assets are recorded at their cash value, which, if not readily available, is calculated by assuming an appropriate rate of interest. They are shown in the balance sheet with an appropriate narration to indicate that the enterprise does not have full ownership thereof.

Where an enterprise owns fixed assets jointly with others (otherwise than as a partner in a firm), the extent of its share in such assets, and the proportion in the original cost, accumulated depreciation and written down value are stated in the balance sheet.

Alternatively, the pro rata cost of such jointly owned assets is grouped together with similar fully owned assets. Details of such jointly owned assets are indicated separately in the fixed assets register. Where several assets are purchased for a consolidated price, the consideration is apportioned to the various assets on a fair basis as determined by competent valuers.

## FIXED ASSETS OF SPECIAL TYPES

Goodwill, in general, is recorded in the books only when some consideration in money or money's worth has been paid for it. Whenever a business is acquired for a price (payable either in cash or in shares or otherwise) which is in excess of the value of the net assets of the business taken over, the excess is termed as 'goodwill'. Goodwill arises from business connections, trade name or reputation of an enterprise or from other intangible benefits enjoyed by an enterprise. As a matter of financial prudence, goodwill is written off over a period. However, many enterprises do not write off goodwill and retain it as an asset.

## DISCLOSURE

Certain specific disclosures on accounting for fixed assets are already required by Accounting Standard 1 on 'Disclosure of Accounting Policies' and Accounting Standard 6 on 'Depreciation Accounting'.

*Further disclosures that are sometimes made in financial statements include*:

- Gross and net book values of fixed assets at the beginning and end of an accounting period showing additions, disposals, acquisitions and other movements;

- Expenditure incurred on account of fixed assets in the course of construction or acquisition; and
- Revalued amounts substituted for historical costs of fixed assets, the method adopted to compute the revalued amounts, the nature of any indices used, the year of any appraisal made, and whether an external valuer was involved, in case where fixed assets are stated at revalued amounts.

## ACCOUNTING FOR GOVERNMENT GRANTS

This Accounting Standard includes paragraphs set in bold italic type and plain type, which have equal authority. Paragraphs in bold italic type indicate the main principles.

### INTRODUCTION

This Standard deals with accounting for government grants. Government grants are sometimes called by other names such as subsidies, cash incentives, duty drawbacks, etc.

*This Standard does not deal with*:

- The special problems arising in accounting for government grants in financial statements reflecting the effects of changing prices or in supplementary information of a similar nature;
- Government assistance other than in the formof government grants;
- Government participation in the ownership of the enterprise.

#### *Definitions*

*The following terms are used in this Standard with the meanings specified*:

- Government refers to government, government agencies and similar bodies whether local, national or international.
- Government grants are assistance by government in cash or kind to an enterprise for past or future compliance with certain conditions. They exclude those forms of government assistance which cannot reasonably have a value placed upon them and transactions with government which cannot be distinguished from the normal trading transactions of the enterprise.

### EXPLANATION

The receipt of government grants by an enterprise is significant for preparation of the financial statements for two reasons. Firstly, if a government grant has been received, an appropriate method of accounting therefor is necessary. Secondly, it is desirable to give an indication of the extent to which the enterprise has benefited from such grant during the reporting period. This facilitates comparison of an enterprise's financial statements with those of prior periods and with those of other enterprises.

### *Accounting Treatment of Government Grants*

### *Capital Approach versus Income Approach*

Two broad approaches may be followed for the accounting treatment of government grants: the 'capital approach', under which a grant is treated as part of shareholders' funds, and the 'income approach', under which a grant is taken to income over one or more periods.

*Those in support of the 'capital approach' argue as follows*:

- Many government grants are in the nature of promoters' contribution, *i.e.*, they are given with reference to the total investment in an undertaking or by way of contribution towards its total capital outlay and no repayment is ordinarily expected in the case of such grants. These should, therefore, be credited directly to shareholders' funds.
- It is inappropriate to recognise government grants in the profit and loss statement, since they are not earned but represent an incentive provided by government without related costs.

*Arguments in support of the 'income approach' are as follows*:

- Government grants are rarely gratuitous. The enterprise earns them through compliance with their conditions and meeting the envisaged obligations. They should therefore be taken to income and matched with the associated costs which the grant is intended to compensate.
- As income tax and other taxes are charges against income, it is logical to deal also with government grants, which are an extension of fiscal policies, in the profit and loss statement.
- In case grants are credited to shareholders' funds, no correlation is done between the accounting treatment of the grant and the accounting treatment of the expenditure to which the grant relates.

It is generally considered appropriate that accounting for government grant should be based on the nature of the relevant grant. Grants which have the characteristics similar to those of promoters' contribution should be treated as part of shareholders' funds. Income approach may be more appropriate in the case of other grants.

It is fundamental to the 'income approach' that government grants be recognised in the profit and loss statement on a systematic and rational basis over the periods necessary to match them with the related costs. Income recognition of government grants on a receipts basis is not in accordance with the accrual accounting assumption.

In most cases, the periods over which an enterprise recognises the costs or expenses related to a government grant are readily ascertainable and thus grants in recognition of specific expenses are taken to income in the same period as the relevant expenses.

### *Recognition of Government Grants*

*Government grants available to the enterprise are considered for inclusion in accounts:*

- Where there is reasonable assurance that the enterprise will comply with the conditions attached to them; and
- Where such benefits have been earned by the enterprise and it is reasonably certain that the ultimate collection will be made.

Mere receipt of a grant is not necessarily a conclusive evidence that conditions attaching to the grant have been or will be fulfilled. An appropriate amount in respect of such earned benefits, estimated on a prudent basis, is credited to income for the year even though the actual amount of such benefits may be finally settled and received after the end of the relevant accounting period. A contingency related to a government grant, arising after the grant has been recognised, is treated in accordance with Accounting Standard (AS) 4, Contingencies and Events Occurring After the Balance Sheet Date. In certain circumstances, a government grant is awarded for the purpose of giving immediate financial support to an enterprise rather than as an incentive to undertake specific expenditure.

Such grants may be confined to an individual enterprise and may not be available to a whole class of enterprises. These circumstances may warrant taking the grant to income in the period in which the enterprise qualifies to receive it, as an extraordinary item if appropriate. Government grants may become receivable by an enterprise as compensation for expenses or losses incurred in a previous accounting period. Such a grant is recognised in the income statement of the period in which it becomes receivable, as an extraordinary item if appropriate.

### *Non-monetary Government Grants*

Government grants may take the form of non-monetary assets, such as land or other resources, given at concessional rates. In these circumstances, it is usual to account for such assets at their acquisition cost. Non-monetary assets given free of cost are recorded at a nominal value.

### *Presentation of Grants Related to Specific Fixed Assets*

Grants related to specific fixed assets are government grants whose primary condition is that an enterprise qualifying for them should purchase, construct or otherwise acquire such assets. Other conditions may also be attached restricting the type or location of the assets or the periods during which they are to be acquired or held. Two methods of presentation in financial statements of grants (or the appropriate portions of grants) related to specific fixed assets are regarded as acceptable alternatives.

Under one method, the grant is shown as a deduction from the gross value of the asset concerned in arriving at its book value. The grant is thus recognised in the profit and loss statement over the useful life of a depreciable asset by way of a reduced depreciation charge. Where the whole, or virtually the whole, of the cost of the asset, the asset is shown in the balance sheet at a nominal value.

Under the other method, grants related to depreciable assets are treated as deferred income which is recognised in the profit and loss statement on a systematic and rational basis over the useful life of the asset. Such allocation to income is usually made over the periods and in the proportions in which depreciation on related assets is charged. Grants related to non-depreciable assets are credited to capital reserve under this method, as there is usually no charge to income in respect of such assets.

However, if a grant related to a non-depreciable asset requires the fulfillment of certain obligations, the grant is credited to income over the same period over which the cost of meeting such obligations is charged to income. The deferred income is suitably disclosed in the balance sheet pending its apportionment to profit and loss account. The purchase of assets and the receipt of related grants can cause major movements in the cash flow of an enterprise. For this reason and in order to show the gross investment in assets, such movements are often disclosed as separate items in the statement of changes in financial position regardless of whether or not the grant is deducted from the related asset for the purpose of balance sheet presentation.

***Presentation of Grants Related to Revenue***

Grants related to revenue are sometimes presented as a credit in the profit and loss statement, either separately or under a general heading such as 'Other Income'. Alternatively, they are deducted in reporting the related expense. Supporters of the first method claim that it is inappropriate to net income and expense items and that separation of the grant from the expense facilitates comparison with other expenses not affected by a grant. For the second method, it is argued that the expense might well not have been incurred by the enterprise if the grant had not been available and presentation

***Presentation of Grants of the Nature of Promoters' Contribution***

Where the government grants are of the nature of promoters' contribution, *i.e.*, they are given with reference to the total investment in an undertaking or by way of contribution towards its total capital outlay (for example, central investment subsidy scheme) and no repayment is ordinarily expected in respect thereof, the grants are treated as capital reserve which can be neither distributed as dividend nor considered as deferred income.

***Refund of Government Grants***

Government grants sometimes become refundable because certain conditions are not fulfilled. A government grant that becomes refundable is treated as an extraordinary item. The amount refundable in respect of a government grant related to revenue is applied first against any unamortised deferred credit remaining in respect of the grant. To the extent that the amount refundable exceeds any such deferred credit, or where no deferred credit exists, the amount is charged immediately to profit and loss statement. The amount refundable in respect of a government grant related to a specific fixed asset is recorded by increasing the book value of the asset or by reducing the capital reserve or the deferred income balance, as appropriate, by the amount refundable.

In the first alternative, *i.e.*, where the book value of the asset is increased, depreciation on the revised book value is provided where a grant which is in the nature of promoters' contribution becomes refundable, in part or in full, to the government on non-fulfillment of some specified conditions, the relevant amount recoverable by the government is reduced from the capital reserve.

***Disclosure***

*The following disclosures are appropriate*:

- The accounting policy adopted for government grants, including the methods of presentation in the financial statements;
- The nature and extent of government grants recognised in the financial statements, including grants of non-monetary assets given at a concessional rate or free of cost.

## ACCOUNTING FOR INVESTMENTS

- *Applicability*: Mandatory for all enterprises. Investments are classified as Long Term Investments and Short Term Investments.
- Current Investment is intended to be held for not more than one year and readily realisable.
- Long term Investment is an investment other than a current investment.

The carrying amount of current investments is lower of cost and fair value. It is prudent to carry investments individually at the lower of cost and fair value. But, such comparison can also be made category-wise. The carrying amount of long-term investments is carried at cost.

However, when there is permanent decline in the value of a long-term investment, the carrying amount is reduced to recognize the decline. The carrying amount of long-term investments should be determined on individual basis. Any reduction or reversal of reduction in value of investment is adjusted through P&L A/c.

### COST OF INVESTMENTS

The cost of an investment should include acquisition charges such as brokerage, fees and duties.

*If an investment is acquired*:

- By issue of shares or other securities; then the investments should be valued at the fair value of the issued security. (*i.e.* Issue price determined by statutory authority)
- By exchange of another asset; then the investments should be valued at fair value of the asset given up or asset acquired, whichever is more clearly evident.

***Investment Property***

Investment Property is investment in land or buildings that is not intended to be occupied substantially for use by, or in the operations of, the investing enterprise. An investment property is classified as long-term investment.

***Disposal of Investments***

On disposal, the difference between the carrying amount and the disposal proceeds, net of expenses, is recognized in the profit and loss statement.

***Reclassification of Investments***

Long-term to short-term: Transfers from one class to another class are made at lower of cost and carrying amount at the date of transfer. Current to long-term: Transfers are made at lower of cost and fair value at the date of transfer.

*Disclosure*:

- Accounting policies for determination of carrying amount
- Classification of Investments
- The amounts included in Profit and loss statement
  - Profits or losses on disposal and changes in carrying amount of current and longterm investments
  - Interest, dividends (showing separately dividends from subsidiary) and rentals on investments showing separately such income from current and long term investments.
  - Gross Income should be disclosed (*i.e.* The amount of TDS should be shown under advance taxes paid)
- Aggregate amount of quoted and unquoted investments giving the aggregate market value of quoted investments.

## ACCOUNTING FOR RETIREMENT BENEFITS

The following is the text of Accounting Standard (AS) 15, 'Accounting for Retirement Benefits in the Financial Statements of Employers', issued by the Council of the Institute of Chartered Accountants of India. The Standard will come into effect in respect of accounting periods commencing on or after 1.4.1995 and will be mandatory in nature.2 The 'Statement on the Treatment of Retirement Gratuity in Accounts' issued by the Institute will stand withdrawn from the aforesaid date.

## INTRODUCTION

- This Statement deals with accounting for retirement benefits in the financial statements of employers.
- *Retirement benefits usually consist of:*
  - Provident fund
  - Superannuation/pension
  - Gratuity
  - Leave encashment benefit on retirement
  - Post-retirement health and welfare schemes
  - Other retirement benefits.

This Statement applies to retirement benefits in the form of provident fund, superannuation/pension and gratuity provided by an employer to employees, whether in pursuance of requirements of any law or otherwise. It also applies to retirement benefits in the formof leave encashment benefit, health and welfare schemes and other retirement benefits, if the predominant characteristics of these benefits are the same as those of provident fund, superannuation/pension or gratuity benefit, *i.e.* if such a retirement benefit is in the nature of either a defined contribution scheme or a defined benefit scheme as described in this Statement. This Statement does not apply to those retirement benefits for which the employer's obligation cannot be reasonably estimated, *e.g.*, ad hoc ex-gratia payments made to employees on retirement.

***Definitions***

*The following terms are used in this Statement with the meanings specified:*

- Retirement benefit schemes are arrangements to provide provident fund, superannuation or pension, gratuity, or other benefits to employees on leaving service or retiring or, after an employee's death, to his or her dependants.
- Defined contribution schemes are retirement benefit schemes under which amounts to be paid as retirement benefits are determined by contributions to a fund together with earnings thereon.
- Defined benefit schemes are retirement benefit schemes under which amounts to be paid as retirement benefits are determinable usually by reference to employee's earnings and/or years of service.
- Actuary means an actuary within the meaning of sub-section (1) of section (2) of the Insurance Act, 1938.
- Actuarial valuation is the process used by an actuary to estimate the present value of benefits to be paid under a retirement benefit scheme and the present values of the scheme assets and, sometimes, of future contributions.
- Pay-as-you-go is a method of recognising the cost of retirement benefits only at the time payments are made to employees on, or after, their retirement.

## EXPLANATION

Retirement benefit schemes are normally significant elements of an employer's remuneration package for employees. It is, therefore, important that retirement benefits are properly accounted for and that appropriate disclosures in respect thereof are made in the financial statements of an employer. Provident fund benefit normally involves either creation of a separate trust to which contributions of both employees and employer are made periodically or remittance of such contributions to the employees' provident fund, administered by the Central Government. Superannuation/ pension benefit (hereinafter referred to as 'superannuation benefit') is basically of two types.

- The first type of benefit is known as defined contribution scheme. Under this type of benefit, the employer makes a contribution once a year (or more frequently in some cases) towards a separately created trust fund or to a scheme administered by an insurer. These contributions earn interest and the accumulated balance of contributions and interest is used to pay the retirement benefit to the employee. Superannuation available under defined contribution scheme has relevance to only total of accumulated contributions and interest and bears no relationship, whatsoever, with the final salary or number of years of service put in by an employee. The defined contribution scheme for superannuation/ pension is, in most respects, similar to the provident fund, so far as the accounting treatment is concerned. It also presupposes payment of contributions every year, either once in a year or more frequently.
- The second type of superannuation scheme is the defined benefit scheme. Under this scheme, the benefit payable to the employee is determined with reference to factors such as a percentage of final salary (*e.g.* the average of one, three or five years' salary), number of years of service and the grade of the employee. The contribution required to finance such a scheme is actuarially determined and is generally expressed as a percentage of salary for the entire group of employees covered by the scheme. For defined benefit superannuation/pension schemes, a trust fund can be created or an arrangement can be negotiated with an insurer so that the annual contributions, calculated actuarially, can be made each year. In such a case, benefits to employees on entitlement would be paid by the trust fund or by the insurer. Alternatively, the superannuation benefit can be paid by the employer as and when an employee leaves.

Gratuity benefit is in the nature of a defined benefit. Gratuity can be paid by the employer as and when an employee leaves. Alternatively, a trust fund can be created, or an arrangement can be negotiated with an insurer so that the annual contributions, calculated actuarially, can be made each year. Benefits to employees on entitlement would in such a case be paid by the trust fund or by the insurer. In certain cases, a retirement benefit scheme may stipulate the basis of contributions on which the benefits are determined and, because of this, may appear to be a defined contribution scheme. However, the provisions of the scheme may also result in the employer being responsible for specified benefits or a specified level of benefits. In this case, the scheme is, in substance, a defined benefit scheme and should be accounted for accordingly. While provident fund schemes are generally contributory schemes from the point of view of employees, gratuity schemes are non-contributory.

The superannuation schemes, on the other hand, can be contributory or noncontributory. Defined benefit schemes, especially those that promise benefits related to remuneration at or near retirement, present significant difficulties in the determination of periodic charge to the statement of profit and loss. The extent of an employer's obligation under such schemes is usually uncertain and requires estimation. In estimating the obligation, assumptions may need to be made regarding future conditions and events which are largely outside the employer's control. As a result of various factors that frequently enter into the computation of retirement benefits under defined benefit schemes and the length of the period over which the benefits are earned, allocation problems arise in determining how the costs of the retirement benefits should be recognised in the financial statements of the employer. Furthermore, long-term uncertainties may give rise to adjustments of estimates of earlier years that can be very significant in relation to current service cost.

The cost of retirement benefits to an employer results from receiving services from the employees who are entitled to receive such benefits. Consequently, the cost of retirement benefits is accounted for in the period during which these services are rendered. Accounting for retirement benefit cost only when employees retire or receive benefit payments (*i.e.*, as per pay-as-you-go method) does not achieve the objective of allocation of those costs to the periods in which the services were rendered.

***Funding***

When there is a separate retirement benefit fund, it is sometimes assumed that the amount paid by an employer to the fund during an accounting period provides an appropriate charge to the statement of profit and loss. While, in many cases, the amount funded may provide a reasonable approximation of the amount to be charged to the statement of profit and loss, there is a vital distinction between the periodic funding of retirement benefits and the allocation of the cost of providing these benefits. The objective of funding is to make available amounts to meet future obligations for the payment of retirement benefits. Funding is a financing procedure and in determining the periodical amounts to be funded, the employermay be influenced by such factors as the availability ofmoney and tax considerations. On the other hand, the objective of accounting for the cost of a retirement benefit scheme is to ensure that the cost of benefits is allocated to accounting periods on a systematic basis related to the receipt of the employees' services.

### *Accounting*

In respect of retirement benefits in the form of provident fund and other defined contribution schemes, the contribution payable by the employer for a year is charged to the statement of profit and loss for the year. Thus, besides the amount of contribution paid, a shortfall of the amount of contribution paid compared to the amount payable for the year is also charged to the statement of profit and loss for the year. On the other hand, if contribution paid is in excess of the amount payable for the year, the excess is treated as a pre-payment. In respect of gratuity benefit and other defined benefit schemes, the accounting treatment depends on the type of arrangement which the employer has chosen to make.

- If the employer has chosen to make payment for retirement benefits out of his own funds, an appropriate charge to the statement of profit and loss for the year is made through a provision for the accruing liability. The accruing liability is calculated just as to actuarial valuation. However, many enterprises which employ only a few persons do not calculate the accrued liability by using actuarial methods. They calculate the accrued liability by reference to some other rational method *e.g.* a method based on the assumption that such benefits are payable to all employees at the end of the accounting year.
- In case the liability for retirement benefits is funded through creation of a trust, the cost incurred for the year is determined actuarially. Many employers undertake such valuations every year while others undertake them less frequently, usually once in every three years. If actuarial valuations are conducted every year, the annual accrual of retirement benefit cost can be easily determined. If, however, the actuarial valuations are not conducted annually, the actuary's report specifies the contributions to be made by the employer on annual basis during the inter-valuation period. This annual contribution (which is in addition to the contribution that may be required to finance unfunded past service cost) reflects proper accrual of retirement benefit cost for each of the years during the inter-valuation period and is charged to the statement of profit and loss for each such year.Where the contribution paid during a year is lower than the amount required to be contributed during the year to meet the accrued liability as certified by the actuary, the shortfall

is charged to the statement of profit and loss for the year. Where the contribution paid during a year is in excess of the amount required to be contributed during the year to meet the accrued liability as certified by the actuary, the excess is treated as a prepayment.

- In case the liability for retirement benefits is funded through a scheme administered by an insurer, it is usually considered necessary to obtain an actuarial certificate or a confirmation from the insurer that the contribution payable to the insurer is the appropriate accrual of the liability for the year. Where the contribution paid during a year is lower than the amount required to be contributed during the year to meet the accrued liability as certified by the actuary or confirmed by the insurer, as the case may be, the shortfall is charged to the statement of profit and loss for the year. Where the contribution paid during a year is in excess of the amount required to be contributed during the year to meet the accrued liability as certified by the actuary or confirmed by the insurer, as the case may be, the excess is treated as a pre-payment.

### *Actuarial Principles*

A number of actuarial valuation methods have been developed by the actuarial profession to estimate employer's obligations under defined benefit schemes. While these methods are primarily designed to calculate funding requirements, they are also frequently used to determine retirement benefit costs for accounting purposes. The actuarial method selected for determining accrual of liability and the assumptions made can have a significant effect on the expense to be recorded in each accounting period. Therefore, in carrying out a periodical valuation, an actuary chooses a suitable valuation method and, in consultation with the employer, makes appropriate assumptions about the variable elements affecting the computations.

The assumptions relate to the expected inflow from future contributions and from investments as well as to the expected outgo for benefits. The uncertainty inherent in projecting future trends in rates of inflation, salary levels and earnings on investments are taken into consideration by the actuary in the actuarial valuations by using a set of compatible assumptions. Usually, these projections are extended until the expected date of death of the last pensioner in case of a superannuation scheme, expected date of death etc. of the beneficiary in case of family pension, and expected service in case of gratuity and are, accordingly, long-term.

### *Past Service Cost and Review of Actuarial Assumptions*

An actuarially determined past service cost arises on the introduction of a retirement benefit scheme for existing employees or on the making of improvements to an existing scheme, etc. This cost gives employees credit for benefits for services rendered before the occurrence of one or more of these events. Views differ as to how to account for this cost. One view is that this cost should be recognised as soon as it has been determined.

Others believe that the entitlement giving rise to past service cost is in return for services to be rendered by employees in future and therefore this cost ought to be allocated over the periods during which the services are to be rendered. In making an actuarial valuation, the actuary may sometimes effect a change in the actuarial method used or in the assumptions adopted for determining the retirement benefit costs.

Any alterations in the retirement benefit costs so arising are charged or credited to the statement of profit and loss for the year or, alternatively, spread over a period not more than the expected remaining working lives of the participating employees. A change in the actuarial method used for determining the retirement benefit costs constitutes a change in an accounting policy and is disclosed accordingly.

### *Retired Employees*

When a retirement benefit scheme for retired employees is amended, due to inflation or for other reasons, to provide additional benefits to retired employees, any additional costs are charged to the statement of profit and loss of the year.

### *Disclosures*

In view of the diversity of practices used for accounting of retirement benefits costs, adequate disclosure of method followed in accounting for them is essential for an understanding of the significance of such costs to an employer. Retirement benefit costs are sometimes disclosed separately for statutory compliance. In other cases, they are considered to be an element of employee remuneration and their separate disclosure is not usually made.

## SEGMENTAL REPORTING

- A Business Segment is a distinguishable component of an enterprise that is engaged in providing an individual product or service or a group of related products or services and that is subject to risks and returns that are different from those of other business segments.
- A Geographical Segment is a distinguishable component of an enterprise that is engaged in providing products or services within a particular economic environment and that is subject to risks and returns that are different from those of components operating in other economic environments.
- The risks and returns of an enterprise are both by the geographical location of production or service facilities and other assets of an

enterprise andlocation of its customers. The definition allows geographical segments to be based on any of the two.

- A Reportable Segment is a business segment or a geographical segment identified on the basis of foregoing definitions for which segment information is required to be disclosed by the standard.
- Enterprise Revenue is revenue is revenue from sales to external customers as reported in the statement of profit and loss. (*i.e.* Sales made to external customers by all segments)
- Segment Revenue is the aggregate of revenue directly attributable to segments revenue reasonably allocated to segment; and revenue from transactions with other segments.
- Segment Expense is the aggregate of operating expense directly attributable to segment expenses reasonably allocated to segment; and expenses relating to transactions with other segments. However, Segment revenue/expense does not include:
  - Extraordinary items as defined in AS-5
  - Interest or dividend (including earned/incurred on loans to other segment) unless the operations of the segment are primarily of a financial nature
  - Gains on sales of investments or on extinguishments of debt (Capital gain/loss) unless the operations of the segment are primarily of a financial nature.
  - General administration expenses, head office expenses and other expenses that arise at the enterprise level and relate to the enterprise as a whole.
- Segment Result is segment revenue less segment expenses.
- Segment Assets are those operating assets that are employed by a segment in its operating activities and that either are directly attributable the segment or can be allocated to the segment on a reasonable basis.
- Segment Liabilities are those operating liabilities that result from operating activities and that either are directly attributable the segment or can be allocated to the segment on a reasonable basis.

## PRIMARY SEGMENT AND SECONDARY SEGMENT

One among the two, Business Segment and Geographical Segment, is primary segment and other becomes secondary segment. The reporting requirements for the primary and secondary segments are different.

## BASIS FOR IDENTIFYING PRIMARY AND SECONDARY SEGMENTS

Risks and returns are the main criteria for identifying primary and secondary segments.

- If the risks and returns of an enterprise are affected predominantly by differences in the products, business segments are recognized as primary segments and geographical segments as secondary segments and vice versa.
- If the risks and returns of an enterprise are affected both by differences in the products as well as differences in the locations in which it operates, then the enterprise should use business segments as its primary segment and geographical segment as its secondary segment.
- If risks and returns of an enterprise are affected neither by differences in products/services nor by differences in geographical areas of operations, the management may elect any of the two as primary with other being secondary segment.

## REPORTABLE SEGMENTS

*A business segment or geographical segment should be identified as reportable segment if*:

- Its revenue from sales to external customers and from transactions with other segments is 10% or more of the total revenue, external and internal, of all segments; or
- Its segment result, whether profit or loss, is 10% or more of- the combined result of all segments in profit, or the combined result of all segments in loss, whichever is greater in absolute amount; or
- Its segment assets are 10% or more of the total assets of all segments.

A business/reportable segment that is not a reportable segment, may be recognized as reportable segment despite its size at the discretion of the management of the enterprise. If total external revenue attributable to reportable segments constitutes less than 75% of the total enterprise revenue, additional segments should be identified as reportable segments, even if they do not meet 10% thresholds, until at least 75% per cent of the total enterprise revenue is included in reportable segments. A segment identified as a reportable segment in the immediately preceding period because it satisfied the relevant 10% thresholds should continue to be a reportable segment for the current period notwithstanding that its revenue, result, and assets no longer meet the 10% thresholds.

## PRIMARY REPORTING FORMAT

*The following disclosures are required for each reportable segment of primary segment*:

- Segment revenue, (with classification of external and internal)
- Segment result
- Total carrying amount of segment assets
- Total amount of segment liabilities
- Total cost incurred during the period to acquire segment assets

- Depreciation and amortisation recognized as expense, and
- Total non cash expenses other than Dep. And amortisation recognized as expense.

Disclosers required pursuant to clause (6) and (7) above, need not be made in respect of a segment, if the enterprise reports cash flows arising from operating, investing and financing activities for such segment. An enterprise should present a reconciliation between the information disclosed for reportable segments and aggregated information in the enterprise financial statements (in respect of clause 1 to 4 above)

**SECONDARY REPORTING FORMAT**

***Where Primary Segments are Business Segments***

Segment revenue from external customers for each geographical segment whose revenue from sales to external customers is 10% or more of enterprise's revenue; The total carrying amount of segment assets for each geographical segment whose segment assets is 10% or more of the total assets of all geographical segments; New assets acquired for each geographical segment whose segment assets is 10% or more of the total assets of all geographical segments.

***Where Primary Segments are Geographical Segments based on Location to Customers***

If locations of assets are different from locations of customers, then the enterprise is required to report the following segment information for each asset based geographical segment whose revenue from sales to external customers is 1% or more of enterprise revenue or whose segment assets are 10% or more of total enterprise assets

- The total carrying amount of segment assets by geographical location of the assets; and
- New segment assets acquired by location of assets.

***Other Disclosures***

In measuring and reporting segment revenue from transactions with other segments, inter-segment transfers should be measured on the basis that the enterprise actually used to price those transfers. The transfer-pricing basis should be disclosed in the financial statements. An enterprise should indicate the types of products and services included in each reported business segment and indicate the composition of each reported geographical segment, primary and secondary, if not otherwise disclosed in the financial statements.

## BORROWING COSTS

This Accounting Standard includes paragraphs set in bold italic type and plain type, which have equal authority. Paragraphs in bold italic type indicate the main principles.

## OBJECTIVE

The objective of this Standard is to prescribe the accounting treatment for borrowing costs.

## SCOPE

- This Standard should be applied in accounting for borrowing costs.
- This Standard does not deal with the actual or imputed cost of owners' equity, including preference share capital not classified as a liability.

## DEFINITIONS

*The following terms are used in this Standard with the meanings specified*:

- Borrowing costs are interest and other costs incurred by an enterprise in connection with the borrowing of funds.
- A qualifying asset is an asset that necessarily takes a substantial period of time to get ready for its intended use or sale.

*Borrowing costs may include*:

- Interest and commitment charges on bank borrowings and other short-term and long-term borrowings;
- Amortisation of discounts or premiums relating to borrowings;
- Amortisation of ancillary costs incurred in connection with the arrangement of borrowings;
- Finance charges in respect of assets acquired under finance leases or under other similar arrangements; and
- Exchange differences arising from foreign currency borrowings to the extent that they are regarded as an adjustment to interest costs.

## RECOGNITION

Borrowing costs that are directly attributable to the acquisition, construction or production of a qualifying asset should be capitalised as part of the cost of that asset. The amount of borrowing costs eligible for capitalisation should be determined in accordance with this Standard. Other borrowing costs should be recognised as an expense in the period in which they are incurred. Borrowing costs are capitalised as part of the cost of a qualifying asset when it is probable that they will result in future economic benefits to the enterprise and the costs can be measured reliably. Other borrowing costs are recognised as an expense in the period in which they are incurred.

### *Borrowing Costs Eligible for Capitalisation*

The borrowing costs that are directly attributable to the acquisition, construction or production of a qualifying asset are those borrowing costs that would have been avoided if the expenditure on the qualifying asset had not been made. When an enterprise borrows funds specifically for the purpose of obtaining a particular qualifying asset, the borrowing costs that directly relate to that qualifying asset can be readily identified. It may be difficult to identify a direct relationship between particular borrowings and a qualifying asset and to determine the borrowings that could otherwise have been avoided. Such a difficulty occurs, for example, when the financing activity of an enterprise is co-ordinated centrally or when a range of debt instruments are used to borrow funds at varying rates of interest and such borrowings are not readily identifiable with a specific qualifying asset.

As a result, the determination of the amount of borrowing costs that are directly attributable to the acquisition, construction or production of a qualifying asset is often difficult and the exercise of judgement is required. To the extent that funds are borrowed specifically for the purpose of obtaining a qualifying asset, the amount of borrowing costs eligible for capitalisation on that asset should be determined as the actual borrowing costs incurred on that borrowing during the period less any income on the temporary investment of those borrowings.

The financing arrangements for a qualifying asset may result in an enterprise obtaining borrowed funds and incurring associated borrowing costs before some or all of the funds are used for expenditure on the qualifying asset. In such circumstances, the funds are often temporarily invested pending their expenditure on the qualifying asset.

In determining the amount of borrowing costs eligible for capitalisation during a period, any income earned on the temporary investment of those borrowings is deducted from the borrowing costs incurred. To the extent that funds are borrowed generally and used for the purpose of obtaining a qualifying asset, the amount of borrowing costs eligible for capitalisation should be determined by applying a capitalisation rate to the expenditure on that asset. The capitalisation rate should be the weighted average of the borrowing costs applicable to the borrowings of the enterprise that are outstanding during the period, other than borrowings made specifically for the purpose of obtaining a qualifying asset. The amount of borrowing costs capitalised during a period should not exceed the amount of borrowing costs incurred during that period.

## EXCESS OF THE CARRYING AMOUNT OF THE QUALIFYING ASSET OVER RECOVERABLE AMOUNT

When the carrying amount or the expected ultimate cost of the qualifying asset exceeds its recoverable amount or net realisable value, the carrying amount is written down or written off in accordance with the requirements of other Accounting Standards. In certain circumstances, the amount of the write-down or write-off is written back in accordance with those other Accounting Standards.

***Commencement of Capitalisation***

*The capitalisation of borrowing costs as part of the cost of a qualifying asset should commence when all the following conditions are satisfied:*

- Expenditure for the acquisition, construction or production of a qualifying asset is being incurred;
- Borrowing costs are being incurred; and
- Activities that are necessary to prepare the asset for its intended use or sale are in progress.

Expenditure on a qualifying asset includes only such expenditure that has resulted in payments of cash, transfers of other assets or the assumption of interest-bearing liabilities. Expenditure is reduced by any progress payments received and grants received in connection with the asset. The average carrying amount of the asset during a period, including borrowing costs previously capitalised, is normally a reasonable approximation of the expenditure to which the capitalisation rate is applied in that period. The activities necessary to prepare the asset for its intended use or sale encompass more than the physical construction of the asset.

They include technical and administrative work prior to the commencement of physical construction, such as the activities associated with obtaining permits prior to the commencement of the physical construction. However, such activities exclude the holding of an asset when no production or development that changes the asset's condition is taking place. For example, borrowing costs incurred while land is under development are capitalised during the period in which activities related to the development are being undertaken. However, borrowing costs incurred while land acquired for building purposes is held without any associated development activity do not qualify for capitalisation.

***Suspension of Capitalisation***

Capitalisation of borrowing costs should be suspended during extended periods in which active development is interrupted. Borrowing costs may be incurred during an extended period in which the activities necessary to prepare an asset for its intended use or sale are interrupted. Such costs are costs of holding partially completed assets and do not qualify for capitalisation.

However, capitalisation of borrowing costs is not normally suspended during a period when substantial technical and administrative work is being carried out. Capitalisation of borrowing costs is also not suspended when a temporary delay is a necessary part of the process of getting an asset ready for its intended use or sale. For example, capitalisation continues during the extended period needed for inventories to mature or the extended period during which high water levels delay construction of a bridge, if such high water levels are common during the construction period in the geographic region involved.

### *Cessation of Capitalisation*

Capitalisation of borrowing costs should cease when substantially all the activities necessary to prepare the qualifying asset for its intended use or sale are complete. An asset is normally ready for its intended use or sale when its physical construction or production is complete even though routine administrative work might still continue. If minor modifications, such as the decoration of a property to the user's specification, are all that are outstanding, this indicates that substantially all the activities are complete.

When the construction of a qualifying asset is completed in parts and a completed part is capable of being used while construction continues for the other parts, capitalisation of borrowing costs in relation to a part should cease when substantially all the activities necessary to prepare that part for its intended use or sale are complete. A business park comprising several buildings, each of which can be used individually, is an example of a qualifying asset for which each part is capable of being used while construction continues for the other parts. An example of a qualifying asset that needs to be complete before any part can be used is an industrial plant involving several processes which are carried out in sequence at different parts of the plant within the same site, such as a steel mill.

## DISCLOSURE

*The financial statements should disclose*:

- The accounting policy adopted for borrowing costs; and
- The amount of borrowing costs capitalised during the period.

# RELATED PARTY DISCLOSURES

Related party is considered to be related if at any time during the reporting period one party has the ability to control the other party or exercise significant influence over the other party in making financial and/or operating decisions. The following related party relationship are covered under AS-18:

Enterprises that directly, or indirectly through one or more intermediaries, control, or are controlled by, or are under common control with the reporting enterprise (*e.g.* Holding companies, subsidiaries and fellow subsidiaries)

Associates and joint ventures of the reporting enterprise Individuals owning, directly or indirectly, an interest in the voting power of the reporting enterprise that gives them control or significant influence over the enterprise, and relatives of any such individual; Key management personnel and relatives of such personnel; and Enterprises over which any person described in (4) or (5) is able to exercise significant influence.

## KEY MANAGEMENT PERSONNEL

Those persons who have the authority and responsibility for planning, directing and controlling the activities of the reporting enterprise.

*The following are not deemed to be related party*:

- Two companies simply because they have common director
- A single customer/supplier with whom an enterprise transacts a significant volume of business merely by virtue of the resulting economic dependence
- Providers of finance
- Trade Unions
- Public Utilities
- Government departments and Government sponsored bodies

***Disclosure***

If there have been transactions between related parties, during the existence of a related party relationships, the reporting enterprise should disclose the followings:

- Name of the transacting related party
- Description of the relationship
- Description of nature of transaction
- Volume of transaction (Amount wise or proportion wise)
- Any other information necessary for understanding financial statements
- Outstanding (Amount wise or proportion wise) and any provision for doubtful debt due from such party
- Amounts written off or written back in respect of debts due from or to related parties.

*The followings are the examples of the related party transactions*:

- Purchase or sale of goods
- Rendering or receiving services
- Purchases or sales of fixed assets
- Licence agreements
- Leasing or hire purchase agreements
- Guarantees and collaterals
- Management contracts including for deputation of employees.

## LEASE

A lease is a contract calling for the lessee (user) to pay the lessor (owner) for use of an asset. A rental agreement is a lease in which the asset is tangible property. Leases for intangible property could include use of a computer programme (similar to a license, but with different provisions), or use of a radio frequency (such as a contract with a cell-phone provider).

A gross lease is when the tenant pays a flat rental amount and the landlord pays for all property charges regularly incurred by the ownership from lawnmowers and washing machines to handbags and jewelry. A cancelable lease is a lease that may be terminated solely by the lessee or solely by the lessor. A non-cancelable lease is a lease that cannot be so terminated. In common parlance, "lease" may connote a non-cancelable lease, whereas "rental agreement" may connote a cancelable lease.

The lease will either provide specific provisions regarding the responsibilities and rights of the lessee and lessor, or there will be automatic provisions as a result of local law. In general, by paying the negotiated fee to the lessor, the lessee (also called a tenant) has possession and use (the rental) of the leased property to the exclusion of the lessor and all others except with the invitation of the tenant. The most common form of real property lease is a residential rental agreement between landlord and tenant. The relationship between the tenant and the landlord is called a tenancy, and the right to possession by the tenant is sometimes called a leasehold interest. A lease can be for a fixed period of time (called the term of the lease) but (depending on the terms of the lease) may be terminated sooner.

A lease should be contrasted to a license, which may entitle a person (called a licensee) to use property, but which is subject to termination at the will of the owner of the property (called the licensor). An example of a licensor/ licensee relationship is a parking lot owner and a person who parks a vehicle in the parking lot. A license may be seen in the form of a ticket to a baseball game. The difference would be that if possession is subject to ongoing, recurrent payments and is generally not subject to termination except for misconduct or nonpayment, it is a lease; if it's a one-time entrance onto someone else's property, it's probably a license. The seminal difference between a lease and a license is that a lease generally provides for regular periodic payments during its term and a specific ending date. If a contract has no ending date then it may be in the form of a perpetual license and still not be a lease.

Under normal circumstances, owners of property are at liberty to do what they want with their property (for a lawful purpose), including dealing with it or handing over possession of the property to a tenant for a limited period of time. If an owner has surrendered possession to another (*i.e.*, the tenant) then any interference with the quiet enjoyment of the property by the tenant in lawful possession is itself unlawful.

Similar principles apply to real property as well as to personal property, though the terminology would be different. Similar principles apply to sub-leasing, that is the leasing by a tenant in possession to a sub-tenant. The right to sub-lease can be expressly prohibited by the main lease, sometimes referred to as a "master lease".

## HISTORY

Over the centuries, leases have served many purposes and the nature of legal regulation has varied just as to those purposes and the social and economic conditions of the times. Leases, for example, were mainly used for agricultural purposes until the late 18th century and early 19th century when the growth of cities in industrialised countries had made leases an important form of landholding in urban areas.

The modern law of landlord and tenant in common law jurisdictions retains the influence of the common law and, particularly, the laissez-faire philosophy that dominated the law of contract and property law in the 19th century. With the growth of consumerism, consumer protection legislation recognised that common law principles, which assume equal bargaining power between the contracting parties, create hardships when that assumption is inaccurate. Consequently reformers have emphasised the need to assess residential tenancy laws in terms of protection they provide to tenants. Legislation to protect tenants is now common.

## GENERAL TERMS

A Lease is a legal contract, and thus enforceable by all parties under the Contract Laws of the applicable jurisdiction. But, since it also represents a conveyance of possessory rights to real estate, it is a hybrid sort of contract that involves qualities of a deed. Some specific kinds of leases may have specific clauses required by statute depending upon the property being lease, and/or the jurisdiction in which the agreement was signed or the residence of the parties.

*Common elements of a lease include*:

- Names of the parties of the agreement.
- The starting date and duration of the agreement.
- Identifies the specific object (by street address, VIN, or make/ model,serial number) being leased.
- Provides conditions for renewal or non-renewal.
- Has a specific consideration (a lump sum, or periodic payments) for granting the use of this object.
- Has provisions for a security deposit and terms for its return.
- May have a specific list of conditions which are therein described as Default Conditions and specific Remedies.
- May have other specific conditions placed upon the parties such as
  - Need to provide insurance for loss
  - Restrictive use
  - Which party is responsible for maintenance

All kinds of personal property (*e.g.*: cars, furniture...) or real property (raw land, apartments, single family homes, and business property (including wholesale and retail)) may be leased. As a result of the lease, the owner (lessor) grants the use of the stated property to the lessee.

## TYPES OF TENANCIES

### *Fixed-term Tenancy or Tenancy for Years*

A fixed-term tenancy or tenancy for years lasts for some fixed period of time. It has a definite beginning date and a definite ending date. Despite the name "tenancy for years", such a tenancy can last for any period of time—even a tenancy for one week may be called a tenancy for years. At Common law the duration did not need to be certain, but could be conditioned upon the happening of some event, (*e.g.*, "until the crops are ready for harvest" or "until the war is over"). In many jurisdictions that possibility has been partially or totally abolished.

A fixed term tenancy comes to an end automatically when the fixed term runs out or, in the case of a tenancy that ends on the happening of an event, when the event occurs. If a holdover tenant remains on the property after the termination of the lease, s/he may become a tenant at sufferance because the lessor/landlord has suffered (or allowed) the tenant to remain as a tenant instead of evicting him or her. Such a tenancy is generally "at will," meaning the tenant or the landlord may terminate it at any time, upon the providing of proper statutory notice.

***Periodic Tenancy***

A periodic tenancy also known as a tenancy from year to year, month to month, or week to week, is an estate that exists for some period of time determined by the term of the payment of rent. An oral lease for a tenancy of years that violates the Statute of Frauds (by committing to a lease of more than—depending on the jurisdiction—one year without being in writing) may actually create a periodic tenancy, depending on the laws of the jurisdiction where the leased premises are located. In many jurisdictions the "default" tenancy, where the parties have not explicitly specified a different arrangement, and where none is presumed under local or business custom, is a month-to-month tenancy.

Either the landlord or the tenant may terminate a periodic tenancy when the period or term is nearing completion, by giving notice to the other party as required by statute or case law in the jurisdiction. Neither landlord nor tenant may terminate a periodic tenancy before the period has ended, without incurring an obligation to pay for the months remaining on the lease. Either party must give notice if it intends to terminate a tenancy from year to year, and the amount of notice is either specified by the lease or by state statute. Notice is usually, but not alway, at least one month, especially for the year to year periodic tenancy.

Durations of less than a year must typically receive notice equal to the period of the tenancy - for example, the landlord must give a month's notice to terminate a tenancy from month to month.

However, many jurisdictions have increased these required notice periods, and some have reduced the capacity of a landlord to use them drastically. For jurisdictions that have local rent control laws, a landlord's ability to terminate a residential tenancy is substantially reduced. For example, in California, the cities of Los Angeles, Santa Monica, West Hollywood, San

Francisco, and Oakland have "rent stabilization ordinances" that limit a landlord's ability to terminate a periodic tenancy, among other restrictions. The notice must also state the effective date of termination, which, in some jurisdictions, must be on the last day of the payment period.

In other words, if a month-to-month tenancy began on the 15th of the month, in a jurisdiction with a last day requirement the termination could not be effective on the 20th of the following month, even though this would give the tenant more than the required one month's notice.

***Tenancy at Will***

A tenancy at will is a tenancy which either the landlord or the tenant may terminate at any time by giving reasonable notice. Unlike a periodic tenancy, it isn't associated with a time period. It may last for many years, but it could be ended at any time by either the lessor or the lessee for any reason, or for no reason at all. Proper notice, as always with landlord/tenant law, must be given, as set forth in the state's statutes. If there is no formal lease, the tenancy at will is the one that usually exists. In rare cases it may occur where the tenancy is not for consideration.

Under the modern common law, a tenancy at will without compensation is very rare, partly because it comes about only if the parties expressly agree that the tenancy is for no rent, commonly where a family member is allowed to live in a home (a nominal consideration may be required) without any formal arrangements. In most residential tenancies for a fixed term, for consideration, the tenant may not be removed except for cause, even if there is no written lease. Many residential leases convert to "at will" tenancy subject to 30-days notice.

Alternatively, a tenancy at will (without a specific time limit) may exist for a temporary period where a tenant wishes to take possession of a property and the landlord agrees, but there is insufficient time in which to negotiate and complete a new lease. In this case, the tenancy at will is terminated as soon as a new lease is negotiated and signed. The parties may also agree on the basis that if the parties fail to enter into a new lease within a reasonable time period, then the tenant must vacate the premises.

If a lease exists at the sole discretion of the landlord, the law of the jurisdiction may imply that the tenant is granted, by operation of law, a reciprocal right to terminate the lease at will. However, a lease that explicitly exists at the will of the tenant (*e.g.* "for as long as the tenant desires to live on this land") generally does not imply that the landlord may terminate the lease; rather, such language may be interpreted as granting the tenant a life estate or even a fee simple.

*A tenancy at will is broken, again by operation of law, if the*:

- Tenant commits waste against the property;
- Tenant attempts to assign the tenancy;
- Tenant uses the property to operate a criminal enterprise;

- Landlord transfers his/her interest in the property;
- Landlord leases the property to another person;
- Tenant or landlord dies.

The specifics of these rules differ from jurisdiction to jurisdiction. Subject to any notice required by law, a tenancy at will also comes to an end when either the landlord or the tenant acts inconsistently with a tenancy. For example, the changing of locks by the landlord is an indication of the end of the tenancy, as is the vacation of the premises by the tenant. However, in some jurisdictions, such as California, a landlord is prohibited from using a "self help" remedy, such as changing the locks, to terminate a tenancy, particularly a residential tenancy. Doing so may constitute a "constructive eviction" and expose the landlord to civil and criminal liability.

### *Tenancy at Sufferance*

A tenancy at sufferance (sometimes called a holdover tenancy) exists when a tenant remains in possession of a property after the expiration of a lease, and until the landlord acts to eject the tenant from the property. Although the tenant is technically a trespasser at this point, and possession of this type is not a true estate in land, authorities recognize the condition in order to hold the tenant liable for rent. The landlord may evict such a tenant at any time, and without notice.

The landlord may also impose a new lease on the holdover tenant. For a residential tenancy, this new tenancy is month to month. For a commercial tenancy of more than a year, the new tenancy is year to year; otherwise it is the same period as the period before the original lease expired. In either case, the landlord can raise the rent, so long as the landlord has told the tenant of the higher rent before the expiration of the original lease.

## FORMALITIES

Formal requirements for a lease are determined by the law and custom of the jurisdiction in which real property is located. In the case of personal property, it is determined by the law and custom of the jurisdiction in which the rental agreement is made. A tenancy for a duration greater than one year must be in writing in order to satisfy the Statute of Frauds.

## TERM

The term of the lease may be fixed, periodic or of indefinite duration. If it is for a specified period of time, the term ends automatically when the period expires, and no notice needs to be given, in the absence of legal requirements. The term's duration may be conditional, in which case it lasts until a specified event occurs, such as the death of a specified individual. A periodic tenancy is one which is renewed automatically, usually on a monthly or weekly basis. A tenancy at will lasts only as long as the parties wish it to, and may be terminated by either party without penalty.

It is common for a lease to be extended on a "holding over" basis, which normally converts the tenancy to a periodic tenancy on a month by month basis. It is also possible for a tenant, either expressly or impliedly, to give up the tenancy to the landlord. This process is known as a "surrender" of the lease.

## RENT

Rent is a requirement of leases in some common law jurisdiction, but not in civil law jurisdiction. In England it was held in the case of Ashburn Anstalt v Arnold that rent was not a requirement for there to be a lease, however the court will more often construe a licence where no rent is paid as it is seen as evidence for no intention to create legal relationship. There is no requirement for the rent to be a commercial amount. "Pepper corn" rent or rent of some nominal amount is adequate for this requirement.

## CAR RENTAL

A car rental agreement may include various restrictions on the way a renter can use a car, and the condition in which it must be returned. For example, some rentals cannot be driven off-road, or out of the country, or towing a trailer, without specific permission. In New Zealand you may have to specifically endorse a promise that the car will not be driven onto Ninety-Mile Beach (because of the hazardous tides).

There will certainly be a requirement to show a driver's license, and only those drivers appearing on the contract may be authorized to drive. It may include an option to purchase auto insurance (motor insurance, UK), if the renter does not already have a policy to cover rentals—another important consideration for multiple drivers. Some agencies may even require a bond payable if the car is not returned in order, often held in the form of a credit-card authorization—voided if the car is returned per agreement.

A renter should be advised that he or she will be responsible for any parking or traffic violations incurred upon the vehicle during the rental period. There should also be advice on handling thefts, accidents, break-downs, and towing. Further terms may include added fees for late returns, drop-off at a different location, or failure to top up the petrol immediately before the return. Finally, there may be provisions for making a non-refundable deposit with a booking, terms for payment of the initial period (with discounts, vouchers, etc.), extended periods, and any damages or other fees that accrue prior to the return.

## REAL ESTATE RENTAL

A rental agreement is often called a lease, especially when real estate is rented. In addition to the basics of a rental (who, what, when, how much), a real estate rental may go into much more detail on these and other issues. The real estate may be rented for housing, parking a vehicle(s), storage, business, agricultural, institutional, or government use, or other reasons.

- *Who*: The parties involved in the contract, the lessor (sometimes called the owner or landlord) and the lessee (sometimes called the renter or tenant) are identified in the contract. A housing lease may specify whether the renter is living alone, with family, children, room-mate, visitors. A rental may delineate the rights and obligations of each of these. For example, a "sub-let" to a stranger might not be permitted without permission of the landlord. This also applies to whether or not pets may be kept by the renter. On the other hand, the renter may also have specific rights against intrusions by the landlord (or other tenants), except under emergency circumstances. A renter is in possession of the property, and a landlord would be trespassing upon the renter's rights if entry is made without proper notice and authority (*e.g.*, 24 hours' notice, daytime, knock first, except for emergency repairs, in case of fire, flood, etc.).
- *What*: Rented real estate may include all or part of almost any real property, such as an apartment, house, building, business office(s) or suite, land, farm, or merely an inside or outside space to park a vehicle, or store things. The premises rented may include not only specific rooms, but also access to other common areas such as off-street parking, basement or attic storage, laundry facility, pool, roof-deck, balconies, etc. The agreement may specify how and when these places may be used, and by whom. There may be detailed description of the current condition of the premises, for comparison with the condition at the time the premises are surrendered.
- *When*: the term of the rental may be for a night (*e.g.*, a hotel room), weeks, months, or years. There may be statutory provisions requiring registration of any rental that could extend for more than a specified number of years (*e.g.*, seven) in order to be enforceable against a new landlord.

  A typical rental is either annual or month-to-month, and the amount of rent may be different for long-term renters (because of lower turnover costs). Leaving a long-term lease before its expiration could result in penalties, or even the cost of the entire agreed period (if the landlord is unable to find a suitable replacement tenant, after diligent pursuit). If a tenant stays beyond the end of a lease for a term of years (one or more), then the parties may agree that the lease will be automatically renewed, or it may simply convert to a tenancy at will (month-to-month) at the pro-rated monthly cost of the previous annual lease. If a tenant at will is given notice to quit the premises, and refuses to do so, the landlord then begins eviction proceedings. In many places it is completely illegal to change locks on doors, or remove personal belongings, let alone forcibly eject a person, without a court order of eviction. There may be strict rules of procedure, and stiff penalties (triple damages, plus attorneys' fees) for violations.

- *How much*: Rent may be payable monthly, annually, or in advance, or as otherwise agreed. A typical arrangement for tenancy at will is "first and last month's rent" plus a security deposit. The "last month's rent" is rent that has yet to be earned by the landlord.

### *Deposit*

The security deposit is often handled as an escrow deposit, owned by the tenant, but held by the landlord until the premises are surrendered in good condition (ordinary wear and tear excepted). In some states, the landlord must provide the tenant with the name and account number of the bank where the security deposit is held, and pay annual interest to the tenant. Other regulations may require the landlord to submit a list of pre-existing damage to the property, or forfeit the security deposit immediately (because there is no way to determine whether a prior tenant was responsible).

### *Insurance*

In order to rent or lease in many apartment buildings, a renter (also referred to as a "lessee") is often required to provide proof of renters insurance before signing the rental agreement. There is a special type of the homeowners insurance in the United States specifically for renters—HO-4. This is commonly referred to as renter's insurance or renter's coverage. Similar to condominium coverage, referred to as a HO-6 policy, a renter's insurance policy covers those aspects of the apartment and its contents not specifically covered in the blanket policy written for the complex. This policy can also cover liabilities arising from accidents and intentional injuries for guests as well as passers-by up to 150' of the domicile. Renter's policies provide "named peril" coverage, meaning the policy states specifically what you are insured against.

*Common coverage areas are*:

- Fire or Lightning
- Windstorm
- Smoke
- Vandalism or Malicious Mischief
- Theft
- Accidental Discharge of Water

Additional events including riot, aircraft, explosion, smoke, hail, falling objects, volcanic eruption, snow, sleet, and weight of ice may also be covered.

## SUBLEASE

In real estate law, sublease (or, less formally, sublet) is the name given to an arrangement in which the lessee in a lease assigns the lease to a third party, thereby making the old lessee the sublessor, and the new lessee the sublessee, or subtenant. This means they are renting the property and renting it out at the same time. For example, the owner of an office building may lease the whole building to a management company. This company may then sublease parts of the building to other people. The management company is said to sublet the property to the individual tenants by means of a sublease. In this event, the management company (which was previously the lessee under the original lease) becomes the sublessor, and the individual tenants are subtenants or sublessees.

The sublessor remains liable to the original lessor for any damage to the property and for payment of rent. Often the original lessee requires a lower rent payment from the sublessee than what he or she may have originally paid, leaving a partial amount of the rent left up to the original lessee.

It is sometimes illegal to charge the subtenant more than the original amount in the sublessee's contract (for instance, in a rent control situation where the rental amount is controlled by law). Subletting of social housing is generally illegal, whatever the rent charged to the subtenant; in the UK it is officially described as a category of housing fraud. A sublease can also apply to vehicles as an alternate type of car rental. In a vehicle sublease, a lessee or vehicle owner can assign a lease to a third party and by way of contractual agreement for specific dates. Although this arrangement is not popular, it is a growing trend in the travel industry as a less expensive alternative for travellers and locals.

### HEAD LEASE

A head lease is a lease between a tenant and a landlord in which overall contractual responsibility is given to one identifiable tenant called the head lessee. This form of lease normally relates to an entire building which is multi-tenanted and subleased, and is usually for a longer term than the subleases.

## EARNINGS PER-SHARE

This Accounting Standard includes paragraphs set in bold italic type and plain type, which have equal authority. Paragraphs in bold italic type indicate the main principles. This Accounting Standard is mandatory for all companies. However, disclosure of diluted earnings per share (both including and excluding extraordinary items) is not mandatory for Small and Medium Sized Companies, as defined in the Notification. Such companies are however encouraged to make these disclosures.

### OBJECTIVE

The objective of this Standard is to prescribe principles for the determination and presentation of earnings per share which will improve comparison of performance among different enterprises for the same period and among different accounting periods for the same enterprise. The focus of this Standard is on the denominator of the earnings per share calculation.

Even though earnings per share data has limitations because of different accounting policies used for determining 'earnings', a consistently determined denominator enhances the quality of financial reporting.

## SCOPE

- This Standard should be applied by all companies. However, a Small and Medium Sized Company, as defined in the Notification, may not disclose diluted earnings per share (both including and excluding extraordinary items).
- In consolidated financial statements, the information required by this Statement should be presented on the basis of consolidated information.

In the case of a parent (holding enterprise), users of financial statements are usually concerned with, and need to be informed about, the results of operations of both the enterprise itself as well as of the group as a whole. In the case of such enterprises, this Standard requires the presentation of earnings per share information on the basis of consolidated financial statements as well as individual financial statements of the parent. In consolidated financial statements, such information is presented on the basis of consolidated information.

## DEFINITIONS

*For the purpose of this Standard, the following terms are used with the meanings specified*:

- An equity share is a share other than a preference share.
- A preference share is a share carrying preferential rights to dividends and repayment of capital.
- A financial instrument is any contract that gives rise to both a financial asset of one enterprise and a financial liability or equity shares of another enterprise.
- A potential equity share is a financial instrument or other contract that entitles, or may entitle, its holder to equity shares.
- Share warrants or options are financial instruments that give the holder the right to acquire equity shares.
- Fair value is the amount for which an asset could be exchanged, or a liability settled, between knowledgeable, willing parties in an arm's length transaction.

Equity shares participate in the net profit for the period only after preference shares. An enterprise may have more than one class of equity shares. Equity shares of the same class have the same rights to receive dividends. A financial instrument is any contract that gives rise to both a financial asset of one enterprise and a financial liability or equity shares of another enterprise.

*For this purpose, a financial asset is any asset that is:*

- Cash;

- A contractual right to receive cash or another financial asset from another enterprise;
- A contractual right to exchange financial instruments with another enterprise under conditions that are potentially favourable; or
- An equity share of another enterprise.

A financial liability is any liability that is a contractual obligation to deliver cash or another financial asset to another enterprise or to exchange financial instruments with another enterprise under conditions that are potentially unfavourable.

*Examples of potential equity shares are*:

- Debt instruments or preference shares, that are convertible into equity shares;
- Share warrants;
- Options including employee stock option plans under which employees of an enterprise are entitled to receive equity shares as part of their remuneration and other similar plans; and
- Shares which would be issued upon the satisfaction of certain conditions resulting from contractual arrangements (contingently issuable shares), such as the acquisition of a business or other assets, or shares issuable under a loan contract upon default of payment of principal or interest, if the contract so provides.

## PRESENTATION

An enterprise should present basic and diluted earnings per share on the face of the statement of profit and loss for each class of equity shares that has a different right to share in the net profit for the period. An enterprise should present basic and diluted earnings per share with equal prominence for all periods presented. This Standard requires an enterprise to present basic and diluted earnings per share, even if the amounts disclosed are negative (a loss per share).

## MEASUREMENT

### *Basic Earnings Per Share*

Basic earnings per share should be calculated by dividing the net profit or loss for the period attributable to equity shareholders by the weighted average number of equity shares outstanding during the period.

### *Earnings–Basic*

For the purpose of calculating basic earnings per share, the net profit or loss for the period attributable to equity shareholders should be the net profit or loss for the period after deducting preference dividends and any attributable tax thereto for the period. All items of income and expense which are recognised in a period, including tax expense and extraordinary items, are included in the determination of the net profit or loss for the period unless an Accounting Standard requires or permits otherwise. The amount of preference dividends and any attributable tax thereto for the period is deducted from the net profit for the period (or added to the net loss for the period) in order to calculate the net profit or loss for the period attributable to equity shareholders.

*The amount of preference dividends for the period that is deducted from the net profit for the period is*:

- The amount of any preference dividends on non-cumulative preference shares provided for in respect of the period; and
- The full amount of the required preference dividends for cumulative preference shares for the period, whether or not the dividends have been provided for. The amount of preference dividends for the period does not include the amount of any preference dividends for cumulative preference shares paid or declared during the current period in respect of previous periods.

If an enterprise has more than one class of equity shares, net profit or loss for the period is apportioned over the different classes of shares in accordance with their dividend rights.

### *Per Share–Basic*

For the purpose of calculating basic earnings per share, the number of equity shares should be the weighted average number of equity shares outstanding during the period. The weighted average number of equity shares outstanding during the period reflects the fact that the amount of shareholders' capital may have varied during the period as a result of a larger or lesser number of shares outstanding at any time. It is the number of equity shares outstanding at the beginning of the period, adjusted by the number of equity shares bought back or issued during the period multiplied by the time-weighting factor. The time-weighting factor is the number of days for which the specific shares are outstanding as a proportion of the total number of days in the period; a reasonable approximation of the weighted average is adequate in many Illustration attached to the Standard illustrates the computation of weighted average number of shares. In most cases, shares are included in the weighted average number of shares from the date the consideration is receivable, for example:

- Equity shares issued in exchange for cash are included when cash is receivable;
- Equity shares issued as a result of the conversion of a debt instrument to equity shares are included as of the date of conversion;
- Equity shares issued in lieu of interest or principal on other financial instruments are included as of the date interest ceases to accrue;

- Equity shares issued in exchange for the settlement of a liability of the enterprise are included as of the date the settlement becomes effective;
- Equity shares issued as consideration for the acquisition of an asset other than cash are included as of the date on which the acquisition is recognised; and
- Equity shares issued for the rendering of services to the enterprise are included as the services are rendered

In these and other cases, the timing of the inclusion of equity shares is determined by the specific terms and conditions attaching to their issue. Due consideration should be given to the substance of any contract associated with the issue Equity shares issued as part of the consideration in an amalgamation in the nature of purchase are included in the weighted average number of shares as of the date of the acquisition because the transferee incorporates the results of the operations of the transferor into its statement of profit and loss as from the date of acquisition.

Equity shares issued during the reporting period as part of the consideration in an amalgamation in the nature of merger are included in the calculation of the weighted average number of shares from the beginning of the reporting period because the financial statements of the combined enterprise for the reporting period are prepared as if the combined entity had existed from the beginning of the reporting period. Partly paid equity shares are treated as a fraction of an equity share to the extent that they were entitled to participate in dividends relative to a fully paid equity share during the reporting period.

## ACCOUNTING FOR TAXES ON INCOME

This Accounting Standard includes paragraphs set in bold italic type and plain type, which have equal authority. Paragraphs in bold italic type indicate the main principles.

### OBJECTIVE

The objective of this Standard is to prescribe accounting treatment for taxes on income. Taxes on income is one of the significant items in the statement of profit and loss of an enterprise. In accordance with the matching concept, taxes on income are accrued in the same period as the revenue and expenses to which they relate. Matching of such taxes against revenue for a period poses special problems arising from the fact that in a number of cases, taxable income may be significantly different from the accounting income. This divergence between taxable income and accounting income arises due to two main reasons. Firstly, there are differences between items of revenue and expenses as appearing in the statement of profit and loss and the items which are considered as revenue, expenses or deductions for tax purposes.

## SCOPE

- This Standard should be applied in accounting for taxes on income. This includes the determination of the amount of the expense or saving related to taxes on income in respect of an accounting period and the disclosure of such an amount in the financial statements.
- For the purposes of this Standard, taxes on income include all domestic and foreign taxes which are based on taxable income.
- This Standard does not specify when, or how, an enterprise should account for taxes that are payable on distribution of dividends and other distributions made by the enterprise.

## DEFINITIONS

*For the purpose of this Standard, the following terms are used with the meanings specified*:

- Accounting income (loss) is the net profit or loss for a period, as reported in the statement of profit and loss, before deducting income tax expense or adding income tax saving.
- Taxable income (tax loss) is the amount of the income (loss) for a period, determined in accordance with the tax laws, based upon which income tax payable (recoverable) is determined.
- Tax expense (tax saving) is the aggregate of current tax and deferred tax charged or credited to the statement of profit and loss for the period.
- Current tax is the amount of income tax determined to be payable (recoverable) in respect of the taxable income (tax loss) for a period.
- Deferred tax is the tax effect of timing differences.
- Timing differences are the differences between taxable income and accounting income for a period that originate in one period and are capable of reversal in one or more subsequent periods.
- Permanent differences are the differences between taxable income and accounting income for a period that originate in one period and do not reverse subsequently.

Taxable income is calculated in accordance with tax laws. In some circumstances, the requirements of these laws to compute taxable income differ from the accounting policies applied to determine accounting income. The effect of this difference is that the taxable income and accounting income may not be the same.

The differences between taxable income and accounting income can be classified into permanent differences and timing differences. Permanent differences are those differences between taxable income and accounting income which originate in one period and do not reverse subsequently. For instance, if for the purpose of computing taxable income, the tax laws allow only a part of an item of expenditure, the disallowed amount would result in a permanent difference. Timing differences are those differences between taxable income and accounting income for a period that originate in one period and are capable of reversal in one or more subsequent periods.

Timing differences arise because the period in which some items of revenue and expenses are included in taxable income do not coincide with the period in which such items of revenue and expenses are included or considered in arriving at accounting income. For example, machinery purchased for scientific research related to business is fully allowed as deduction in the first year for tax purposes whereas the same would be charged to the statement of profit and loss as depreciation over its useful life. The total depreciation charged on the machinery for accounting purposes and the amount allowed as deduction for tax purposes will ultimately be the same, but periods over which the depreciation is charged and the deduction is allowed will differ. Another example of timing difference is a situation where, for the purpose of computing taxable income, tax laws allow depreciation on the basis of the written down value method, whereas for accounting purposes, straight line method is used.

Some other examples of timing differences arising under the Indian tax laws are given in Illustration I. Unabsorbed depreciation and carry forward of losses which can be setoff against future taxable income are also considered as timing differences and result in deferred tax assets, subject to consideration of prudence.

# 3

# Computer and Computerised Accounting System

With the expansion of business the number of transactions increased. The manual method of keeping and maintaining records was found to be unmanageable. With the introducton of computers in business, the manual method of accounting is being gradually replaced. And finally, the database technology has revolutionised the accounts department of the business. organisations. In this lesson, we will study about characteristics of computer, role of computers in accounting, need of computerised accounting, etc.

## COMPUTER AND ITS CHARACTERISTICS

Computer is an electronic device that can perform a variety of operations in accordance with a set of instructions called programme. It is a fast data processing electronic machine. It can provide solutions to all complicated situations.

It accepts data from the user, converts the data into information and gives the desired result. Therefore, we may define computer as a device that transforms data into information. Data can be anything like marks obtained in various subjects. It can also be name, age, sex, weight, height, etc. of all the students, savings, investments, etc., of a country. Computer is defined in terms of its functions.

### CHARACTERISTICS OF COMPUTER

*A Computer is better than human being. It possesses some characteristics. These are as follows*:

- *Speed*: It can access and process data millions times faster than humans can. It can store data and information in its memory, process them and produce the desired results. It is used essentially as a data processor. All the computer operations are caused by electrical pulses and travels at the speed of light. Most of the modern computers are capable of performing 100 million calculations per second.

- *Storage*: Computers have very large storage capacity. They have the capability of storing vast amount of data or information. Computers have huge capacity to store data in a very small physical space. Apart from storing information, today's computers are also capable of storing pictures and sound in digital form.
- *Accuracy*: The accuracy of computer is very high and every calculation is performed with the same accuracy. Errors occur because of human beings rather than technological weakness; main sources of errors are wrong program by the user or inaccurate data.
- *Diligence*: A computer is free from tiredness and lack of concentration. Even if it has to do 10 million calculations, it will do even the last one with the same accuracy and speed as the first.
- *Versatility*: Computer can perform wide range of jobs with speed, accuracy, and diligence. In any organisation, often it is the same computer that is used for diverse purposes such as accounting, playing games, preparing electric bills, sending e-mail and so on.
- *Communication*: Computers are being used as powerful communication tools. All the computers within an office are connected by cable and it is possible to communicate with others in the office through the network of computer.
- *Processing Power*: Computer has come a long way today. They began as mere prototypes at research laboratories and went on to help the business organisations, and today, their reach is so extensive that they are used almost everywhere. In the course of this evolution, they have become faster, smaller, cheaper, more reliable and user friendly.

## COMPONENTS OF COMPUTER

A computer consists of the major components i.e., Input Unit, Central Processing Unit and Output Unit. Diagrammatically, these components may be presented as follows:

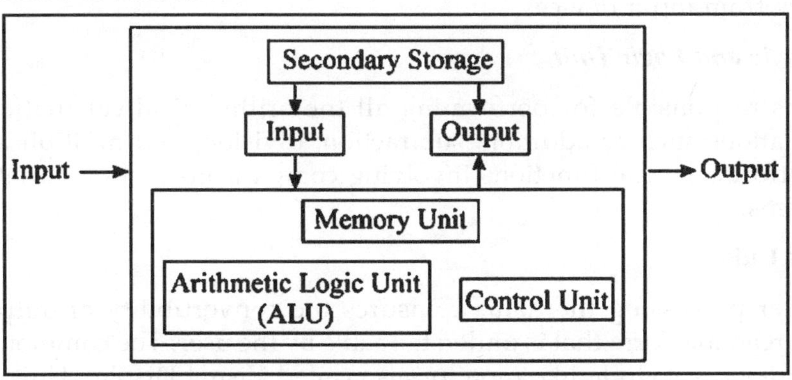


**Fig.** Components of Computer

## Input Unit

Input unit is controlling the various input devices which are used for entering data into the computer. The mostly used input devices are keyboard, mouse, and scanner. Other such devices are magnetic tape, magnetic disk, light pen, bar code reader, smart card reader, etc. Besides, there are other devices which respond to voice and physical touch. Physical touch system is installed at airport for obtaining the online information about departure and arrival of flight. The input unit is responsible for taking input and converting it into binary system.

## Central Processing Unit (CPU)

The CPU is the control centre for a computer. It guides, directs and governs its performance. It is the brain of the computer. The main unit inside the computer is the Central Processing Unit. Central Processing Unit is to computer as the brain is to human body. This is used to store program, photos, graphics, and data and obey the instructions in program.

*It is divided into three subunits*:

- Control Unit
- Memory Unit
- Arithmetic Logic Unit (ALU)

### *Control Unit*

Control unit controls and co-ordinates the activities of all the components of the computer. This unit accepts input data and converts it into computer binary system.

### *Memory Unit*

This unit stores data before being actually processed. The data so stored is accessed and processed according to instructions which are also stored in the memory section of computer well before such data is transmitted to the memory from input devices.

### *Arithmetic and Logic Unit*

It is responsible for performing all the arithmetical calculations and computations such as addition, subtraction, division, and multiplication. It also performs logical functions involving comparisons among variable and data items.

## Output Unit

After processing the data, it ensures the convertibility of output into human readable form that is understandable by the user. The commonly used output devices include like monitor also called Visual Display Unit, printer etc.

## LIMITATIONS OF A COMPUTER AND COMPURISED ACCOUNTING

The limitations of computer are depending upon the operating environment they work in.

*These limitations are given below as:*

- *Cost of Installation*: Computer hardware and software needs to be updated from time to time with availability of new versions. As a result heavy cost is incurred to purchase a new hardware and software from time to time.
- *Cost of Training*: To ensure efficient use of computer in accounting, new versions of hardware and software are introduced. This requires training and cost is incurred to train the staff personnel.
- *Self Decision Making*: The computer cannot make a decision like human beings. It is to be guided by the user.
- *Maintenance*: Computer requires to be maintained properly to help maintain its efficiency. It requires a neat, clean and controlled temperature to work efficiently.
- *Dangers for Health*: Extensive use of computer may lead to many health problems such as muscular pain, eyestrain, and backache, etc. This affects adversely the working efficiency and increasing medical expenditure.

## ROLE OF COMPUTERS IN ACCOUNTING

The most popular system of recording of accounting transactions is manual which requires maintaining books of accounts such as Journal, Cash Book, Special purpose books, ledger and so on. The accountant is required to prepare summary of transactions and financial statements manually. The advanced technology involves various machines capable of performing different accounting functions, for example, a billing machine. This machine is capable of computing discount, adding net total and posting the requisite data to the relevant accounts.

With substantial increase in the number of transactions, a machine was developed which could store and process accounting data in no time. Such advancement leads to number of growing successful organisations. A newer version of machine is evolved with increased speed, storage, and processing capacity. A computer to which they were connected operated these machines. As a result, the maintenance of accounting data on a real-time basis became almost essential. Now maintaining accounting records become more convenient with the computerised accounting.

The computerised accounting uses the concept of databases. For this purpose an accounting software is used to implement a computerised accounting system. It does away the necessity to create and maintain journals, ledgers, etc., which are essential part of manual accounting. Some of the commonly used accounting softwares are Tally, Cash Manager, Best Books, etc. Accounting software is used to implement a computerised accounting. The computerised accounting is based on the concept of database. It is basic software which allows access to the data contained in the data base. It is a system to manage collection of data insuring at the same time that it remains reliable and confidential. Following are the components of Computerised accounting software.

**Preparation of Accounting Documents**

Computer helps in preparing accounting documents like Cash Memo, Bills and invoices etc., and preparing accounting vouchers.

**Recording of Transactions**

Every day business transactions are recorded with the help of computer software. Logical scheme is implied for codification of account and transaction. Every account and transaction is assigned a unique code. The grouping of accounts is done from the first stage. This process simplifies the work of recording the transactions.

**Preparation of Trial Balance and Financial Statements**

After recording of transaction, the data is transferred into Ledger account automatically by the computer. Trial Balance is prepared by the computer to check accuracy of the records. With the help of trial balance the computer can be programmed to prepare Trading, Profit and Loss account and Balance Sheet. These components can be shown as :

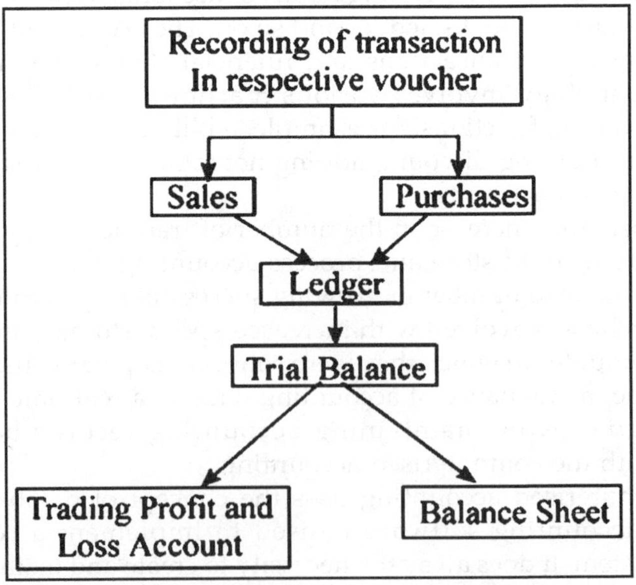


**Fig.** Components of Computerised Accounting Software

## COMPUTERISED ACCOUNTING

Transaction processing system (TPS) is the first stage of computerised accounting system. The purpose of any TPS is to record, process, validate and store transactions that occur in various functional areas of a business for subsequent retrieval and usage. TPS involves following steps in processing a transaction: Data Entry, Data Validation, Processing and Revalidation, Storage, Information and Reporting. It is one of the transaction processing systems which is concerned with financial transactions only. When a system contains only human resources it is called manual system; when it uses only computer resources, it is called computerised system and when it uses both human and computer resources, it is called computer-based system.

*These steps can be explained with an example making use of Automatic Teller Machine (ATM) facility by a Bank-Customer*:

- *Data Entry*: Processing presumes data entry. A bank customer operates an ATM facility to make a withdrawal. The actions taken by the customer constitute data which is processed after validation by the computerised personal banking system.
- *Data Validation*: It ensures the accuracy and reliability of input data by comparing the same with some predefined standards or known data. This validation is made by the 'Error Detection' and 'Error Correction' procedures. The control mechanism, wherein actual input data is compared with predetermined norm is meant to detect errors while error correction procedures make suggestions for entering correct data input. The Personal Identification Number (PIN) of the customer is validated with the known data. If it is incorrect, a suggestion is made to indicate the PIN is invalid. Once the PIN is validated, the amount of withdrawal being made is also checked to ensure that it does not exceed a prespecified limit of withdrawal.
- *Processing and Revalidation*: The processing of data occurs almost instantaneously in case of Online Transaction Processing (OLTP) provided a valid data has been fed to the system. This is called check input validity. Revalidation occurs to ensure that the transaction in terms of delivery of money by ATM has been duly completed. This is called check output validity.
- *Storage*: Processed actions, as described above, result into financial transaction data i.e. withdrawal of money by a particular customer, are stored in transaction database of computerized personal banking system. This makes it absolutely clear that only valid transactions are stored in the database.
- *Information*: The stored data is processed making use of the Query facility to produce desired information.
- *Reporting*: Reports can be prepared on the basis of the required information content according to the decision usefulness of the report.

## NEED AND REQUIREMENTS OF COMPUTERSIED ACCOUNTING

The need for computerised accounting arises from advantages of speed, accuracy and lower cost of handling the business transactions.

### NUMEROUS TRANSACTIONS

The computerised accounting system is capable of handling large number of transactions with speed and accuracy.

### INSTANT REPORTING

The computerised accounting system is capable of offering quick and quality reporting because of its speed and accuracy.

### REDUCTION IN PAPER WORK

A manual accounting system requires large physical storage space to keep accounting records/books and vouchers/ documents. The requirement of stationery and books of accounts along with vouchers and documents is directly dependent on the volume of transactions beyond a certain point. There is a dire need to reduce the paper work and dispense with large volumes of books of accounts. This can be achieved by introducing computerised accounting system.

### FLEXIBLE REPORTING

The reporting is flexible in computerised accounting system as compared to manual accounting system. The reports of a manual accounting system reveal balances of accounts on periodic basis while computerised accounting system is capable of generating reports of any balance as when required and for any duration which is within the accounting period.

### ACCOUNTING QUERIES

There are accounting queries which are based on some external parameters. For example, a query to identify customers who have not made the payments within the permissible credit period can be easily answered by using the structured query language (SQL) support of database technology in the computerised accounting system. But such an exercise in a manual accounting system is quite difficult and expensive in terms of manpower used. It will still be worse in case the credit period is changed.

### ON-LINE FACILITY

Computerised accounting system offers online facility to store and process transaction data so as to retrieve information to generate and view financial reports.

## SCALABILITY

Computerised accounting system are fully equipped with handling the growing transactions of a fast growing business enterprise. The requirement of additional manpower in Accounts department is restricted to only the data operators for storing additional vouchers. There is absolutely no additional cost of processing additional transaction data.

## ACCURACY

The information content of reports generated by the computerised accounting system is accurate and therefore quite reliable for decisionmaking. In a manual accounting system the reports and information are likely to be distorted, inaccurate and therefore cannot be relied upon. It is so because it is being processed by many people, especially when the number of transactions to be processed to produce such information and report is quite large.

## SECURITY

Under manual accounting system it is very difficult to secure such information because it is open to inspection by any eyes dealing with the books of accounts. However, in computerised accounting system only the authorised users are permitted to have access to accounting data. Security provided by the computerised accounting system is far superior compared to any security offered by the manual accounting system.

## BASIC REQUIREMENTS OF THE COMPUTERISED ACCOUNTING SYSTEM

*The basic requirements of any computerised accounting system are the followings*:

- *Accounting framework*: It is the application environment of the computerised accounting system. A healthy accounting framework in terms of accounting principles, coding and grouping structure is a pre-condition for any computerized accounting system.
- *Operating procedure*: A well-conceived and designed operating procedure blended with suitable operating environment of the enterprise is necessary to work with the computerised accounting system.

The computerised accounting is one of the database-oriented applications wherein the transaction data is stored in well- organized database. The user operates on such database using the required interface and also takes the required reports by suitable transformations of stored data into information. Therefore, the fundamentals of computerised accounting include all the basic requirements of any database-oriented application in computers.

# 4

# Morality in Accounting

## CONCEPT OF JUSTICE IN ACCOUNTING

Fairness judgments are taken for granted in accounting although their clear meaning is not well specified. Two generally accepted meanings concern the idea of neutrality in preparation and presentation of financial reports and the idea of justice in outcome. While both notions play a useful role in accounting, the expansion of the notion of fairness to deal with distribution considerations links it to alternative philosophical concepts more compatible with moral concepts of justice.

Basically, fairness may be viewed as a moral concept of justice subject to three different interpretations of the notions of distributive justice. Accordingly, the accounting discussion of fairness by introducing the main philosophical concepts of distributive justice in the accounting contest. The end result is the possibility to view and compare the concept of fairness through different distributive justice frameworks.

## FAIRNESS IN ACCOUNTING

### Fairness as Neutrality in Presentation

Fairness is best understood in the professional accounting literature and pronouncements as an expression of the neutrality of the accountant in the preparation of financial reports. The first suggestion of the use of fairness in accounting was made by D. R. Scott in 1941 when he listed it as a prin-ciple of accounting and stated: "Accounting rules, procedures, and tech-niques should be fair, unbiased and impartial.

They should not serve a special interest." Since then, the fairness concept has become an implicit ethical norm. In general, the fairness concept implies that accounting state-ments have not been subject to undue influence or bias. Fairness implies that the preparers of accounting information have acted in good faith and employed ethical business practices and sound accounting judgment in the pre-sentation, production, and auditing of accounting results.

Fairness is a value statement that is variously applied in accounting. James Patillo, who made fairness the subject of a book, ranks it as a basic standard to be used in the evaluation of other standards because it is the only standard that implies "ethical considerations."

From contrasting the connotation of justice, truth, and fairness, the current social concept of fairness is selected as the basic standard by which to measure the propri-ety of accounting principles and rules which purports to be the means of attaining the objective. Fairness to all parties, therefore, is formulated to be the single basic standard of accounting, that criterion or test which all accounting propositions must reflect before being included in the accounting structure.

The importance of fairness was also evident when C. T. Devine gave preserving equity among conflicting groups a central place among accounting concerns. And in spite of contentions that fairness is subjective, ambiguous, and therefore cannot serve as a basis for developing accounting the-ory. It has become one of the basic objectives of accounting. A first evidence of this importance is the reference by the American Institute of Certified Public Accountants' (AICPA) Committee on Auditing Procedures to the criteria of "fairness of presentation" as conformity with generally accepted accounting principles, disclosure, consistency, and comparability. In an unqualified report, "present fairly" connotes compliance with generally accepted accounting principles and generally accepted auditing standards.

The reference to a true and fair view in auditors' reports, under laws on the English pattern, is similar to the U.S. connotation. It implies that the audi-tor, by being fair, has complied with protocol largely of his own creation. Under both laws however, the term fairness is given dominance although not well specified. R. C. Chambers attributes the situation to the loose rein of the law. He states: "The vagueness of the law may be attributed to the belief of legislators or of lawyers that the terms used in the statutes are terms of art, peculiar to accounting and accountants, which should properly be left to accountants to elucidate."

Without mentioning fairness explicitly, Baruch Lev advocated a concept of equity as equality of opportunity in the sense of an equal access to infor-mation relevant for asset valuation. Absence of equity implies systematic and significant information asymmetries leading to adverse private and social consequences in the form of high transaction costs, thin markets, low liquidity, and decreased gains from trade. Operationally, Lev suggests the decrease of information asymmetries by a search for those specific information items that are at the disposition of some informed investors while not of others, favoring thereby the interests of the less informed over those of the more informed.

The equity criterion as espoused by Lev and others in this section are forms of fairness in presentation aimed at decreasing information asymmetries between various classes of investors and financial statement users to en- sure an equal endowment of information. It is very much in line with the argument that equality of opportunity, as opposed to equality of actual out- comes, is the sole principle of justice guiding government decisions. It is also appealing to those who may intuitively see a link between increasing equality of opportunity and equality of outcomes, and to those who as-sume that the ex-ante equality of opportunity concept conflicts less with ef-ficiency incentives than do the egalitarian ex-post concepts of equity.

**Fairness as Justice in Outcome**

The view of fairness as neutrality in presentation of an equality of opportunity is not without its critics. Paul Williams characterized it as an evalua-tion process with the following two attributes:

- That the evaluator is aware of the condition that any consequences of his or her actions will be judged as fair or unfair,
- That the evaluation attempts to adopt a perspective of impartiality. Williams argued that given the concern in accounting with efficiency and the link between efficiency and distribution, distributive judgments are fairness judgments. Therefore, fairness derives also from a concept of distributive justice. The problems of distribution have almost been ignored in the conventional view of fairness as neutrality in presentation as a matter beyond the scope of their concern. The concern was with merely the final production and disclosure of accounting results rather than their distribution.

There are, however, three notable exceptions in the accounting literature that have shown concern with distributive questions:

The first exception emanates from the social accounting concern with ac-counting for externalities and reporting some forms of social report. A first example includes Scott's view of the social role of accounting in the resolu-tion of conflicting social interest: "The compromise of conflicting interests is a process of valuation.

It accomplishes social organization and results in a distribution of economic incomes. Value and distribution constitute a sim- ple problem and accounting theory is especially and peculiarly a treatment of that problem." A second example includes the various calls for the role of social account-ing in some form of rectification of society's ills. It is best stated by H. Schreuder and K. V. Ramanathan as follows: "In the context of traditional economic analysis, the issue boils down to a distributional problem, namely the apportionment in a society of the costs and benefits of economic activity. Economists have long recognized that such distributional issues cannot be addressed without taking a normative position."

Fairness in the social accounting literature becomes a matter of the distri-bution of social responsibility in general and social responsiveness as the capacity of a corporation to respond to social pressures. Thus, corporate social responsiveness, as an expression of fairness, goes beyond the moral and ethical connotation of social responsibility to the managerial process of response. The response to be fair involves the identification, measurement, and disclosure, where necessary, of the social costs and benefits created by the economic activities of the firm, as well as the adequate responses to these problems.

The second exception emanates from advocates of the political economy of accounting, and the critical and Marxist approach to accounting. They advocate a political economy approach that recognizes power and conflict in society and the effects of accounting reports on the distribution of income, wealth, and power in society. The third exception emanates from the positive theory of accounting view that accounting can be used to optimally resolve conflicts over resource allo-cation to a limited set of participants. Fairness in this context is ultimately in the shareholders' interest.

## FAIRNESS

### Rawls' Theory of Justice

The goal of Rawls' theory of justice is to develop a moral theory about justice in the form of principles to apply to the development of the basic structure of society, and that presents a direct challenge to utilitarianism. As an egalitarian theory, its main contention is the distribution of all eco-nomic goods and services equally except where an unequal distribution would actually work to everyone's advantage, or at least would benefit the worst-off society. Using what he calls the "Kantian concept of equality," Rawls starts by comparing life to a game of chance where nature bestows on each individual a generation, a culture, a social system, a family, and a set of personal attributes that determines his or her happiness.

Accepting this ran-dom allocation is viewed as unjust and a set of just institutions is required. To establish just institutions, Rawls suggests that individuals step behind a "veil of ignorance" that eliminates any knowledge about potential positions and benefits under a given set of principles. Then, to reach a social contract, they must choose from this original position principles of justice leading to the just society. From this original position and under the veil of ignorance, individuals will choose two principles of justice:

*First*: Each person is to have an equal right to the most extensive basic liberty com-patible with a similar liberty for others.

*Second*: Social and economic inequalities are to be arranged so that they are both,

- Reasonably expected to be to everyone's ad- vantage,
- Attached to positions and offices open to all.

Rawls maintains that the two principles are lexicographically ordered, the first one over the second.

*He states*: Now it is possible, at least theoretically, that by giving up some of their fundamental liberties men are sufficiently compensated by the resulting social and economic gains. The general conception of justice implies no restrictions on what sort of in- equalities; it only requires that everyone's position be improved.... Imagine... that men forgo certain political rights when the economic returns are significant and their capacity to influence the course of policy by the exercise of these rights would be marginal in any case. It is this kind of exchange which the two principles as stated rule out; being arranged in serial order they do not permit exchanges between basic liberties and economic and social gains.

The first principle shows that emphasis placed by Rawls on liberty and the precedence of liberty over the second principle of justice. Liberty can only be restricted when it is formulated as follows: "The principles of justice are to be ranked in lexical order and therefore, liberty can be restricted only for the sake of liberty.

*There are two cases*:

- A less restrictive liberty shared by all,
- A less than equal liberty must be acceptable to those citizens with the lesser liberty."

The second principle of justice, which Rawls labeled the difference prin-ciple, contains a second lexicographic ordering of the welfare of the individuals from lowest to highest, where the welfare of the worst-off individual is to be maximized first before proceeding to higher levels. In its most general form, the difference principle states:

In a basic structure with no relevant representatives, first maximize the welfare of the worst-off representative, minimize the welfare of the second worst-off man, and so on until the last case which is, for equal welfare of all the preceding n-1 representatives, maximize the welfare of the best-off representative man. We think of this as the lexical difference principle.

These two principles show a democratic conception that eliminates those aspects of the social world that seem arbitrary from a moral point of view. This does not necessarily eliminate economic inequality. Rawls justifies some difference in income first: as incentives to attract people in certain positions and motivate them to perform; and as a guarantee that certain public-interest positions will be filled. To implement Rawls' theory, the idea of "basic structure" may be "a constitutional democracy," which preserves equal basic liberties, with a government that promotes equality of opportu-nity and guarantees a social minimum and a market-based economic system. Rawls suggests that this social minimum be established before allowing the rest of the total income to be settled by the price system.

It is to be settled by special payments for sickness and unemployment and monetary transfer sys-tems such as negative income tax. Rawls, however, gives little attention to the identification of the worst-off representative.

*He offers only two alterna-tives*:

- To choose a particular social position, say that of the unskilled worker, and then to count as the least advantaged all those with the average income of this group, or less;
- To focus on the relative income and wealth with no reference to social position — that is, all persons with less than half of the median income and wealth may be taken as the least advantaged segment. With regard to redistribution, Rawls finds large inequalities to be permissible if lowering them would make the working class even worse- off. Basically, with the raising of expectations of the more advantaged, the situation of the worst-off is continuously improved. Inequalities will tend to be leveled down by the increasing availability of educated talent and ever- widening expectations. However, Rawls calls for the establishment of social minimums through various transfers and redistributive mechanisms. But would Rawls' difference principle assure an adequate level of the necessary goods and services? There are a lot of disagreements on this issue.

Derek Phillips joins the opposite chorus: The major reason for this concerns Rawls' emphasis on incentives. With the difference principle... an unequal distribution of wealth and income is justified if and only if it will maximize benefits to the least advantaged segments within a society. But if, as Rawls assumes, these inequalities must be rather large, then it seems likely that the actual benefits — even if maximized — will not be sufficient to provide an ade-quate level for the least advantaged segment, they will fail to do so for those persons who require extra medical care, protection and other basic goods. This is a consequence of the fact... that the difference principle makes no allowances for the par-ticular needs of especially disadvantaged individuals."

While better criteria still need to be developed to resolve these issues, Gerwith asserts that what is needed is a drastic redistribution of wealth and an effective exercise of the fundamental rights to freedom and well-being. Basically, Rawls and Gerwith disagree on how the needs of the disadvan-taged are to be met. While Rawls is willing to accept an unequal distribution of economic rewards, if it benefits the least advantaged, Gerwith maintains that the wealthy have an obligation to assist the disadvantaged.

## Fairness in Accounting According to Rawls

Rawls' contract theory — a theory of just social institutions — may be offered as a concept of fairness in accounting. Applied to accounting, it sug-gests first the potential reliance on the veil of ignorance in all the situations calling for an accounting choice eventually to yield solutions that are neutral, fair, and socially just. Second, it also suggests the expanded role of ac- counting in the creation of just institutions and the definition of the social minimum advocated by Rawls. This role, as also espoused by advocates of accounting, will lead to the elimination of those aspects of the social world in general, and the accounting world in particular, that seem arbitrary from a moral point of view. This view of fairness would be most welcome to advocates of social accounting. As stated by Williams:

Rawlsian principles also may prove to be a useful set of premises for speculation about alternative accounting systems. For example, one plausible reason for the slow theoretical development of social accounting, at least in the United States, could be the constraining effect of conventional accounting premises about character and legitimacy of institutions, both public and private. Accounting scholars with interests in social accounting are certainly free to generate and test hypotheses about measuring and reporting, in Rawlsian, or any other, institutional setting.

**Nozick's Theory of Justice**

While Rawls is interested in the justice of one or another pattern of distribution, Nozick is interested in the process through which distribution comes about. He first argued that Rawls' theory of justice violates people's rights, and consequently cannot be morally justified; that it ignores people's entitlements and is, like most other theories of justice, patterned. Patterned theories of justice imply that a distribution is to vary along some natural dimension, weighted sum of natural dimensions, or lexicographic ordering of natural dimensions.

Examples of such distributions include those based on need, merit, or work. Nozick maintains: "To think that the task of a theory of justice is to fill in the blank in each according to his —— is to be predis-posed to search for a pattern; and separate treatment from each according to his —— treats production and distribution as two separate and independent issues." Nozick argues that such theories of justice, based on the patterned and end-state principles, violate people's rights and exclude recognition of an entitlement principle of distributive justice, whereby individuals are entitled to their possessions as long as they acquired them by legitimate means, including voluntary transfers, exchanges, and cooperative productive activity. No- zick's theory focuses on the importance of historical principles, in the sense that a distribution is just or not depending on how it came about. He justiies his theory as follows:

- A person who acquires a holding in accordance with the principle of justice in acquisition is entitled to that holding.
- A person who acquires a holding in accordance with the principle of justice in transfer, from someone else entitled to that holding, is entitled to the holding.
- No one is entitled to a holding except by (repeated) applications of 1. and 2.

The principles involve, respectively, the question of original acquisition of holdings, and the rectification of injustices in holdings. Nozick introduced a proviso, however, to ensure that an individual's entitlements do not result in a net loss in what remains for other persons to use. Nozick's theory is then a theory of justice in holdings. It is a very special kind of theory of distributive justice, as Nozick emphasizes:

The term "distributive justice" is not a neutral one. Hearing the term "distribution," most people presume that some thing or mechanism uses some principle or criterion to give out a supply of things.... However, we are not in the position of children who have been given portions of pie by someone who now makes last-minute adjustments to rectify careless cutting. There is no central distribution, no person or group entitled to control all the resources, jointly deciding how they are to be doled out. What each person gets, he gets from others who give it to him in exchange for some- thing, or as a gift. In a free society, diverse persons control different resources, and new holdings arise out of the voluntary exchanges and actions of persons. There is no more a distribution of shares than there is a distribution of mates in a society in which persons choose whom they shall marry. The total result is the product of many individuals' decisions which the different individuals involved are entitled to make.

Although some criteria remain to be used, Nozick's theory has been criticized for its failure to recognize the right to well-being. The question generally asked is: Is it just to tie the socioeconomic standing of other family members entirely to the moral acceptability of historical process through which the breadwinner has acquired his or her holdings? Those answering "no" argue that it may appear to anyone involved with a sense of justice and concerned about some family members reducing their standard of living radically, when, in other cases, correction is required because of someone else's unjust acquisition; and feeling something morally unsatisfactory about some people being very well compared to others.

**Fairness in Accounting According to Nozick**

The use of the economic man theory in accounting and the decision usefulness criterion used in empirical accounting research link fairness and dis-tributive justice to a free market mechanism. Accounting is viewed as essential to the efficient running of an organization, and the mere reaching of efficiency is presumed to make everybody better off in possession of their just share. Fairness to the positivists and the rationality theorists is linked to an efficient market that allows a just transfer to shareholders. It is essentially a libertarian theory of distribution a la Nozick, based on a principle of justice in acquisition and in transfer. This concept of distributive justice with its reliance on a free market mechanism does not allow for dealing adequately with fairness as a distributive function, because it is assumed to fail the discussion of the social obligations of humans to each other, perpetuate past violations of principles of acquisition and transition, and distort the meaning of well offness in a world of scarcity.

The reliance on the market mechanism, the absence of a moral language to discuss the social obligations, as well as the absence of a concept of redistributive justice are the fans of the cited failures of the libertarian theory of justice. In addition, the growing importance of meritocracy in the context of a basically market system has created problems for a Nozickean theory of justice. The conflicting rules of distribution are not well accepted in our contemporary culture. Most often, members of the organization demand to receive what they justly deserve.

Under the tutoring of the school system, and reinforced by other meritocratic organizations, a person has been socialized to feel that he or she ought to get what has been earned and to be protected from the vagaries and irrationalities of the market. Basically, stakeholders and other shareholders may not be satisfied by the conventional reporting emphasis on returns to shareholders. For example, labour may feel that the profit generated dictates a different distribution than the one dictated by justice in holding and transfer, and a reporting system emphasizing the "mere" just distribution is warranted.

**Gerwith's Theory of Justice**

The goal of Gerwith's theory of justice was to provide a rational justification for moral principles to objectively distinguish morally right actions and institutions from morally wrong ones. The necessary content of morality is in actions and their generic features. The actions are distinguished in terms of two categorical features: voluntariness and purposiveness. Given the importance of action as the necessary and universal matter of all moral and other practical precepts, Gerwith presents his doctrine of the structure of actions in three main steps: First, every agent implicitly makes evaluative judgments about the goodness of his purposes and hence about the necessary goodness of the freedom and well-being that are necessary conditions of his acting to achieve his purposes. Second, because of this necessary goodness, every agent implicitly makes a deontic judgment in which he claims that he has rights to freedom and well-being.

Third, every agent must claim these rights for the sufficient reason that he is a prospective agent who has purposes he wants to fulfill, so that he logically must accept the generalization that all prospective agents have rights to freedom and well-being.

The rights to freedom and well-being are seen as generic, fundamental, and universal. As a result Gerwith asserts that every agent logically must acknowledge certain generic obligations: Negatively, he ought to refrain from coercing and from harming his recipients; positively, he ought to assist them to have freedom and well-being whenever they cannot otherwise have the necessary goods and he can help them at no comparable loss to himself.

The general principle of these obligations and rights may be expressed as the following precepts addressed to every agent: Act in accord with the generic rights of your recipients as well as yourself.

I call this the Principle of Generic Consistency (PGC) since it combines the formal consideration of rights to the generic features or goods of action. Gerwith calls the PGC the supreme moral principle, as it requires the agents not to interfere with the freedom and well-being of others. It remains that the PGC has both direct and indirect application.

The direct application concerns the requirement for agents to act in accord with rights to freedom and well-being of all other persons. The indirect application concerns the requirement that institutional arrangements must express or serve the freedom and well-being of all other persons.

The indirect application involves specifically social rules and arrangements to be implemented in a static and dynamic phase. The static phase generates rules to protect an existing equality of generic rights, while the dynamic phase calls for redistributive justice to eliminate inequalities through a "supportive state."

*The social rules between two extremes are as follows*:

- A certain libertarian extreme that would defend the existing distribution of wealth, arising presumably from just acquisition,
- An egalitarian extreme that calls for a drastic redistribution to be guided solely by the aim of maximally benefiting those who are the least advantaged. Both extremes appear deficient:

The former extreme does not recognize the independent right to well-being, including additive goods, on the part of those whose initial position in life subjects them to serious advantages. The latter extreme does not recognize the independent right to freedom as applied in the production of valued commodities and the consequent earnings in income. Thus the two extremes overlook, respectively, the claims of severe economic need and the claims of worthiness as based on voluntary effort and accomplishment. Naturally the two extremes are Nozick's and Rawls' positions, as they are seen as ignoring the independent right to well-being and the independent right to freedom.

# 5

# Trend Toward Globalization

The United States emerged as the world's most dynamic commercial power after World War II. Winning the war without any battles being fought on its soil, and with much of Europe and Japan lying in ruins, American industrial might was unchallenged for a decade or so after the war. This position of preeminence bred overconfidence. As an example, the term "international business" was parochially understood to mean a U.S. firm opening up a branch office, say, in France, to assist the parent in selling American goods in the European market.

As Europe recovered from the devastation of war, the concept of international business expanded from a marketing function of U.S. products sold overseas to a manufacturing function of U.S licensed products made, and sold, overseas. This was an early, generally unrecognized, step in the process of globalization, a word that has only fairly recently entered into the business vocabulary. Globalization of commerce and trade took another step forward when the intent of building a manufacturing plant in Europe was the marketing of the goods not just within Europe but outside Europe, including the United States itself.

This exceeded the boundaries of meaning implied by the phrase "international business." This new variant of international business required a new name: the "multinational corporation." The designation multinational corporation, according to a professor at a prestigious institution, could be achieved if a company was a Fortune 500 company with at least a 25 percent equity investment in manufacturing facilities in at least six different nations. This was still a rather parochial view of international or multinational, because the company must be a U.S. domiciled company numbered among the Fortune 500.

By this definition, the multinational company did not come into existence after World War II, but in the latter half of the nineteenth century. Isaac Singer, the inventor of the sewing machine, was both a mechanical and a marketing genius who first recognized the value of advertising, demonstrations, training, and selling on credit. He created an effective sales force of women trained on Singer sewing machines, who, in turn, created a market for Singer machines by teaching other women how to sew using a Singer machine. Singer knew that women trained on a Singer sewing machine would be most likely to buy a Singer sewing machine, which goes a long way toward explaining why Apple computers are so often found in elementary schools today.

Most families did not have sufficient cash to purchase a sewing machine outright. Singer responded to this impediment to sales by introducing the hire purchase method of buying a sewing machine. All he required was a small down payment followed by monthly payments thereafter, with ownership transferred to the purchaser with the last payment. This gave birth to buying on credit, an indispensable aspect of modern marketing embodied in credit cards. Singer built the world's largest factory of its time in Elizabeth, New Jersey, for the efficient "assembly" of a half million sewing machines per year.

Some have maintained that the Elizabeth factory deserved the appellation of "mass production," which is a term invented later to describe the size of Henry Ford's assembly operations. Isaac Singer also recognized the potential for marketing sewing machines on a worldwide basis. He opened a large factory in Scotland to sell sewing machines in England and built manufacturing plants on other continents and marketed his sewing machines on a global basis.

Virtually no village, no matter how remote from the mainstream of civilization, was without a hand- or foot-powered sewing machine. The Singer sewing machine, prominently displayed in the front window of many a cottage, was the symbol of prosperity—not unlike having a luxury automobile parked in one's driveway today. Singer achieved multinational status in the nineteenth century. If he had a decentralized operation, his might have been the first global company.

## GLOBAL BUSINESS

What is new is not international or multinational business, but global business. Global business implies that the parent, or founding, company has become indistinguishable in relative importance from the other operating affiliates. It means that the dominating culture within a global business enterprise is not necessarily American or French or any other nationality. An imaginary global company may be domiciled in the Netherlands Antilles. The home office may be not much more than a communications centre tying the various corporate entities together.

The choice of the Netherlands Antilles may be for local reporting requirements (minimal), tax advantages (little or no taxes for activities carried out by the home office), access to the international banking community (easy in this age of instant communications), and access to a recognized legal system for the resolution of corporate matters and disputes and to an accepted set of accounting principles for the issuance of consolidated financial reports (the Dutch legal and accounting systems). The choice of the Netherlands Antilles as the corporate headquarters may also be a way of communicating to the world that no particular nation can lay claim as being the nation of domicile or as being the dominant culture within the corporation.

Below the corporate parent would be divisions representing the interests of the company in broad areas of the world, such as continents. Below these would be another layer of organizations representing the business interests of the global corporation in various countries on the continent. Herein lie the beginnings of complications both in operational, organizational, and marketing matters and in financial reporting. The European organization may be headquartered in Switzerland, which may also handle Swiss sales.

The Swiss organization may own 75 percent of the company conducting business in Spain and Portugal. This company may conduct business in Morocco through an operating affiliate that is 50 percent owned by a Moroccan company. The Moroccan affiliate may, in turn, own a partial interest in the organization's activities in France, and the French affiliate, in turn, may end up owning a partial interest in another company in Switzerland, which, in effect, competes with the Swiss corporate entity that is supposed to be running matters in Europe.

A common problem for multinational companies conducting business through various operational affiliates is the matter of jurisdiction, the drawing of boundary lines separating the activities of one corporate entity from another. The nature of the corporate organization may be simple when the parent organization sets up manufacturing and marketing affiliates dedicated to serving the company's interests within the borders of a nation. At other times, it may be more convoluted, not to confuse outsiders but to ensure a degree of ownership and, therefore, active involvement of managers responsible for the corporation's operations in their locality.

This, in turn, is usually a consequence of a company expanding into a new area where a corporate beachhead has to be first established. This can be accomplished by forming a new affiliate partly owned by key persons, or a local company, to ensure the success of the new venture.

A truly global company probably does not yet exist. The business that is nearest to being organized in this fashion is shipping. A shipping company may have its headquarters domiciled in Bermuda, its marketing organization in New York, its operational organization in London, its manning of vessels conducted through companies in Italy and Pakistan, and may operate its principal assets, ships, under Panamanian and Liberian companies.

The company's business is global, moving goods and commodities from one part of the world to another. The orientation of management is global, with little association with any particular country. Many shipping companies, although not all, exhibit little reluctance to move their operations from one country to another, if local government regulations make it uncomfortable for them to remain. This global attitude toward the organization and the operation of a company exists because the corporate assets float. Most companies have assets solidly fixed to land. Most companies are understandably organized in a more provincial fashion because their assets are not easily moved from the jurisdiction of one country to that of another.

However, there certainly is a tendency for companies to conduct their business on a more global basis. No company is forever fixed to any one nation as long as it enjoys the right to build new factories in whatever nation provides the most attractive and stable environment. Therefore, over a long period of time, a company can, and often will, redeploy its assets from one nation to many nations.

## THE PROGRESS OF GLOBALIZATION

To examine the nature of the organization of companies operating on a worldwide basis, and to sense the trend of companies becoming more global in their activities, we reviewed annual reports of two arbitrarily selected American companies. One is a major pharmaceutical company and the other a major oil services and chemical company. The pharmaceutical company has operations within the United States, which are conducted through thirty wholly owned corporate entities.

These, in turn, have wholly owned operating affiliates in different countries. For instance, Canada is served by eight wholly owned operating affiliates reporting directly to various wholly owned subsidiaries of the U.S. parent organization. In other words, the operating affiliates in Canada do not report directly to the parent organization but to various corporate entities beneath the parent. Thus, there appears to be no direct corporate link between a non-U.S. operating affiliate and the parent organization.

From one to three wholly owned operating affiliates represent the company's business in manufacturing, marketing, and distribution in each of thirteen Latin American countries. From one to ten operating affiliates do business in each of seventeen European countries including Poland, Hungary, Turkey, and Yugoslavia. Anywhere from one to five operating affiliates are in each of twenty-one nations in Australia, the Far and Middle East, and Africa.

Presumably, other nations without operating affiliates within their borders are served by those in nations that do have such representation. Perhaps there is cooperative sharing of the market by different operating affiliates. Perhaps they compete for business as though there were no common ownership of the company's shares. Anything is possible in the operations of a multinational company.

The corporate parent issues one income statement and balance sheet. Yet the company consists, from an operating point of view, of over 170 independent companies listed in the company's annual report. Each of these companies may have its own set of subsidiary companies performing marketing and distribution functions in different locales. Even if there is only an average of three such subsidiaries per listed affiliate, there are over five hundred separate entities whose financial reports have to be consolidated or combined, one way or another, into a single annual report to the shareholders.

In a three-year period, the share of revenues for this company in the United States compared to the total revenues fell from 51 percent to 48 percent. Whereas the share of U.S. operating profit rose during this particular three-year period, the percentage of identifiable assets in the United States fell from 54 percent to 52 percent. Although these are not spectacular changes, the trend, if it continues for a decade or so, will certainly make the company less American and more global.

The second example is an oil service and chemical company. Its chemical division is headquartered in the United States with eleven operating affiliates in Europe. However, these are not all wholly owned. Two are 70 percent owned and another is only 15 percent owned by the American parent. The company's petroleum services business is handled by ten separate American corporations that are wholly owned, plus thirty-five others scattered on every continent of the world. Ownership in these operating affiliates varies from 25 percent to 100 percent. About half of the operating affiliates outside the United States are not wholly owned by the U.S. parent.

Owning less than 100 percent of an operating affiliate casts a different light on the role of management. The parent organization cannot manage a partially owned operating affiliate without taking into consideration the minority or majority shareholders. These minority or majority holdings are there for a reason, usually associated with the founding of the affiliate or the expansion of its sphere of activity. The company's annual report, a single set of figures on its income statement and balance sheet, has to reflect not only the large number of operating affiliates making up the whole company, and their respective subsidiaries, but also the fact that these operating affiliates, through which the company conducts its business, are not wholly owned.

For this particular company, an arbitrarily selected three-year period shows that U.S. revenues remained flat at 57 percent of total revenues and assets in the United States remained flat at 51 percent of all assets. However, nearly all operating profit was made outside of the United States. If this is where the profits lie, then this is where new capital investments will be made. With time, this company, too, will become less American.

In some respects, both of these companies, with about a half share of their assets and revenues in the United States, may be more global than one may surmise. In the past, a U.S. subsidiary on non-U.S. soil was headed by an American corporate management team, with local nationals restricted to manning the lower rungs of the management ladder. Decision making was somewhat centralized, with the parent organization playing a decisive role in the operations of an affiliate. Now a corporate entity at a non-U.S. location is apt to be manned from top to bottom by local nationals. Decision making is far more decentralized, with greater emphasis on financial reporting as the primary control mechanism. Although it is true that U.S. corporate headquarters retains the right to approve major capital expenditure top executive positions, day-to-day operational, marketing, and personnel decisions are usually made at the local level.

True globalization of these companies may occur when the U.S. corporate parent becomes the U.S. operating affiliate of a company whose headquarters has been moved to Bermuda. The headquarters itself may be no more than a coordination and financial reporting centre. A global company is no longer an American or a French company with a large number of foreign subsidiaries. Rather, it is a collection of corporate entities each concentrating in pursuing the company's business in a geographic area. There is no dominant culture within the company, because there is no dominant national corporate entity within the company.

A manager of any nationality has a chance to achieve the ranks of top management. The role of top management is to guide the overall direction of the company in pursuit of an agreed on set of corporate objectives. The role of top management has not changed—it is just that when they do meet around a table, they may not be all of one nationality. They may not even meet around a table. Teleconferencing can electronically create a conference without the physical presence of the participants. Modern means of communications can tie together the top management team no matter where they are located. The orientation of top management may not be bound by the political or economic considerations of any one nation.

The quintessential American company, Coca-Cola, has banned the words "domestic" and "foreign" from corporate communication. Although Americans are still the largest per capita consumers of Coca-Cola, the United States only has about 5 percent of the world's population. That means that 95 percent of the potential market is outside the United States. The U.S. market, in 1991, represented one third of sales and one fifth of the operating income for CocaCola. Not only is four fifths, or 80 percent, of operating income outside the United States, but the non-U.S. share is growing and is expected to reach 90 percent in a few years.

Top management is increasingly non-American. This is intentional because Coca-Cola wants to become a global company with global management. Coca-Cola is even thinking of global advertising, one commercial to be aired throughout the world. The higher growth rates in Coca-Cola consumption in non-U.S. areas of the world than in the United States. A comparison of the ten-year with the five-year figures indicates that this trend is accelerating. The market highlights reveal the company's orientation to penetrating the global market. Clearly, with the passage of time, Coca-Cola's being American in origin will be an historic footnote.

## GLOBALIZATION IN OCEAN AND MONMOUTH COUNTIES

Globalization does not only mean American companies becoming less American. Globalization also means non-American companies becoming more American. Ocean and Monmouth counties are two typical New Jersey counties, as American as apple pie. Yet, many people in these two counties work for corporate entities that are owned by non-U.S. companies. A&P is a food retailer employing one thousand people in the two counties. Once A&P was an all-American institution known as the Great Atlantic and Pacific Tea Company, with retail food

*Unit case equals 24 8-ounce drinks Excludes Soviet Union and ChinaIncludes Japanese non-carbonated soft drinks*

United States Most developed market, with great opportunity ahead... key bottle/can growth channels: mass merchandisers, drug store chains, petroleum retailers, warehouse dubs... incremental fountain growth through several new major accounts...share gain of 0.6 points to 41 percent and the largest share advantage ever over our main U.S. competitor...one share point is 74 million unit cases Philippines San Miguel joint venture global model since 1981 formation...14 percent average annual unit case growth since 1981...new Santa Rosa superplant helped meet Manila demand...significant post-mix opportunity...three- year average post-mix growth of nearly 25 percent

Germany Focus on Coca-cola, Coke light, Sprite and Fanta... bottling efficiencies gained through continued system rationalization...64 bottling entities consolidated into 37 in 1990...incremental growth provided by new eastern German market Norway Fanta mandarin rollout sparked growth...1.5 liter returnable/refillable PET launching extended packaging innovation...12 percent Coke light share is among world's highest

Great Britain Coca-Cola & Schweppes Beverages highly successful joint venture...four-year average unit case growth 22 percent...larger PET packages and can multipacks support volume advances...new production plant planned for southern England Austria Value pricing strategy and point-of-sale merchandising generated double-digit unit case growth... Sprite light rollout boosted diet segment sales...returnable-refillable PET packaging introduced

France Company-owned bottler handles 91 percent of volume... production rationalized...reorganized total sales function to provide national account service... 16,000 vending machines and 5,000 post-mix dispensers placed in 1990... aggressive merchandising added 20,000 displays, 700 coolers in 5,000 supermarkets Turkey Company-owned Ankara bottler set growth pace... larger one-way packages, post-mix development, vending placement should drive continued strong growth

Brazil Solid growth as prices held firm and costs were contained... merchandising and larger packages empha-sized...post-mix currently only 7 percent of total volume, representing significant opportunity

Australia Highest per capita consumption in Pacific...86 percent share of cola segment...growth forged by aggressive marketing, expanded availability...vending machines to double to 50,000 by end of decade Colombia Larger packages stimulate growth despite overall higher prices...1.5 liter glass bottle introduced...diet Coke relaunched with 100 percent aspartame

Japan Coca-Cola leads cola segment with 80 percent share... Company products lead world's largest non-carbonated segment...world's highest vending machine per capita... more than 750,000 in place Mexico Per capita consum-ption second only to U.S....focus on advancing infrastructure, large-size packaging innovation... more than 30,000 coolers/refrigerators placed in 1990... 25 new wareho-uses opened...new bottling lines commissioned

stores stretching from coast to coast. The company was dominant in the national food retail chain store business from the nineteenth century until after World War II. There may be employees at A&P today who think they are working for an American company, but they are not. The majority of shares are owned by German investors.

The one thousand employees at the various franchise outlets of Pearl Vision Centers, Haagen Daas, Bennigan's, Steak & Ale, and Burger King may think they are working for American companies, but they are not.

These franchises are owned by Grand Metropolitan, an English firm. Although the 650 workers at Ciba-Geigy and the 370 workers at Nestle Foods are probably aware that they are working for U.S. subsidiaries of Swiss companies, this insight may, or may not, be shared by the 450 workers at Air Cruisers, a manufacturer of inflatable rafts, which is owned by a French company.

The 400 workers at Dialight, a maker of electronic parts, may not be aware that they are really working for a Dutch company, and the 900 workers at A&S and Sterns may, or may not, be aware that they are employees of a U.S. subsidiary of a Canadian retailer. The 350 workers at New Jersey Steel or the 90 workers at Container Corporation of America may be misled by the American sounding names of their companies into thinking that they are working for U.S. companies. They are not. They are actually working for subsidiaries of a Swiss and an Irish company, respectively. And the list goes on.

## AMERICA NO LONGER THE DRIVING FORCE

As American firms have, at least historically, gobbled up overseas companies, American firms are now free game in the worldwide pursuit of companies desiring to extend their markets by buying companies not located on their native soil, or in building factories on American soil. Indeed, the Japanese have largely taken over the mantle of what was once worn by American corporate raiders: the ugly American is now the ugly Japanese. American managers are being warned about the high probability of having to report to Japanese superiors and of how difficult it will be for Americans to achieve the upper echelons of corporate positions at Japanese owned enterprises. Learning Japanese cultural practices and etiquette, even to the extent of learning the Japanese language, are now viewed as ways for the overachievers to overachieve. A decade or so ago, one merely had to substitute "European" for "American" and "American", for "Japanese" and the statements would have been just as applicable.

The globalization of business may be more rapid than one might imagine. Of the largest one hundred companies in the world, 60 percent were U.S. firms in 1960, 56 percent in 1970, and 44 percent in 1980. In 1990, of the one hundred largest companies in the world, fifty-four were Japanese, thirty-four American, seven British, and the remaining six were scattered among other nations. Where the world's largest companies are domiciled is of interest because the top one thousand companies produce one quarter of the entire world's economic output of goods and services.

## HISTORIC ROOTS OF GLOBALIZATION

The globalization of the conduct of business is part of the process of globalization of the world political and economic systems. This is not a recent phenomenon. Globalization of the world's political and economic systems has a long history; driven by the desire to superimpose the will of one nation over others by warfare it goes back to the dawn of civilization. The Roman Empire, although built on military conquest, created a single integrated political and economic system of government covering much of the then known civilized world.

Political integration was achieved on a personal level, with the emperor selecting the provincial governors. Like-minded thinking by the provincial governors was encouraged by the presence of units of the Roman army who reported to, and were controlled by, the emperor, thus establishing Pax Romana. The Roman peace was maintained also by cultural integration with the adoption of Roman customs, dress, language, and religion by the indigenous peoples.

Economic integration was fostered by building a system of roads that was not exceeded in length and scope until the construction of the U.S. interstate highway system after World War II. Accompanying the road system to enhance economic integration was a common currency, uniform weights and measurements, and a judicial system for resolving commercial disputes. Traders were able to roam the entire Roman Empire exchanging goods in one region for those of another without much in the way of tariffs, customs, border inspections, and other impediments to free trade such as thieves, marauding bandits, and toll collectors.

The Dark Ages in the western part of the Roman Empire has been described as a thousand-year depression brought on by the cessation of free trade caused by thieves, marauding bandits, and toll collectors.

Ultimately, the Roman Empire fell, although it took its time. But the dream of a universal empire never died. Charlemagne and Napoleon attempted to revive the dream of a single nation state encompassing all of Europe. The Hapsburg Empire kept the dream of free trade within the open frontiers of its domain alive. All of these attempts failed, but the dream did not. Unfortunately, for the first half of the twentieth century, the dream lived on with Hitler and Mussolini.

Now, during the second half of the twentieth century, the dream of a global political and economic system may be achieved without military action. In fact, the idea is advancing faster than any army can march. There are no serious obstacles facing the advance of globalization. No one seems to object. Unlike in the past, there appears to be no single charismatic leader. After World War II, the United States appeared to be leading the process, but it is difficult to say that a particular American was leading the process. Today, one might argue that Europe, in forming the European Community and in taking the first steps to bring eastern Europe into the European Community, has assumed the mantle of leadership. However, as before, there does not seem to be an individual leader.

All the leaders of the industrialized nations are marching to the same drum beat. It might be more accurate to say that any national leader who obstructs the process of globalization will not remain in power for long. The words "new world order" (*Novus Ordo Seclorum*) have been on the back of the U.S. dollar bill for a long time without much public mention. Now the words "new world order," along with "global island" and "global community," are bandied about in such a way that one must conclude that there is no opposition to globalization. This is quite remarkable considering that the supposed benefits of the universal state have often been the excuse to justify military conquest.

## GLOBALIZATION AND THE U.S. CONSTITUTION

Military aggression with one nationality dominating others was never a popular means to achieve political and economic integration, except for the winners. The losers were unwilling participants and eventually undid what the winners had achieved. Now a new way has been found. The new world political order is to be based on a relationship similar to that which exists among the fifty individual states making up the United States and the nation called the United States. After the American Revolution, the Articles of Confederation bound the thirteen colonies too loosely, so to speak, for any concerted action to be undertaken by the newly independent nation.

One might liken the Articles of Confederation to the League of Nations, which came into being after World War I. Both were ineffectual in binding together sovereign states into a single community of not-so-sovereign states. The Constitution arose from the failure of the Articles of Confederation to weld a single nation from the independent states. This was also the essential reason for abandoning the League of Nations in favour of forming the United Nations after World War II. Unlike the charter of the United Nations, the Constitution contained a mechanism to create a single nation out of thirteen sovereign states, without the use of force or the submergence of individual cultures. The United Nations has not been so successful.

The Constitution is well known for creating a system of checks and balances among the judicial, legislative, and executive branches of government to ensure that no branch of the government and, therefore, no individual would dominate the other branches, or the nation. However, another challenge facing the founders of the United States was dealing with the problem of the sovereignty of the various states. Each state jealously guarded its natural rights as a sovereign state. For example, goods could not cross state borders without paying tariffs and being subject to quotas and other impediments to free trade. Money was defined by each state. Some way had to be found to honour the rights of states while yet binding them into a single nation in order for the Constitution to be ratified by the states. This was achieved in the Tenth Amendment to the Bill of Rights:

"The powers not delegated to the United States [i.e., the national government) by the Constitution, nor prohibited by it to the states, are reserved to the states respectively, or to the people."

The Constitution was ratified on the basis that the states ratifying the Constitution knew exactly what degree of sovereignty was being transferred to the national government, and what acts of sovereignty were prohibited to them. Therefore, any other act of sovereignty not specifically mentioned or prohibited was left in the hands of the state, or its people. This division of sovereign power between national and state governments, and the rights given to the people with respect to speech, press, assembly, and to bear arms, made it difficult for the central government to become too intrusive in the lives of the people. The limits placed on governmental powers encouraged a free exchange of ideas.

General prohibitions on the rights of states to interfere with interstate trade and commerce, and subsequent legislation against the formation of trusts, such as the Sherman Anti-Trust Act, fostered a free market economy. Some variant of the principles incorporated in the Constitution, and some variant of the free market economy, is present in every nation in the industrialized world. Moreover, democracy and the free market economy are the goals of those nations who are tying to escape from the inefficiencies, capriciousness, and arbitrariness of overbearing bureaucracies or dictatorships.

The true worth of the Constitution is its capacity to amalgamate a single nation out of a community of nations without resorting to force, or to the submergence of individual cultures to a dominant culture. It is interesting to note that the United Nations, the outgrowth of the League of Nations, is not a primary mover in this amalgamation of sovereign and independent nations into vast economic and political units. Perhaps it is the veto, a definitively nondemocratic concept, that permits the superpowers to maintain their sovereignty in world affairs, that prevents the United Nations from fully playing out its intended role.

Economic amalgamation accompanies political integration, or it may be the other way around. Who knows, for it is often difficult to separate the two. Indeed, one may argue that economic integration seems to precede political amalgamation. The G eneral Agreement on Tariffs and Trade (GATT) talks have been continually held since its founding after World War II. The purpose of GATT is to reduce tariffs and remove trade barriers; that is, to set the stage for the economic integration of its member nations. The organization for promoting economic integration is the OECD, the acronym for the Organization of Economic Cooperation and Develop-ment, whose name eloquently describes its purposes.

The OECD encompasses much of the industrialized world. In the Far East, its members are Australia, New Zealand, and Japan. In North America, the member nations are Canada and the United States. The European members are Austria, Belgium, Finland, France, Germany, Greece, Iceland, Ireland, Italy, Luxembourg, Netherlands, Norway, Portugal, Spain, Sweden, Switzerland, Turkey, and the United Kingdom.

Despite fits and starts, and occasional breakdowns in talks, the efforts of GATT have resulted in a significant reduction in trade barriers and tariffs among

The industrialized nations in the Far East, North America, and Europe. Once trade barriers are removed, nations become interested in avoiding ruinous trade wars. The European Coal and Steel Community was formed to coordinate the activities of the coal and steel industry within the member nations. This led to the formation of the European Economic Community, or Common Market, an effort to coordinate a much wider sphere of economic activity with political implications. The European Economic Community was transformed in 1992 to a single market, the European Community, which performs, or administrates, those economic and political functions that have been given up by the individual nations.

The European Community differs from the Common Market in that there is to be total freedom of the movement of goods, services, and people throughout the member states. Border stations within the European Community for customs inspections of goods crossing national borders for compliance with quotas and the payment of tariffs, along with the checking of passports, will eventually be relegated to the dustbin of history.

The movement of goods, services, and people between Germany and France will be no different, in principle, than between Massachusetts and

Connecticut. Moreover, the European Community has been given broad responsibilities to integrate the communication and transportation systems, organize a common European programme on energy and environmental issues, bring about a common currency and a European banking system, and harmonize taxation and financial reporting. Much of this activity is associated with the European Parliament, and its various ministries, in Brussels.

## GLOBAL MONEY

Globalization requires a global currency. After World War II, the "global" currency was the U.S. dollar. With the recovery of nations after the war, other currencies transformed themselves from soft to hard; that is, from undesirable to desirable currencies in the conduct of international trade. A desirable, or hard, currency is one that is an acceptable medium of exchange and a storehouse of value, characteristics not found in many currencies.

There has been a relative decline of the United States as a world economic power, caused not so much by its industrial decline as by the industrial emergence of the powerhouses in Germany, Japan, and other nations along the Pacific rim. This has dimmed the former luster of the U.S. greenback. As yet, however, a truly global currency has not taken the place of the U.S. dollar. Special Drawing Rights (SDRs), issued by the International Monetary Fund, represent a basket of currencies of the industrial nations of the world. However, SDRs have not been a practical substitute for the role of the U.S. dollar in settling accounts between nations and as a currency for world trade. But that is not stopping the movement toward a global currency.

In late 1991, the members of the European Community more or less agreed to a common central bank and a single currency by 1997, or possibly, by 1999. The European Currency Unit, or ECU, is intended to replace all European currencies. If this is approved by the member nations of the European Community, then the sovereign power associated with each nation issuing its own money and determining interest rates will be turned over to a common central bank.

European nations that have habitually devalued their currencies to make their products more price competitive will then have to directly address the causes of their non-competitiveness. The nations of Europe will not have the freedom to generate large budget deficits because they will lose the sovereign power to print money to paper over the deficits. These may be considered the disadvantages of a common currency. The chief advantage is not having to exchange currencies when goods cross a border. Businesses will no longer have to worry about the repercussions of adverse currency exchange rate fluctuations between the time of shipping goods and collecting revenue. Nor are goods crossing borders subject to inspection, tariffs, and quotas. Therefore, the cost of conducting business will fall, and presumably, living standards will rise.

To most Europeans, the advantages seem to outweigh the disadvantages. Efforts are already underway among the European nations to reduce budget deficits to ease the pressure on inflation and interest rates in preparation for the day when a new ECU currency will be exchanged for existing European national currencies. The anticipated timetable will not be long once the Maastricht Treaty is approved by the member nations. The European Monetary Institute is to be organized in 1994 and is anticipated to be transformed into the embryonic European Central Bank by 1996. At that time, national budgets are to be more or less in line with one another, in order to have comparable interest and inflation rates among the European nations. This will allow the establishment of a permanent exchange rate among the various currencies, and hopefully, the ultimate step of permitting the exchange of all the currencies for one single currency, the ECU.

In the meantime, there is close coordination between the various central banks of Europe, Japan, and the United States with regard to controlling the trading range of currency exchange rates. If the trading range between all the hard currencies remains sufficiently narrow, then the major currencies, in the aggregate, can be treated as a global currency. Trading ranges among the hard currencies, however, have fluctuated widely, although not nearly as much as the trading ranges among the soft currencies. This makes the reporting of financial results for companies with operating affiliates located in one hundred different countries more difficult because these operations are conducted in one hundred different currencies. This leads to transaction and translation gains and losses resulting from fluctuating currency exchange rates: a sure sign that there is no global currency at the moment.

## SOVEREIGNTY AT BAY

Globalization of the world's political and economic activities has not yet been achieved. In some respects, it is still a dream. On the surface, the world still operates under a system of sovereign nations where "the king can do no wrong." However, its appearance may be more superficial than real. The presidents and prime ministers of states gather frequently and their photographs seem to reveal a gathering of governors of states or mayors of cities rather than sovereign rulers "who can do no wrong." Perhaps no one can better attest to the degree of political integration than Saddam Hussein, who made the sovereign decision that Kuwait should be the nineteenth province of Iraq. Never in modern history has there been an instance of all the nations of the world uniting in a common cause. Although some nations were more active, and others more passive or even resistant, the point was that Saddam Hussein had to face a united world community of nations intent on preserving the independence of oil rich Kuwait. This is something that neither Saddam Hussein nor the leaders of the community of nations, thought possible.

## TECHNICAL UNDERPINNINGS OF GLOBALIZATION

There is a technical side to the progress being made in global political and economic integration. Certainly, technical advances in communications have helped to integrate the nations of the world. It took a month for the Duke of Palma in the Netherlands to send a message to his master, Philip II of Spain, asking permission to pursue a course of action against the rebelling people of the Netherlands. It also took a month for Philip to communicate his decision back to the duke. Therefore, two months passed before the duke received, or was denied permission, to act. If the duke did not care for Philip's response, add another two months before a decision could be reached. And two more for another round of letters to be exchanged if the two still did not see eye to eye. Even when agreement was reached, circumstances usually had changed sufficiently to start the process over again.

The same approximate passage of time separated George III of England from his colonial governors in the thirteen colonies. The decisions of both kings were largely irrelevant by the time they were received—events had long since passed them by. Today, a retired person in Illinois can be kept abreast with events of a war in the Middle East just as currently as those at the scene. During the Iraq War, he could share the fear of an approaching Scud missile with the people of Tel Aviv. There were several occasions when representatives of governments, including Saddam Hussein himself, relied on the Cable News Network as a source of current information about what was going on in the Middle East in preference to their own official channels of communication.

A common source of information that is current and shared among the governments of the world tends to coordinate and integrate courses of action to be undertaken by the world community of nations. In a sense, the world's leaders are reacting to a common information base while, more or less, sharing the same economic and political goals. This encourages like decisions being made by like minded leaders. The sovereignty of nations in terms of "the king can do no wrong" has lost most, if not all, of its meaning in today's world.

Logistical systems have been integrated to permit a low-cost and flexible system of moving goods between, and within, nations. The millions of ubiquitous containers can be as easily transported by truck as by barge, rail, and vessel.

For certain high-valued and lightweight cargoes, air can be added to the list. Therefore, as long as a river, road, or railroad track connects a factory with a port terminal, the factory is connected to the world. A container can be loaded at a factory and its doors sealed shut. The container can be lifted onto one mode of transport and shifted to another without the expense of off-loading and on loading the contents of the container.

It is the container itself, with its contents untouched, that is moved from one mode of transport to another. The cost of lifting a container off a truck and loading it on a vessel is minuscule. Therefore, the preferred mode of transport is one of convenience and cost. The contents of a container are not off-loaded until it has arrived at its final destination.

Inter modalism is the realization of the concept of the globalization of the world's logistical systems. A factory in Japan can load a container with its goods on a truck or railway car. The container can be trucked or railed down to a port terminal. It is then loaded on a container vessel and can reach France by a choice of routes. For instance, the container can be shipped to a West Coast U.S. or Canadian port. Special dedicated container trains transverse the North American continent for loading the container on another vessel from an East Coast U.S. or Canadian port for movement to a French port. North America becomes a land bridge connecting the Pacific and Atlantic oceans. The final leg from the French, or any European port, to the container's destination in France can be by truck, rail or barge, or combination thereof.

The concept of North America being a land bridge for the movement of containers is matched by the land bridge system that connects east coast Russian ports with Europe. The Trans-Siberian railroad offers direct service from Vladivostok to Vienna. From Vienna, other railroad lines and trucks, with, perhaps, a side trip on a barge towed up the Danube, can carry the container to its final destination. Naturally, the container loaded on a vessel in Japan can reach Europe without the use of land bridges. But the vessel has a choice of transversing the world either through the Suez or the Panama Canals, or bypassing both by sailing around the southern tip of Africa. The vessel can stop at any European port, not necessarily in France, for off-loading the container on a flatbed truck, railcar, barge, or a smaller container vessel for the final leg of its journey.

Containerized freight using inter modal means of transport provides a globalized transport system whose cost is relatively low compared to the value of a container filled with finished, or semi finished, goods. Containers can be shipped from nearly any point to another point on the globe for a cost that adds anywhere from 2 percent to 5 percent to the value of the goods in a container. This is truly a low shipping cost.

This means that any location on the globe that offers 2 percent to 5 percent savings in manufacturing costs, be it in the form of labour, material, or financing, can be considered a potential site for a factory. Small wonder that the Ford Escort is assembled from parts made in forty different nations. The globalization of logistics would not have been possible without a worldwide telecommunications and data processing system to keep track of the millions of containers. An individual container can be on any railroad car, truck, barge, vessel, and possibly airplane, in any nation, or crossing any ocean.

The knowledge of the current location of each individual container, and the identification of the carrier, is a sine qua non condition for the functioning of an inter modal containerized freight system. A worldwide telecommunications system that links computers programmed to handle the necessary "paperwork" is an integral part of the workings of a globalized logistics system.

## GLOBAL LANGUAGE AND CULTURE

The global language for communication in world commerce is English, or some might say, American. This is a legacy of the times when Great Britain, as progenitor nation of the industrialized world, ruled a quarter of the world's land surface. Although it might be advantageous for a businessman to understand the native language of another businessman with whom he is negotiating a transaction, it is not necessary. In fact, a company that attempts to transact business on a global scale without the ability to communicate in English would be at a competitive disadvantage. One can also sense the rise of a global culture. With much misgivings among individuals, the global culture appears to be American. American TV shows and movies provide much of the entertainment fare for the world's population. The golden arches of McDonald's can be found in every part of the world along with showings of "Married, With Children" and video tapes of Madonna, which to some is a rather gruesome thought.

## GLOBAL FINANCE AND TRADE

Another area of globalization is the world financial system. Precious metals, currencies, and securities are traded on a twenty-four-hour basis. A trader in gold can have his account automatically shifted from Tokyo to Hong Kong to trading centers in Europe and then to the United States, and trade gold twenty four hours a day without sleeping. Major currency exchange centers coordinate their opening and closing times, permitting currencies to be traded twenty-four hours a day. The world's stock markets are moving in this direction.

Single country mutual funds are being organized so that investors can diversify their holdings in Germany, Spain, Mexico, New Zealand, Singapore, Japan, and other nations to suit their global tastes. This is a modern version of investors once being advised to diversify their holdings in different industries within their nation of domicile; 40 percent in steel and 30 percent in computers may now be 40 percent in Japan in 30 percent in Germany. Other global mutual funds are,

**Table. GDP Compared with Merchandise Trade Exports**

| Gross Domestic Trade Exports | Merchandise Percent Of Gdp | Exports As | Product |
|---|---|---|---|
| Singapore | $ 28.4 | $ 44.6 | 157% |
| Belgium | 126.5 | 100.7 | 80 |
| Hong Kong | 52.5 | 28.7 | 55 |
| Netherlands | 221.7 | 107.8 | 49 |
| Venezuela | 43.8 | 13.0 | 30 |

| | | | |
|---|---|---|---|
| Germany | 1189.0 | 340.6 | 29 |
| Korea | 211.9 | 62.3 | 29 |
| Portugal | 44.9 | 12.8 | 29 |
| Canada | 488.6 | 114.1 | 23 |
| Israel | 46.0 | 10.7 | 23 |
| New Zealand | 41.4 | 8.6 | 21 |
| United Kingdom | 717.9 | 152.4 | 21 |
| Yugoslavia | 71.8 | 13.3 | 19 |
| Greece | 39.9 | 7.4 | 18 |
| France | 955.8 | 172.6 | 18 |
| South Africa | 80.4 | 13.5 | 17 |
| Italy | 865.7 | 140.7 | 16 |
| Australia | 281.9 | 33.2 | 12 |
| Spain | 379.4 | 44.5 | 12 |
| Brazil | 319.2 | 34.4 | 11 |
| Japan | 2818.5 | 275.0 | 10 |
| Iran | 150.3 | 13.0 | 9 |
| United States | 5156.4 | 346.9 | 7 |

already diversified, with holdings spread over various nations. This represents an enormous shift in portfolio management focus from companies to countries.

One measure of the degree of globalization that has already been achieved is the ratio of a nation's exports in relation to its gross domestic product. In the table, merchandise trade exports are all exports such as food, fuel, commodities, and manufactured goods. The gross domestic product (GDP) is a measure of total commercial activity within a nation. Figures are in billions of dollars for the year 1989 and were taken from the *1991 World Development Report* published by The World Bank.

This list of selected nations shows that many nations have exports that are a significant portion of their total domestic economic output, which is a measure of the extent of globalization of world commerce. The Far Eastern trading nations of Singapore, Hong Kong, and Korea are about where one might expect, because their economies are export oriented. One surprise is Japan, which is actually far down the list of exporting nations with regards to the relationship of its exports to its domestic economy. Japan is certainly a major world exporting nation, but its exports in relation to its domestic economy are about the same as those of the United States.

This is indicative of the robustness of the Japanese domestic market and the size and living standards of its population. The issue in the financial press is not the size of Japanese exports as such, because both Germany and the United States exceed the dollar volume of Japanese exports. The issue is the size of the trade surplus, which in 1989, was about $68 billion. For the United States, the discussion is on the ramifications of the nation's trade deficit, which in 1989 was $145 billion. Much of the world trade imbalance is between these two countries.

Moreover, in reviewing the list, one can see the impetus for the economic integration of the European Community. The size of individual European exports and imports to and from other European nations in relation to their domestic economy is probably on the same scale of magnitude as individual states in the United States. In 1992, the European Community consisted of Belgium, Denmark, Germany, France, Greece, Ireland, Italy, Luxembourg, Netherlands, Portugal, Spain, and the United Kingdom. The list of participating countries in the European Community is expected to grow with the possible inclusion of Scandinavian and eastern European nations. If Poland, Czechoslovakia, and Hungary join, the potential of member status being given to the nations making up the former Soviet Union becomes more feasible. This may well lead to the "United States of Europe," which like the United States of America, would stretch from the Atlantic to the Pacific.

President Bush's support of a free trade zone encompassing Canada, the United States, and Mexico may be a precursor to the " United States of North America." The " United States of North America," along with the " United States of Europe," may be the precursor to the " United States of the Northern Hemisphere." Japan and other Far Eastern centers of industry could hardly refrain from joining a market that encompasses so much of the world. As preposterous as all this may sound, it is not nearly as preposterous in 1992 as it was in 1982.

Everything is becoming globalized, homogenized, and pasteurized as a new world system of mutual integration of human activity becomes ever more quickly a reality. There is, however, one remaining activity that has somewhat, but not entirely, escaped the onslaught of sameness. That is accounting and financial reporting.

# 6

# Development of Network Technology

The development of digital technologies and the convergence of broadcasting, telecommunications and informatics offer sizeable opportunities for the implementation of appropriate new technologies by developing countries.

The World Telecommunication Development Conference (WTDC) held in Hyderabad (India) from 24 May to 4 June 2010 adopted, among others, the Programme 1: "Information and Communication Infrastructure and Technology Development".

The programme assists Member States and ITU-D Sector Members to maximise the utilization of appropriate new technologies in the development of their information and communication infrastructure.

The programme also assists developing countries to plan, build, operate, upgrade, manage and maintain technologies applicable in their networks and services. This includes the development of the Telecommunications and Information infrastructure and applications. Applied research and the transfer of technological know-how will be an indispensable part of the task of expediting the access to new technologies on a non-discriminatory basis for developing countries and countries with economies in transition.

The programme will be carried out by various means, including symposia, workshops, conferences, seminars and expert advice as well as information sharing, creation of tools and training material. As issues of network reliability and quality of service continues to be of considerable interest to developing countries, the programme focuses on management issues, marketing techniques and the introduction of new services, taking into account the recent trends in the development of telecommunications, broadcasting and informatics.

## THE DEVELOPMENT OF COMPUTER NETWORKS

The development of computer technologies and its applications has been extremely rapid in the eighties and nineties. Computer networks belong to the most significant fields of technical development.

*This is a consequence of two development paths:*

1. The growing importance of PCs due to the rapidly increasing computing capacity.
2. The organizational and communicative advantages of electronic networks have led to the widespread use of private networks, not only within companies and its subsidiaries but also in customer-supplier-relations.

The main impulse came from a public network - the Internet. It is generally believed that computer networks like the Internet will fundamentally change economy and society. Castells (1996) even compares this new development with the Industrial Revolution. In order to understand what consequences computer networks will have on society and economy it seems necessary to first understand why and how such networks develop.

In this chapter we try to take a step in this direction. We attempt to find key economic factors that may have driven the rapid international diffusion of networking over the past years, and to identify the conditions that may stimulate or hamper this development. We will do this by developing a conceptual framework and a simple economic model that captures the key factors.

In this chapter we apply a microeconomic perspective. Rational agents are assumed to decide about whether to connect to another agent through a network link or not based on a comparison of their costs and benefits of this step. In order to keep the analysis manageable we use relatively simple concepts of costs and benefits in this context. Most importantly, we assume that all the costs and benefits materialize in the current period so that we don't have to take into account discounting and expectations about the future development of the network.

Of course, in reality there are different components of the costs of a network link: installation costs, fixed and variable telecommunication costs, provider fees, etc. In our analysis we assume only the costs of establishing the network link. A similar argument holds for benefits as well. Here we assume that the main effect of a computer network link lies in the reduction of distance friction. This, in turn, allows for an increased level of interaction between actors. The actors are assumed to derive utility from this interaction.

A major economic element of any network infrastructure lies in the existence of network externalities. In our simple model network externalities originate from the fact that when an actor connects to another actor who is already on a network, distance friction between all actors already on the network and the new member is reduced.

These network externalities are the main driving force behind network development. They also raise the question of optimality and individual vs. social valuation.

## THE ROLE OF COMPUTER NETWORKS IN DEVELOPMENT

The good news is that the Internet has grown like a weed, and many welcome it as a tool for productivity and enlightenment; the bad news is that it is almost unknown in developing nations. This chapter offers the hypothesis that computer networks can improve life in developing nations at a relatively low cost. We begin with a brief discussion of development, followed by some of the ways computer networks might help, and conclude with a look at what can be done.

## DIMENSIONS OF DEVELOPMENT

"Development" is an imprecise concept. Economists once equated it with economic productivity—GDP per capita—but that is too simple a formulation. Rising GDP might be accompanied by environmental damage, anger over growing disparity in income distribution, disappointment when expectations rise faster than they are fulfilled, displacement of traditional values and customs, crowded cities, and so forth. Furthermore, GDP counts many painful transactions as positive, for example, bypass surgery, buying a second home after a divorce, or the paycheck of a housewife who is forced into the labour market to make ends meet.

A broader conception of human development is used in the United Nations Development Programme (UNDP) Reports on Human Development, published annually since 1992, e.g. their concept of development includes human autonomy and breadth of choice, equity, sustainability, and empowerment as well as productivity. In an attempt to capture this multidimensional concept of development, UNDP computes a comprehensive Human Development Index (HDI) as a function of productivity, health, and education. It is reassuring that this index shows less variance among nations than GDP per capita, still there are major disparities between nations.

With the comprehensive, UNDP concept of development in mind, let us turn to some of contributions networks might make in economic productivity, health, education, democracy, and quality of life.

### Economic Productivity

Communication pays. In recent telecommunication investments in developing nations, the World Bank expects rates of return between 13 and 20 percent, averaging about 20 percent. In addition to return on investment, they estimate 15-30 percent return to the general economy. They also find "very large economic returns" from the telecommunications components in other sectors such as railways, power, tourism, banking, and rural development.. Computer networks run over telephone infrastructure at relatively small marginal cost, providing increased economic benefit. Consider the success of the Relcom (RELiable COMmunications) network in the ex-Soviet Union. Relcom was established in April, 1989, using a Microvax in

Moscow and PC compatible (286 and 386) computers connected with dial-up lines and 2400 and 9600 bps modems. On August 22, 1990, they started international Internet connectivity with hourly phone calls from Helsinki to Moscow for batch transfer of e-mail and Usenet news. By September, 1993, Relcom served nearly 7,000 organizations and an estimated 200,000 users connecting 162 regions and cities.

In spite of having begun under a communist regime, Relcom carried commercial traffic from the start, and was heavily commercial a year after it began. The network was used for markets and business communication within the nation, and for international transactions and coordination. In a 1994 Usenet News posting, Relcom co-founder Vadim Antonov said he believed the social and business impact of Relcom had been greater than that of the Internet in the US. Relcom is unusual since networks in developing nations have usually started in the university and research community. However it is not the only example. One of the newer networks, in Ghana, accepted commercial traffic from its inception, and 36 of its 89 customers were businesses 8 months after it began.

Networks enable international communication with suppliers, customers, and other stakeholders. Much of the economic success of the US is attributable to our lead in establishing a mass, tariff-free market supported by good communication and transportation. Networks can help open mass, global markets to developing nations. This of course raises the specter of reduced wages and environmental destruction in developed nations.

The entrance of new competition will surely hurt certain industries and workers, but can this globalization be stopped? I do not think so. If that is the case, we in developed nations should console ourselves by noting the positive implications—increased investment opportunity and trade, increased efficiency, lower-cost goods, service and distribution jobs, a more just, peaceful, humane world, and so forth. Economists since Ricardo have insisted that the economic pie is largest when every person (and nation) does what he or she does best. At the same time, we should work against the negative side effects, for example, by seeking international environmental and labour standards.

**Education**

In 1992, Pedro Hepp and his colleagues at the Catholic University in Chile began a five-year project to develop and evaluate an elementary school network called Enlaces (links). Their goals were to enhance efficiency, quality and equity in education and to "integrate the children into the culture." They began with a pilot in six locations, and today there are 144 networked schools. Initially, each school had two computers and a 2400 bps modem. Today, there are between 3 and 10 computers and an Ethernet in each school. They began with batch transfer, making interactive access impossible, but a dozen schools are now getting IP connectivity to the Internet on a pilot basis.

Enlaces provides a variety of services—student and teacher newsletters, educational software, curriculum notes, computer conferences, e-mail, and database access. It has been formally evaluated, for example, they have shown a statistically significant effect on student creativity, and the government has decided to expand nationwide. With World Bank funding, the goal is to reach 100% of the secondary schools and 50% of the primary schools by 2000.

The support structure has been decentralized through the (long) country with 15 universities participating. One of their strong beliefs is that the teachers are at the centre of the network, and their training and support budget is 25% of the total project. From the beginning, Hepp understood the importance of supporting low income, rural and outlying areas. A project like this not only benefits Chile, we can all learn from it. (What proportion of the schools in your community have Ethernets)?

One might argue that Chile is a prosperous developing nation, and therefore atypical. That is so, but even poor nations can make progress. The Cuban economy was dealt a debilitating blow by the fall of Communism in Eastern Europe, but has continued allocating resources to a small education network.

Cuba's networking project is based in the Cuban Youth Computing Clubs (YCCs). Begun in 1987, the YCCs are typically Cuban in their stress on grass roots participation. The centres are reminiscent of Bob Albrecht's People's Computer Company (PCC) and similar experiments dating back to the 1960s in the United States. Like the PCC, they have computers running games, drawing programmes, and other software, which the children may use in a relatively unstructured manner. Additionally, the YCCs offer classes on using application packages and programming. There are now 150 YCCs spread throughout the nation. Eighty of these have 2,400 bps modems which are used to dial into shell accounts on a PC running Unix in Havana. That computer makes UUCP transfers to Canada twice daily, connecting rural Cuba to the world.

It is not coincidental that Cuba and Chile provide examples of education networks in developing nations. Both have strong records of investment in human capital—education and health care. (Cuban and Chilean adult literacy and infant mortality are both above the averages for the UNDP "highly-developed" nations).

These examples have stressed primary and secondary schools, but networks in developing nations generally begin in the university and research community. The advantages of networks to academia are obvious—databases are shared, conferences organized, papers circulated and discussed, collaborative research and writing undertaken, and so forth. It should be noted that this is not a one- way street. Scientists in developing nations, for example, Cuban biotechnologists have much to contribute to the rest of the world.

Universities and research in developing nations will be strengthened, and the "brain drain" diminished as the Net reduces pressure on professionals to move abroad. Early in the century, physics research was concentrated in a few centres. Increased international communication—journals and conferences—led to worldwide dispersion of physics research. International meetings and journals grew, but not as rapidly as domestic activity. The Net will accelerate the spread of excellence.

**Health Care**

We are also seeing early application of networks to health care in developing nations. For example, HealthNet links health care workers in 16 African nations and 4 Asian nations with each other and with colleagues and databases in developed nations using a variety of communication protocols over leased and switched land lines and terrestrial and satellite packet radio. It provides e-mail, a listserver, electronic publications, database access, distance learning, Internet consulting and support, and facilitates cooperation between libraries.

As an example application, consider the use of the ProMED (Programme for Monitoring Emerging Diseases) mailing list during the recent Ebola virus outbreak in Zaire. ProMED was established by 60 researchers in September 1993, and now has over 1,600 members in 80 countries. The list first heard of the outbreak from member Dr. Karl Johnson, the man who discovered and named the Ebola virus in Zaire in 1976. They circulated information from the U.S. Centers for Disease Control & Prevention.

The World Health Organization, The Canadian Health Department, Health Canada, The Swiss Tropical Medicine Institute, The South African National Institute of Virology, and other organizations and Web sites. Subscribers provided sources and bibliographies for information about the Ebola virus and disease and reports of local reaction in Cameroon, Uganda and other countries neighbouring Zaire. They got information to and from effected nations, helping control the spread of the virus and treat the disease, and they provided objective news to the general public.

Today, most HealthNet communication is international, since intranational connectivity is still very sparse in developing nations. But, one can imagine many networking applications in healthcare in a nation like Cuba or China where "barefoot doctors" and other paramedical people serve poor communities and rural areas.

Note that HealthNet uses satellite technology, which may have great promise for developing nations. They do not use the heavy, geostationary satellites that carry television or long distance telephony, but small, low-earth-orbit (LEO) satellites. The current HealthNet satellite is capable of full-duplex, 9,600 bps communication.

Several users may request messages at the same time, but only two can be sending. The satellite is in polar orbit, so it covers the globe, with locations near the equator getting 4 daily passes of about 13 minutes. The ground stations are PC- compatibles with a controller, radio and antenna. Messages may go to any HealthNet user, satellite station, or the Internet, with Internet routing through a gateway at the Memorial University of Newfoundland. The system as typical off-line e-mail with file attachments.

Thirteen-minute uplinks at 9,600 bps will not solve the world's health communication problems, but this is an experiment which hopefully scales up. Several consortia are raising capital and beginning work on LEO satellite networks. Most ambitious is Teledesic, a venture financed by Bill Gates and cellular entrepreneur Craig McCaw. They plan a network of 840 LEO satellites in 21, 435-mile high orbital planes, optimized for digital communication—routers in space. They are targeting two million simultaneous connections and T1 speeds, which would enable connectivity in rural clinics and villages. While many feel this is overly ambitious, they are counting on mass-produced components and technological progress for success.

HealthNet also uses terrestrial radio links, running IP over paths up to 1,000 km. Again, they are operating at a very small scale, but entrepreneurs are investing in terrestrial wireless infrastructure in developing nations. For example, the International Telecommunication Union has established WorldTel, an ambitious organization that is raising capital and beginning pilot installations for wireless telephone links to rural communities in developing nations.

**Democracy and Human Rights**

One might expect networks to encourage democracy by providing people living under dictatorship with outside information and ideas, and by enabling them to share ideas and coordinate political activity within their nations. For example, the Net was used for both inter and intranational communication during the failed Soviet Coup attempt, and it carried news and discussion of events in Tian An Men Square, Chiapas, and so forth. Indeed, we have a dictator's dilemma - - the Net is good for economic development, but may undermine control.

Going beyond anecdote, Kedzie presents multivariate statistical analysis showing that interconnectivity is a better predictor of democracy than schooling, GDP, life expectancy, ethnic homogeneity, or population, particularly in regions of newly emerging democracy. He also analysed the data looking for causality, finding stronger evidence for networks leading to democracy than democracy leading to networks or a spurious correlation of the two with development. Still, he concludes that "the most plausible relationship between democracy and networked communication (and perhaps economic development) may be a virtuous circle with positive feedbacks in both directions".

Many organizations supporting human rights and democracy in developing nations use the Net. The Association for Progressive

Communication (APC) has been a leader in this effort since 1989, coordinating the operation and development of networks devoted to peace, ecology, human rights, and other "progressive" causes. By August 1995, there were 18 member networks, serving over 31,000 activists, educators, nonprofits and non-governmental organizations (NGOs) in over 133 countries.

APC also exchanges e-mail and selected conferences with 40 partner networks. In September, 1995, APC was granted Consultative Status, Category 1, with the Economic and Social Council of the United Nations. This means they can have a permanent representative at the UN, and are entitled to submit written statements to the Council, to be granted hearings, and to propose agenda items for consideration by the Council and its subsidiary bodies.

**Quality of Life**

The environment is under stress everywhere. We have pollution, and energy and other resources are limited. To the extent that networks enable us to substitute communication for transportation, they will have helped. We normally think of this effect with telecommuters in developed nations, but it may also save a rural farmer, labourer or craftsman a trip to town. More important, rural people may not move.

The humanity is flocking to cities in search of better education, health care, and employment. They joke that the national bird of China is now the "crane" because so many high rise buildings are under construction, but can the environment stand the strain of 100 new high-rise Hong Kong's? And, what of congestion, traffic, crime and other side-effects of urbanization? This is not a simple defence of the noble rural life. When allowed, rural people move to the city because it provides a better life. If rural or town life can be improved, fewer may feel compelled to move.

It emphasized Hanoi and Ho Chi Minh City, as opposed to, say, networking regional capitals and fanning out from there. Implicitly or explicitly, infrastructure planning is social planning. Could a Vietnamese Net help curb urbanization while providing urban advantages in towns and rural areas? This issue is tied to productivity—prosperous nations involve a high percentage of the population in intellectual and economic life. Perhaps breadth of choice is at the heart of quality of life. A simpler, rural life may be desirable if it is freely chosen, rather than imposed by necessity. Choice implies awareness, and communication technology expands horizons, making us aware of vocational, political, and value issues and alternatives.

## THE ADVANTAGES (BENEFITS) OF NETWORKING

You have undoubtedly heard the "the whole is greater than the sum of its parts". This phrase describes networking very well, and explains why it has become so popular. A network isn't just a bunch of computers with wires running between them. Properly implemented, a network is a system that provides its users with unique capabilities, above and beyond what the individual machines and their software applications can provide. Most of the benefits of networking can be divided into two generic categories: *connectivity* and *sharing*. Networks allow computers, and hence their users, to be connected together. They also allow for the easy sharing of information and resources, and cooperation between the devices in other ways. Since modern business depends so much on the intelligent flow and management of information, this tells you a lot about why networking is so valuable.

*Here, in no particular order, are some of the specific advantages generally associated with networking*:

- *Connectivity and Communication*: Networks connect computers and the users of those computers. Individuals within a building or work group can be connected into *local area networks (LANs)*; LANs in distant locations can be interconnected into larger *wide area networks (WANs)*. Once connected, it is possible for network users to communicate with each other using technologies such as electronic mail. This makes the transmission of business (or non-business) information easier, more efficient and less expensive than it would be without the network.
- *Data Sharing*: One of the most important uses of networking is to allow the sharing of data. Before networking was common, an accounting employee who wanted to prepare a report for her manager would have to produce it on his PC, put it on a floppy disk, and then walk it over to the manager, who would transfer the data to her PC's hard disk. (This sort of "shoe-based network" was sometimes sarcastically called a "sneakernet".)

True networking allows thousands of employees to share data much more easily and quickly than this. More so, it makes possible applications that rely on the ability of many people to access and share the same data, such as databases, group software development, and much more. Intranets and extranets can be used to distribute corporate information between sites and to business partners.

- *Hardware Sharing*: Networks facilitate the sharing of hardware devices. For example, instead of giving each of 10 employees in a department an expensive colour printer (or resorting to the "sneakernet" again), one printer can be placed on the network for everyone to share.
- *Internet Access*: The Internet is itself an enormous network, so whenever you access the Internet, you are using a network. The significance of the Internet on modern society is hard to exaggerate, especially for those of us in technical fields.
- *Internet Access Sharing*: Small computer networks allow multiple users to share a single Internet connection. Special hardware devices allow the bandwidth of the connection to be easily allocated to

various individuals as they need it, and permit an organization to purchase one high-speed connection instead of many slower ones.

- *Data Security and Management*: In a business environment, a network allows the administrators to much better manage the company's critical data. Instead of having this data spread over dozens or even hundreds of small computers in a haphazard fashion as their users create it, data can be centralized on shared servers. This makes it easy for everyone to find the data, makes it possible for the administrators to ensure that the data is regularly backed up, and also allows for the implementation of security measures to control who can read or change various pieces of critical information.
- *Performance Enhancement and Balancing*: Under some circumstances, a network can be used to enhance the overall performance of some applications by distributing the computation tasks to various computers on the network.
- *Entertainment*: Networks facilitate many types of games and entertainment. The Internet itself offers many sources of entertainment, of course. In addition, many multi-player games exist that operate over a local area network. Many home networks are set up for this reason, and gaming across wide area networks (including the Internet) has also become quite popular. Of course, if you are running a business and have easily-amused employees, you might insist that this is really a *disadvantage* of networking and not an advantage!

## NETWORKING BASICS

As companies rely on applications like electronic mail and database management for core business operations, computer networking becomes increasingly more important. This tutorial helps to explain Ethernet and Fast Ethernet, which are two of the most popular technologies used in networking.

### LANS (LOCAL AREA NETWORKS)

A network is any collection of independent computers that communicate with one another over a shared network medium. LANs are networks usually confined to a geographic area, such as a single building or a college campus. LANs can be small, linking as few as three computers, but often link hundreds of computers used by thousands of people. The development of standard networking protocols and media has resulted in worldwide proliferation of LANs throughout business and educational organizations.

### WANS (WIDE AREA NETWORKS)

Often a network is located in multiple physical places. Wide area networking combines multiple LANs that are geographically separate. This is accomplished by connecting the different LANs using services such as dedicated leased phone lines, dial-up phone lines (both synchronous and asynchronous), satellite links, and data packet carrier services. Wide area networking can be as simple as a modem and remote access server for employees to dial into, or it can be as complex as hundreds of branch offices globally linked using special routing protocols and filters to minimize the expense of sending data sent over vast distances.

## INTERNET

The Internet is a system of linked networks that are worldwide in scope and facilitate data communication services such as remote login, file transfer, electronic mail, the World Wide Web and newsgroups. With the meteoric rise in demand for connectivity, the Internet has become a communications highway for millions of users. The Internet was initially restricted to military and academic institutions, but now it is a full-fledged conduit for any and all forms of information and commerce. Internet websites now provide personal, educational, political and economic resources to every corner of the planet.

## INTRANET

With the advancements made in browser-based software for the Internet, many private organizations are implementing intranets. An intranet is a private network utilizing Internet-type tools, but available only within that organization. For large organizations, an intranet provides an easy access mode to corporate information for employees.

## ETHERNET

Ethernet is the most popular physical layer LAN technology in use today. Other LAN types include Token Ring, Fast Ethernet, Fiber Distributed Data Interface (FDDI), Asynchronous Transfer Mode (ATM) and LocalTalk. Ethernet is popular because it strikes a good balance between speed, cost and ease of installation. These benefits, combined with wide acceptance in the computer marketplace and the ability to support virtually all popular network protocols, make Ethernet an ideal networking technology for most computer users today. The Institute for Electrical and Electronic Engineers (IEEE) defines the Ethernet standard as IEEE Standard 802.3. This standard defines rules for configuring an Ethernet network as well as specifying how elements in an Ethernet network interact with one another. By adhering to the IEEE standard, network equipment and network protocols can communicate efficiently.

### Fast Ethernet

For Ethernet networks that need higher transmission speeds, the Fast Ethernet standard (IEEE 802.3u) has been established. This standard raises the Ethernet speed limit from 10 Megabits per second (Mbps) to 100 Mbps with only minimal changes to the existing cable structure. There are three types of Fast Ethernet: 100BASE-TX for use with level 5 UTP cable, 100BASE-FX for use with fibre-optic cable, and 100BASE-T4 which utilizes an extra two wires for use with level 3 UTP cable.

The 100BASE-TX standard has become the most popular due to its close compatibility with the 10BASE-T Ethernet standard. For the network manager, the incorporation of Fast Ethernet into an existing configuration presents a host of decisions. Managers must determine the number of users in each site on the network that need the higher throughput, decide which segments of the backbone need to be reconfigured specifically for 100BASE-T and then choose the necessary hardware to connect the 100BASE-T segments with existing 10BASE-T segments. Gigabit Ethernet is a future technology that promises a migration path beyond Fast Ethernet so the next generation of networks will support even higher data transfer speeds.

**Token Ring**

Token Ring is another form of network configuration which differs from Ethernet in that all messages are transferred in a unidirectional manner along the ring at all times. Data is transmitted in tokens, which are passed along the ring and viewed by each device. When a device sees a message addressed to it, that device copies the message and then marks that message as being read. As the message makes its way along the ring, it eventually gets back to the sender who now notes that the message was received by the intended device.

The sender can then remove the message and free that token for use by others. Various PC vendors have been proponents of Token Ring networks at different times and thus these types of networks have been implemented in many organizations.

**Protocols**

Network protocols are standards that allow computers to communicate. A protocol defines how computers identify one another on a network, the form that the data should take in transit, and how this information is processed once it reaches its final destination. Protocols also define procedures for handling lost or damaged transmissions or "packets." TCP/IP (for UNIX, Windows NT, Windows 95 and other platforms), IPX (for Novell NetWare), DECnet (for networking Digital Equipment Corp. computers), AppleTalk (for Macintosh computers), and NetBIOS/NetBEUI (for LAN Manager and Windows NT networks) are the main types of network protocols in use today.

Although each network protocol is different, they all share the same physical cabling. This common method of accessing the physical network allows multiple protocols to peacefully coexist over the network media, and allows the builder of a network to use common hardware for a variety of protocols. This concept is known as "protocol independence," which means that devices that are compatible at the physical and data link layers allow the user to run many different protocols over the same medium.

**Media**

An important part of designing and installing an Ethernet is selecting the appropriate Ethernet medium. There are four major types of media in use today: Thickwire for 10BASE5 networks, thin coax for 10BASE2 networks, unshielded twisted pair (UTP) for 10BASE-T networks and fibre optic for 10BASE-FL or Fiber-Optic Inter-Repeater Link (FOIRL) networks. This wide variety of media reflects the evolution of Ethernet and also points to the technology's flexibility. Thickwire was one of the first cabling systems used in Ethernet but was expensive and difficult to use. This evolved to thin coax, which is easier to work with and less expensive.

The most popular wiring schemes are 10BASE-T and 100BASE-TX, which use unshielded twisted pair (UTP) cable. This is similar to telephone cable and comes in a variety of grades, with each higher grade offering better performance. Level 5 cable is the highest, most expensive grade, offering support for transmission rates of up to 100 Mbps. Level 4 and level 3 cable are less expensive, but cannot support the same data throughput speeds; level 4 cable can support speeds of up to 20 Mbps; level 3 up to 16 Mbps. The 100BASE-T4 standard allows for support of 100 Mbps Ethernet over level 3 cable, but at the expense of adding another pair of wires (4 pair instead of the 2 pair used for 10BASE-T); for most users, this is an awkward scheme and therefore 100BASE-T4 has seen little popularity. Level 2 and level 1 cables are not used in the design of 10BASE-T networks.

For specialized applications, fibre-optic, or 10BASE-FL, Ethernet segments are popular. Fiber-optic cable is more expensive, but it is invaluable for situations where electronic emissions and environmental hazards are a concern. Fiber-optic cable is often used in interbuilding applications to insulate networking equipment from electrical damage caused by lightning. Because it does not conduct electricity, fibre-optic cable can also be useful in areas where large amounts of electromagnetic interference are present, such as on a factory floor. The Ethernet standard allows for fibre-optic cable segments up to 2 kilometres long, making fibre optic Ethernet perfect for connecting nodes and buildings that are otherwise not reachable with copper media.

**Topologies**

A network topology is the geometric arrangement of nodes and cable links in a LAN, and is used in two general configurations: bus and star. These two topologies define how nodes are connected to one another. A node is an active device connected to the network, such as a computer or a printer. A node can also be a piece of networking equipment such as a hub, switch or a router. A bus topology consists of nodes linked together in a series with each node connected to a long cable or bus. Many nodes can tap into the bus and begin communication with all other nodes on that cable segment. A break anywhere in the cable will usually cause the entire segment to be inoperable until the break is repaired. Examples of bus topology include 10BASE2 and 10BASE5.

10BASE-T Ethernet and Fast Ethernet use a star topology, in which access is controlled by a central computer. Generally a computer is located at one end of the segment, and the other end is terminated in central location with a hub. Because UTP is often run in conjunction with telephone cabling, this central location can be a telephone closet or other area where it is convenient to connect the UTP segment to a backbone. The primary advantage of this type of network is reliability, for if one of these 'point-to-point' segments has a break, it will only affect the two nodes on that link. Other computer users on the network continue to operate as if that segment were nonexistent.

**Collisions**

Ethernet is a shared media, so there are rules for sending packets of data to avoid conflicts and protect data integrity. Nodes determine when the network is available for sending packets. It is possible that two nodes at different locations attempt to send data at the same time. When both PCs are transferring a packet to the network at the same time, a collision will result. Minimizing collisions is a crucial element in the design and operation of networks. Increased collisions are often the result of too many users on the network, which results in a lot of contention for network bandwidth. This can slow the performance of the network from the user's point of view. Segmenting the network, where a network is divided into different pieces joined together logically with a bridge or switch, is one way of reducing an overcrowded network.

**Ethernet Products**

The standards and technology that have just been discussed help define the specific products that network managers use to build Ethernet networks. The following text discusses the key products needed to build an Ethernet LAN.

**Transceivers**

Transceivers are used to connect nodes to the various Ethernet media. Most computers and network interface cards contain a built-in 10BASE-T or 10BASE2 transceiver, allowing them to be connected directly to Ethernet without requiring an external transceiver. Many Ethernet devices provide an AUI connector to allow the user to connect to any media type via an external transceiver. The AUI connector consists of a 15-pin D-shell type connector, female on the computer side, male on the transceiver side. Thickwire

(10BASE5) cables also use transceivers to allow connections. For Fast Ethernet networks, a new interface called the MII (Media Independent Interface) was developed to offer a flexible way to support 100 Mbps connections. The MII is a popular way to connect 100BASE-FX links to copper-based Fast Ethernet devices.

### Network Interface Cards

Network interface cards, commonly referred to as NICs, are used to connect a PC to a network. The NIC provides a physical connection between the networking cable and the computer's internal bus. Different computers have different bus architectures; PCI bus master slots are most commonly found on 486/Pentium PCs and ISA expansion slots are commonly found on 386 and older PCs. NICs come in three basic varieties: 8-bit, 16-bit, and 32-bit.

The larger the number of bits that can be transferred to the NIC, the faster the NIC can transfer data to the network cable. Many NIC adapters comply with Plug-n-Play specifications. On these systems, NICs are automatically configured without user intervention, while on non-Plug-n-Play systems, configuration is done manually through a setup programme and/or DIP switches.

Cards are available to support almost all networking standards, including the latest Fast Ethernet environment. Fast Ethernet NICs are often 10/100 capable, and will automatically set to the appropriate speed. Full duplex networking is another option, where a dedicated connection to a switch allows a NIC to operate at twice the speed.

### Hubs/Repeaters

Hubs/repeaters are used to connect together two or more Ethernet segments of any media type. In larger designs, signal quality begins to deteriorate as segments exceed their maximum length. Hubs provide the signal amplification required to allow a segment to be extended a greater distance.

A hub takes any incoming signal and repeats it out all ports. Ethernet hubs are necessary in star topologies such as 10BASE-T. A multi-port twisted pair hub allows several point-to-point segments to be joined into one network. One end of the point-to-point link is attached to the hub and the other is attached to the computer.

If the hub is attached to a backbone, then all computers at the end of the twisted pair segments can communicate with all the hosts on the backbone. The number and type of hubs in any one-collision domain is limited by the Ethernet rules. A very important fact to note about hubs is that they only allow users to share Ethernet. A network of hubs/repeaters is termed a "shared Ethernet," meaning that all members of the network are contending for transmission of data onto a single network (collision domain).

This means that individual members of a shared network will only get a percentage of the available network bandwidth. The number and type of hubs in any one collision domain for 10Mbps Ethernet is limited by the following rules:

| Network Type | Max Nodes Per Segment | Max Distance Per Segment |
|---|---|---|
| 10BASE-T | 2 | 100m |
| 10BASE2 | 30 | 185m |
| 10BASE5 | 100 | 500m |
| 10BASE-FL | 2 | 2000m |

## RESEARCH NETWORKING

Research Networking (RN) is about using web-based tools to discover and use research and scholarly information about people and resources. Research Networking tools (RN tools) serve as knowledge management systems for the research enterprise.

RN tools connect institution-level/enterprise systems, national research networks, publicly available research data (*e.g.*, grants and publications), and restricted/proprietary data by harvesting information from disparate sources into compiled expertise profiles for faculty, investigators, scholars, clinicians, community partners, and facilities.

RN tools facilitate the development of new collaborations and team science to address new or existing research challenges through the rapid discovery and recommendation of researchers, expertise, and resources. RN tools differ from search engines such as Google in that they access information in databases and other data not limited to web pages. They also differ from social networking systems such as LinkedIn or Facebook in that they represent a compendium of data ingested from authoritative and verifiable sources rather than predominantly individually-asserted information, making RN tools more reliable.

Yet, RN tools have sufficient flexibility to allow for profile editing. RN tools also provide resources to bolster human connector systems: they can make non-intuitive matches, they do not depend on serendipity, and they do not have a propensity to return only to previously identified collaborations/ collaborators. RN tools also generally have associated analytical capabilities that enable evaluation of collaboration and cross-disciplinary research/ scholarly activity, especially over time.

Importantly, data harvested into robust RN tools is accessible for broad repurposing, especially if available as linked open data (RDF triples). Thus RN tools enhance research support activities by providing data for customized, up-to-date web pages, CV/biosketch generation, and data tables for grant proposals.

## IMPROVE NETWORKING SKILLS

For many of us, networking skills are not something we are born with. You may have to work hard to come out of your shell and make the contacts you need to improve your chances on your career path. With a little practice and the willingness to get out of your "comfort zone," you can improve your networking skills.

**START NETWORKING WITH CONFIDENCE**

- Compose a brief introduction for yourself. You may need to compose several versions of this speech, each customized to particular situations. For example, if you are interested in finding a new position or starting a new business, you might write two versions of your speech—one for employment contacts and one for venture capitalists.
- Practice your introduction by standing before a mirror and paying close attention to your posture and stance. You should try to exude confidence by keeping your shoulders back and your eyes up.
- Find a friend or someone you feel comfortable rehearsing your short introduction in front of. This should be someone who is willing to listen and give constructive criticism to help you perfect your introduction or icebreaker.
- Find a networking opportunity that is low key and low pressure at which to unveil your introductory speech. This can be anything from a casual party to an alumni event for your college or university.
- Dress the part. Your appearance makes up a large part of the first impression for a new contact. When networking for your career or business, choose professional attire that is suitable to the occasion and avoid over- or under-dressing.
- Introduce yourself to at least one new person during your first networking event. By overcoming your fear or shyness, you will find the next introduction that much easier.
- Improve the likelihood that the contacts you make will be fruitful by following up. Send a brief e-mail or make a couple of calls, especially if you promised or were promised information or job leads during your initial conversation.
- Keep getting out there. The best way to improve your networking skills is through real-world experience.

# 7

# Status of Security in Computing

## UNDERSTANDING SECURITY AND SAFE COMPUTING

If you connect to the Internet, allow other people to use your computer, or share files with others, you should take steps to protect your computer from harm. Why? Because there are computer criminals (sometimes called *hackers* or *crackers*) who attack other people's computers. These people can attack directly, by breaking into your computer through the Internet and stealing your personal information, or indirectly, by creating malicious software (or *malware*) designed to harm your computer. Fortunately, you can protect yourself by taking a few simple precautions. This chapter describes the threats and what you can do to defend against them.

## CHECK YOUR SECURITY STATUS WITH WINDOWS SECURITY CENTER

Windows Security Center is your headquarters for computer security. It shows your computer's current security status and recommends anything that you should do to help make your computer more secure.

*To open it:*

- Open Security Center by clicking the Start button, clicking Control Panel, clicking Security, and then clicking Security Center.

*Security Center checks your computer for these security essentials:*

- *Firewall.* A firewall can help protect your computer by preventing hackers or malicious software from gaining access to it.
- *Automatic updating.* Windows can routinely check for updates for your computer and install them automatically.
- *Malware protection.* Antivirus software can help protect your computer against viruses, worms, and other security threats. Antispyware software can help protect your computer from spyware and other potentially unwanted software.
- *Other security settings.* Security Center checks for proper Internet security settings and whether User Account Control is turned on.

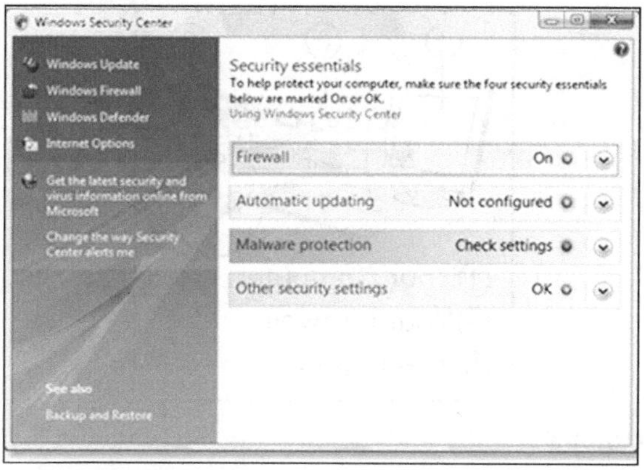


**Windows Security Center**

If any of the security items have a red or yellow background, your computer might be vulnerable to security threats. To fix the problem, click an item to expand it, and then follow the instructions.

**Security Alerts**

If Windows detects that your computer might need enhanced security in any one of the security areas—firewall, automatic updating, malware protection, or other security settings—you will see a notification every time you log on until the problem is fixed. Notifications are displayed in the notification area of the taskbar.

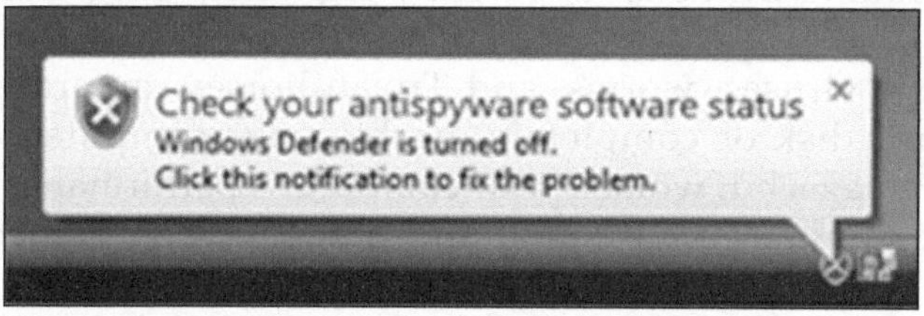


**Security Notification**

Click the notification to open Security Center, where you can learn how to fix the problem.

**Use a Firewall**

A firewall is software or hardware that checks information coming from the Internet or a network and then either turns it away or allows it to pass through to your computer, depending on your firewall settings. In this way, a firewall helps prevent hackers and malicious software from gaining access to your computer. Windows Firewall is built into Windows and is turned on automatically.

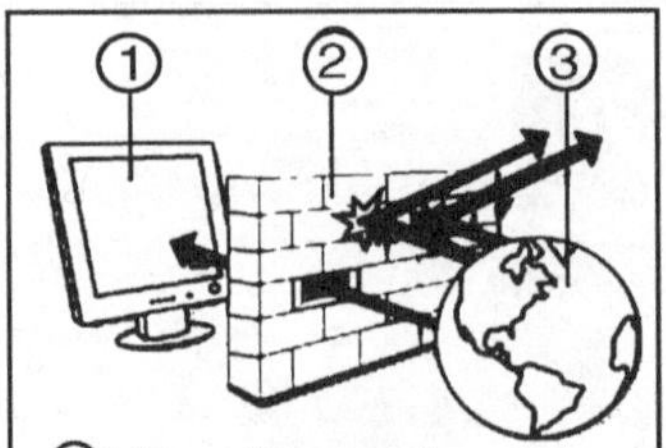


**How a Firewall Works**

If you run a programme such as an instant messaging programme or a multiplayer network game that needs to receive information from the Internet or a network, the firewall asks if you want to block or unblock (allow) the connection. If you choose to unblock the connection, Windows Firewall creates an exception so that the firewall won't bother you when that programme needs to receive information in the future.

**Use Virus Protection**

Viruses, worms, and Trojan horses are programmes created by hackers that use the Internet to infect vulnerable computers. Viruses and worms can replicate themselves from computer to computer, while Trojan horses enter a computer by hiding inside an apparently legitimate programme, such as a screen saver.

Destructive viruses, worms, and Trojan horses can erase information from your hard disk or completely disable your computer. Others don't cause direct damage, but worsen your computer's performance and stability. Antivirus programmes scan e-mail and other files on your computer for viruses, worms, and Trojan horses. If one is found, the antivirus programme either *quarantines* (isolates) it or deletes it entirely before it damages your computer and files.

Windows does not have a built-in antivirus programme, but your computer manufacturer might have installed one. Check Security Center to find out if your computer has antivirus protection. If not, go to the Microsoft Antivirus Partners webpage to find an antivirus programme.

Because new viruses are identified every day, it's important to select an antivirus programme with an automatic update capability. When the antivirus software is updated, it adds new viruses to its list of viruses to check for, helping to protect your computer from new attacks. If the list of viruses is out of date, your computer is vulnerable to new threats. Updates usually require an annual subscription fee. Keep the subscription current to receive regular updates.

**Use Spyware Protection**

Spyware is software that can display advertisements, collect information about you, or change settings on your computer, generally without appropriately obtaining your consent. For example, spyware can install unwanted toolbars, links, or favourites in your web browser, change your default home page, or display pop-up ads frequently. Some spyware displays no symptoms that you can detect, but it secretly collects sensitive information, such as which websites you visit or text that you type. Most spyware is installed through free software that you download, but in some cases simply visiting a website results in a spyware infection.

To help protect your computer from spyware, use an antispyware programme. This version of Windows has a built-in antispyware programme called Windows Defender, which is turned on by default. Windows Defender alerts you when spyware tries to install itself on your computer. It also can scan your computer for existing spyware and then remove it. Because new spyware appears every day, Windows Defender must be regularly updated to detect and guard against the latest spyware threats. Windows Defender is updated as needed whenever you update Windows. For the highest level of protection, set Windowsto install updates automatically.

**Update Windows Automatically**

Microsoft regularly offers important updates to Windows that can help protect your computer against new viruses and other security threats. To ensure that you receive these updates as quickly as possible, turn on automatic updating. That way, you don't have to worry that critical fixes for Windows might be missing from your computer.

Updates are downloaded behind the scenes when you're connected to the Internet. The updates are installed at 3:00 A.M. unless you specify a different time. If you turn off your computer before then, you can install updates before shutting down. Otherwise, Windowswill install them the next time you start your computer.

*To turn on automatic updating:*

- Open Windows Update by clicking the Start button, clicking All Programmes, and then clicking Windows Update.
- Click Change settings.
- Make sure Install updates automatically (recommen-ded) is selected. Windowswill install important updates for your computer as they become available. Important updates provide significant benefits, such as improved security and reliability.
- Under Recommended updates, make sure the Include recommended updates when downloading, installing, or notifying me about updates check box is selected, and then click OK. Recommended updates can address non-critical problems and help enhance your

computing experience. If you are prompted for an administrator password or confirmation, type the password or provide confirmation.

**Use a Standard User Account**

When you log on to your computer, Windows grants you a certain level of rights and privileges depending on what kind of user account you have. There are three different types of user accounts: standard, administrator, and guest. Although an administrator account provides complete control over a computer, using a standard account can help make your computer more secure. That way, if other people (or hackers) gain access to your computer while you are logged on, they can't tamper with the computer's security settings or change other user accounts.

*To determine your account type:*

- Open User Accounts by clicking the Start button, clicking Control Panel, User Accounts and Family Safety (or clicking User Accounts, if you are connected to a network domain), and then clicking User Accounts.

The account type appears under your name.

**User Account Information**

If you are currently using an administrator account, see Change a user's account type to learn how to change it to a standard account.

## SYMANTEC ANTIVIRUS: CHECKING STATUS

An option in Symantec antivirus virus protection check status is available as a security centre and it provides information on how a security tool is protecting the computer at home or at work. Read on to find out more!

**Status of Symantec Antivirus or Norton Antivirus**

Symantec Antivirus for home users is called Norton Antivirus while business users have Symantec Endpoint Protection security as antivirus protection. Both editions provide a Symantec antivirus virus protection status. It is important that the antivirus programmes in any computers, at home or a network, are protecting and securing the PC from viruses or any type of malware attacks, including intrusions.

The image at the left displays a Symantec antivirus virus protection check status as "secure" which is what end-users or business customers of Symantec should find. However, if the status requires attention or is at risk, it means that there is a problem with the Norton or Symantec antivirus settings, a protection has been disabled, or the product is not up-to-date, or has expired.

**Status of Symantec or Norton Antivirus**

If the status of Symantec or Norton antivirus shows an "Attention," you should immediately check the cause. The image at right is an example of when Symantec antivirus virus protection requires attention because the e-mail protection has been disabled. It does not mean that your computer is at risk from viruses, Trojans, worms, spyware, adware or other types of malware, but does mean the protection by Symantec to scan incoming and outgoing emails will not be scanned for malicious codes within the messages or the e-mail attachments.

This type of problem on Norton's security status is easy to fix. Manually enabling any disabled protection should bring back the "Secure" status message, or by clicking on the "Fix" button to automate the process of enabling the protection offered by Symantec. A computer can be "At risk," because one of the important protection modules in the Symantec product that protects the computer against malware, has been disabled:

This can be fixed as well by enabling the disabled protection. However, if enabling the protection continues to display a "At risk" or "Attention" status in the Norton antivirus programme, the user needs to try and restart the computer and then check the product's security centre status again.

**The Symantec Antivirus Virus Protection Check Status Is Still Problematic**

In most cases, a PC restart should resolve or refresh the status of Norton or Symantec antivirus, but if the problem continues, the product includes an interactive support module to automate a fix. In the Norton product, you can click the Support > Get Support from the user interface and it will open the integrated and interactive support options.

This is called One Click Support and it will autofix any problems in Norton products *e.g.* corrupted or damaged installation, corrupted virus definitions, expired subscription and/or activation issues: If a PC restart and autofix session using Norton One Click Support has failed to resolve the problem, the user may need to contact Symantec support using the same option by clicking the "Continue" button in the Norton One Click Support in order to start using the interactive troubleshooter, or by contacting Symantec technical support directly.

If the troubleshooter has detected problems in Symantec antivirus programme, there will be resolutions for each problem: If the PC is at risk and the Symantec product has been disabled by virus or malware, you have to disinfect the computer before you can fix the security status of Norton.

## SECURITY PROBLEM IN COMPUTING

How do we protect our most valuable assets? One option is to place them in a safe place, like a bank. We seldom hear of a bank robbery these days, even though it was once a fairly lucrative undertaking. In the American Wild West, banks kept large amounts of cash on hand, as well as gold and silver, which could not be traced easily. In those days, cash was much more commonly used than checks.

Communications and transportation were primitive enough that it might have been hours before the legal authorities were informed of a robbery and days before they could actually arrive at the scene of the crime, by which time the robbers were long gone.

To control the situation, a single guard for the night was only marginally effective. Should you have wanted to commit a robbery, you might have needed only a little common sense and perhaps several days to analyse the situation; you certainly did not require much sophisticated training. Indeed, you usually learned on the job, assisting other robbers in a form of apprenticeship. On balance, all these factors tipped very much in the favour of the criminal, so bank robbery was, for a time, considered to be a profitable business. Protecting assets was difficult and not always effective.

Today, however, asset protection is easier, with many factors working against the potential criminal. Very sophisticated alarm and camera systems silently protect secure places like banks whether people are around or not. The techniques of criminal investigation have become so effective that a person can be identified by genetic material (DNA), fingerprints, retinal patterns, voice, a composite sketch, ballistics evidence, or other hard-to-mask characteristics. The assets are stored in a safer form. For instance, many bank branches now contain less cash than some large retail stores because much of a bank's business is conducted with checks, electronic transfers, credit cards, or debit cards.

Sites that must store large amounts of cash or currency are protected with many levels of security: several layers of physical systems, complex locks, multiple-party systems requiring the agreement of several people to allow access, and other schemes. Significant improvements in transportation and communication mean that police can be at the scene of a crime in minutes; dispatchers can alert other officers in seconds about the suspects to watch for. From the criminal's point of view, the risk and required sophistication are so high that there are usually easier ways than bank robbery to make money.

### Protecting Valuables

This book is about protecting our computer-related assets, not about protecting our money and gold bullion. That is, we plan to discuss security for computing systems, not banks. But we can learn from our analysis of banks because they tell us some general principles about protection. In other words, when we think about protecting valuable information, we can learn a lot from the way we have protected other valuables in the past. The differences between how people protect computing systems and how banks protect money. The table reinforces the point that we have many challenges to address when protecting computers and data, but the nature of the challenges may mean that we need different and more effective approaches than we have used in the past.

Protecting our valuables, whether they are expressed as information or in some other way, ranges from quite unsophisticated to very sophisticated. We can think of the Wild West days as an example of the "unsophisticated" end of the security spectrum. And even today, when we have more sophisticated means of protection than ever before, we still see a wide range in how people and businesses actually use the protections available to them.

**Table. Protecting Money vs. Protecting Information**

| Characteristic | Bank Protecting Money | People Protecting Information |
|---|---|---|
| Size and portability | Sites storing money are large, unwieldy, not at all portable. Buildings require guards, vaults, many levels of physical security to protect money. | Items storing valuable assets are very small and portable. The physical devices in computing can be so small that thousands of dollars' worth of computing gear can fit comfortably in a briefcase. |
| Ability to avoid physical contact | Difficult. When banks deal with physical currency, a criminal must physically demand the money and carry it away from the bank's premises. | Simple. When information is handled electronically, no physical contact is necessary. Indeed, when banks handle money electronically, almost all transactions can be done without any physical contact. Money can be transferred through computers, mail, or telephone. |
| Value of assets | Very high. | Variable, from very high to very low. Some information, such as medical history, tax payments, investments, or educational background, is confidential. Other information, about troop movements, sales strategies, buying patterns, can be very sensitive. Still other information, such as address and phone number, may be of no consequence and easily accessible by other means. |

In fact, we can find far too many examples of computer security that seem to be back in the Wild West days. Although some organizations recognize computers and their data as valuable and vulnerable resources and have applied appropriate protection, others are dangerously deficient in their security measures. In some cases, the situation is even worse than that in the Wild West. And as software consumers, we find that the lack of protection is all the more dangerous when we are not even aware that we are susceptible to software piracy or corruption.

The possibility of crime is bad enough. But worse yet, in the event of a crime, some organizations neither investigate nor prosecute for fear that the revelation will damage their public image. For example, would you feel safe depositing your money in a bank that had just suffered a several million-dollar loss through computer-related embezzlement? In fact, the breach of security makes that bank painfully aware of all its security weaknesses. Once bitten, twice shy; after the loss, the bank will probably enhance its security substantially, quickly becoming safer than a bank that had not been recently victimized.

Even when organizations want to take action against criminal activity, criminal investigation and prosecution can be hindered by statutes that do not recognize electromagnetic signals as property.

The news media sometimes portrays computer intrusion by teenagers as a prank no more serious than tipping over an outhouse. But, as we see in later chapters, computer intrusion can hurt businesses and even take lives. The legal systems around the world are rapidly coming to grips with the nature of electronic property as intellectual property critical to organizational or mission success; laws are being implemented and court decisions declared that acknowledge the value of information stored or transmitted via computers. But this area is still new to many courts, and few precedents have been established.

Throughout this book, we look at examples of how computer security affects our lives directly and indirectly. And we examine techniques to prevent security breaches or at least to mitigate their effects. We address the security concerns of software practitioners as well as those professionals, managers, and users whose products, services, and well-being depend on the proper functioning of computer systems. By studying this book, you can develop an understanding of the basic problems underlying computer security and the methods available to deal with them.

*In particular, we do the following:*

- Examine the risks of security in computing
- Consider available countermeasures or controls
- Stimulate thought about uncovered vulnerabilities
- Identify areas where more work is needed.

In this chapter, we begin by examining what kinds of vulnerabilities computing systems are prone to. We then consider why these vulnerabilities are exploited: the different kinds of attacks that are possible. This chapter's third focus is on who is involved: the kinds of people who contribute to the security problem. Finally, we introduce how to prevent possible attacks on systems.

### Characteristics of Computer Intrusion

Any part of a computing system can be the target of a crime. When we refer to a computing system, we mean a collection of hardware, software, storage media, data, and people that an organization uses to perform computing tasks. Sometimes, we assume that parts of a computing system are not valuable to an outsider, but often we are mistaken. For instance, we tend to think that the most valuable property in a bank is the cash, gold, or silver in the vault. But in fact the customer information in the bank's computer may be far more valuable. Stored on paper, recorded on a storage medium, resident in memory, or transmitted over telephone lines or satellite links, this information can be used in myriad ways to make money illicitly.

A competing bank can use this information to steal clients or even to disrupt service and discredit the bank. An unscrupulous individual could move money from one account to another without the owner's permission. A group of con artists could contact large depositors and convince them to invest in fraudulent schemes. The variety of targets and attacks makes computer security very difficult. Any system is most vulnerable at its weakest point. A robber intent on stealing something from your house will not attempt to penetrate a two-inch-thick metal door if a window gives easier access. Similarly, a sophisticated perimeter physical security system does not compensate for unguarded access by means of a simple telephone line and a modem. We can codify this idea as one of the principles of computer security.

This principle implies that computer security specialists must consider all possible means of penetration. Moreover, the penetration analysis must be done repeatedly, and especially whenever the system and its security change. People sometimes underestimate the determination or creativity of attackers. Remember that computer security is a game with rules only for the defending team: The attackers can (and will) use any means they can. Perhaps the hardest thing for people outside the security community to do is to think like the attacker. One group of creative security researchers investigated a wireless security system and reported a vulnerability to the system's chief designer, who replied "that would work, but no attacker would try it". Don't believe that for a minute: No attack is out of bounds.

Strengthening one aspect of a system may simply make another means of penetration more appealing to intruders. For this reason, let us look at the various ways by which a system can be breached.

## THE MEANING OF COMPUTER SECURITY

We have seen that any computer-related system has both theoretical and real weaknesses. The purpose of computer security is to devise ways to prevent the weaknesses from being exploited. To understand what preventive measures make the most sense, we consider what we mean when we say that a system is "secure."

## SECURITY GOALS

We use the term "security" in many ways in our daily lives. A "security system" protects our house, warning the neighbours or the police if an unauthorized intruder tries to get in.

"Financialsecurity" involves a set of investments that are adequately funded; we hope the investments will grow in value over time so that we have enough money to survive later in life. And we speak of children's "physical security," hoping they are safe from potential harm. Just as each of these terms has a very specific meaning in the context of its use, so too does the phrase "computer security."

When we talk about computer security, we mean that we are addressing three important aspects of any computer-related system: confidentiality, integrity, and availability.

- Confidentiality ensures that computer-related assets are accessed only by authorized parties. That is, only those who should have access to something will actually get that access. By "access," we mean not only reading but also viewing, printing, or simply knowing that a particular asset exists. Confidentiality is sometimes called secrecy or privacy .
- Integrity means that assets can be modified only by authorized parties or only in authorized ways. In this context, modification includes writing, changing, changing status, deleting, and creating.
- Availability means that assets are accessible to authorized parties at appropriate times. In other words, if some person or system has legitimate access to a particular set of objects, that access should not be prevented. For this reason, availability is sometimes known by its opposite, denial of service.

Security in computing addresses these three goals. One of the challenges in building a secure system is finding the right balance among the goals, which often conflict. For example, it is easy to preserve a particular object's confidentiality in a secure system simply by preventing everyone from reading that object.

However, this system is not secure, because it does not meet the requirement of availability for proper access. That is, there must be a balance between confidentiality and availability. But balance is not all. In fact, these three characteristics can be independent, can overlap and can even be mutually exclusive. For example, we have seen that strong protection of confidentiality can severely restrict availability. Let us examine each of the three qualities in depth.

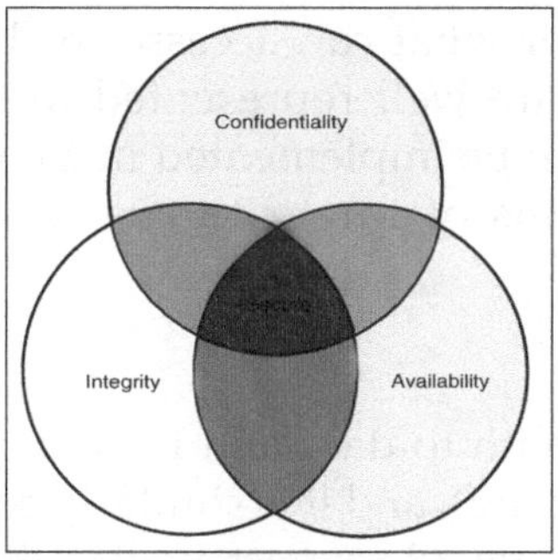


**Fig.** Relationship between Confidentiality, Integrity, and Availability.

## Confidentiality

You may find the notion of confidentiality to be straightforward: Only authorized people or systems can access protected data. However, as we see in later chapters, ensuring confidentiality can be difficult. For example, who determines which people or systems are authorized to access the current system? By "accessing" data, do we mean that an authorized party can access a single bit? the whole collection? pieces of data out of context? Can someone who is authorized disclose those data to other parties? Confidentiality is the security property we understand best because its meaning is narrower than the other two. We also understand confidentiality well because we can relate computing examples to those of preserving confidentiality in the real world.

## Integrity

Integrity is much harder to pin down. As Welke and Mayfield point out, integrity means different things in different contexts. When we survey the way some people use the term, we find several different meanings. For example, if we say that we have preserved the integrity of an item, we may mean that the item is:

- Precise
- Accurate
- Unmodified
- Modified only in acceptable ways
- Modified only by authorized people
- Modified only by authorized processes
- Consistent
- Internally consistent
- Meaningful and usable.

Integrity can also mean two or more of these properties. Welke and Mayfield recognize three particular aspects of integrity authorized actions, separation and protection of resources, and error detection and correction. Integrity can be enforced in much the same way as can confidentiality: by rigorous control of who or what can access which resources in what ways. Some forms of integrity are well represented in the real world, and those precise representations can be implemented in a computerized environment. But not all interpretations of integrity are well reflected by computer implementations.

**Availability**

Availability applies both to data and to services (that is, to information and to information processing), and it is similarly complex. As with the notion of confidentiality, different people expect availability to mean different things.

*For example, an object or service is thought to be available if:*

- It is present in a usable form.
- It has capacity enough to meet the service's needs.
- It is making clear progress, and, if in wait mode, it has a bounded waiting time.
- The service is completed in an acceptable period of time.

*We can construct an overall description of availability by combining these goals. We say a data item, service, or system is available if:*

- There is a timely response to our request.
- Resources are allocated fairly so that some requesters are not favoured over others.
- The service or system involved follows a philosophy of fault tolerance, whereby hardware or software faults lead to graceful cessation of service or to work-arounds rather than to crashes and abrupt loss of information.
- The service or system can be used easily and in the way it was intended to be used.
- Concurrency is controlled; that is, simultaneous access, deadlock management, and exclusive access are supported as required.

The expectations of availability are far-reaching. Indeed, the security community is just beginning to understand what availability implies and how to ensure it. A small, centralized control of access is fundamental to preserving confidentiality and integrity, but it is not clear that a single access control point can enforce availability. Much of computer security's past success has focused on confidentiality and integrity; full implementation of availability is security's next great challenge.

## VULNERABILITIES

When we prepare to test a system, we usually try to imagine how the system can fail; we then look for ways in which the requirements, design, or code can enable such failures. In the same way, when we prepare to specify, design, code, or test a secure system, we try to imagine the vulnerabilities that would prevent us from reaching one or more of our three security goals.

It is sometimes easier to consider vulnerabilities as they apply to all three broad categories of system resources (hardware, software, and data), rather than to start with the security goals themselves. The types of vulnerabilities we might find as they apply to the assets of hardware, software, and data. These three assets and the connections among them are all potential security weak points. Let us look in turn at the vulnerabilities of each asset.

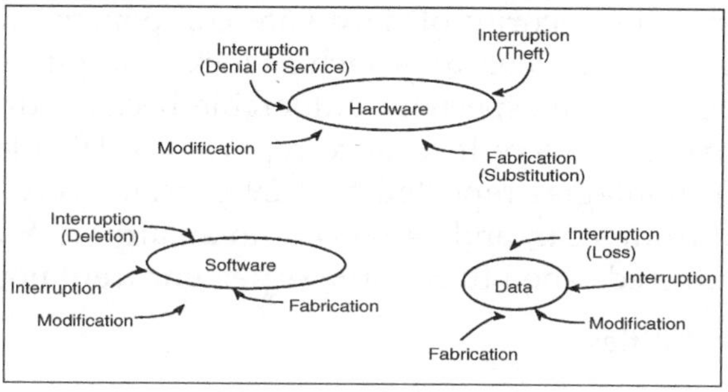


**Fig.** Vulnerabilities of Computing Systems.

## Hardware Vulnerabilities

Hardware is more visible than software, largely because it is composed of physical objects. Because we can see what devices are hooked to the system, it is rather simple to attack by adding devices, changing them, removing them, intercepting the traffic to them, or flooding them with traffic until they can no longer function. However, designers can usually put safeguards in place.

But there are other ways that computer hardware can be attacked physically. Computers have been drenched with water, burned, frozen, gassed, and electrocuted with power surges. People have spilled soft drinks, corn chips, ketchup, beer, and many other kinds of food on computing devices. Mice have chewed through cables. Particles of dust, and especially ash in cigarette smoke, have threatened precisely engineered moving parts. Computers have been kicked, slapped, bumped, jarred, and punched. Although such attacks might be intentional, most are not; this abuse might be considered "involuntary machine slaughter": accidental acts not intended to do serious damage to the hardware involved.

A more serious attack, "voluntary machine slaughter" or "machinicide," usually involves someone who actually wishes to harm the computer hardware or software. Machines have been shot with guns, stabbed with knives, and smashed with all kinds of things. Bombs, fires, and collisions have destroyed computer rooms. Ordinary keys, pens, and screwdrivers have been used to short-out circuit boards and other components. Devices and whole systems have been carried off by thieves. The list of the kinds of human attacks perpetrated on computers is almost endless.

In particular, deliberate attacks on equipment, intending to limit availability, usually involve theft or destruction. Managers of major computing centres long ago recognized these vulnerabilities and installed physical security systems to protect their machines. However, the proliferation of PCs, especially laptops, as office equipment has resulted in several thousands of dollars' worth of equipment sitting unattended on desks outside the carefully protected computer room. (Curiously, the supply cabinet, containing only a few hundred dollars' worth of pens, stationery, and paper clips, is often locked.) Sometimes the security of hardware components can be enhanced greatly by simple physical measures such as locks and guards.

Laptop computers are especially vulnerable because they are designed to be easy to carry. Safe ware Insurance reported 600,000 laptops stolen in 2003. Credent Technologies reported that 29 percent were stolen from the office, 25 percent from a car, and 14 percent in an airport. Stolen laptops are almost never recovered: The FBI reports 97 percent were not returned.

**Software Vulnerabilities**

Computing equipment is of little use without the software (operating system, controllers, utility programmes, and application programmes) that users expect. Software can be replaced, changed, or destroyed maliciously, or it can be modified, deleted, or misplaced accidentally. Whether intentional or not, these attacks exploit the software's vulnerabilities. Sometimes, the attacks are obvious, as when the software no longer runs. More subtle are attacks in which the software has been altered but seems to run normally. Whereas physical equipment usually shows some mark of inflicted injury when its boundary has been breached, the loss of a line of source or object code may not leave an obvious mark in a programme. Furthermore, it is possible to change a programme so that it does all it did before, and then some. That is, a malicious intruder can "enhance" the software to enable it to perform functions you may not find desirable. In this case, it may be very hard to detect that the software has been changed, let alone to determine the extent of the change.

A classic example of exploiting software vulnerability is the case in which a bank worker realised that software truncates the fractional interest on each account. In other words, if the monthly interest on an account is calculated to be .5467, the software credits only .54 and ignores the $.0067. The worker amended the software so that the throwaway interest (the $.0067) was placed into his own account. Since the accounting practices ensured only that all accounts balanced, he built up a large amount of money from the thousands of account throw-aways without detection. It was only when he bragged to a colleague of his cleverness that the scheme was discovered.

**Software Deletion**

Software is surprisingly easy to delete. Each of us has, at some point in our careers, accidentally erased a file or saved a bad copy of a programme, destroying a good previous copy. Because of software's high value to a commercial computing centre, access to software is usually carefully controlled through a process called configuration management so that software cannot be deleted, destroyed, or replaced accidentally. Configuration management uses several techniques to ensure that each version or release retains its integrity. When configuration management is used, an old version or release can be replaced with a newer version only when it has been thoroughly tested to verify that the improvements work correctly without degrading the functionality and performance of other functions and services.

**Software Modification**

Software is vulnerable to modifications that either cause it to fail or cause it to perform an unintended task. Indeed, because software is so susceptible to "off by one" errors, it is quite easy to modify. Changing a bit or two can convert a working programme into a failing one. Depending on which bit was changed, the programme may crash when it begins or it may execute for some time before it falters.

With a little more work, the change can be much more subtle: The programme works well most of the time but fails in specialized circumstances. For instance, the programme may be maliciously modified to fail when certain conditions are met or when a certain date or time is reached. Because of this delayed effect, such a programme is known as a logic bomb. For example, a disgruntled employee may modify a crucial programme so that it accesses the system date and halts abruptly after July 1. The employee might quit on May 1 and plan to be at a new job miles away by July. Another type of change can extend the functioning of a programme so that an innocuous programme has a hidden side effect. For example, a programme that ostensibly structures a listing of files belonging to a user may also modify the protection of all those files to permit access by another user.

*Other categories of software modification include:*

- Trojan horse: a programme that overtly does one thing while covertly doing another
- Virus: a specific type of Trojan horse that can be used to spread its "infection" from one computer to another
- Trapdoor: a programme that has a secret entry point
- Information leaks in a programme: code that makes information accessible to unauthorized people or programmes.

Of course, it is possible to invent a completely new programme and install it on a computing system. Inadequate control over the programmes that are installed and run on a computing system permits this kind of software security breach.

**Software Theft**

This attack includes unauthorized copying of software. Software authors and distributors are entitled to fair compensation for use of their product, as are musicians and book authors. Unauthorized copying of software has not been stopped satisfactorily. The legal system is still grappling with the difficulties of interpreting paper-based copyright laws for electronic media.

**Data Vulnerabilities**

Hardware security is usually the concern of a relatively small staff of computing centre professionals. Software security is a larger problem, extending to all programmers and analysts who create or modify programmes. Computer programmes are written in a dialect intelligible primarily to computer professionals, so a "leaked" source listing of a programme might very well be meaningless to the general public.

Printed data, however, can be readily interpreted by the general public. Because of its visible nature, a data attack is a more widespread and serious problem than either a hardware or software attack. Thus, data items have greater public value than hardware and software because more people know how to use or interpret data.

By themselves, out of context, pieces of data have essentially no intrinsic value. For example, if you are shown the value "42," it has no meaning for you unless you know what the number represents. Likewise, "326 Old Norwalk Road" is of little use unless you know the city, state, and country for the address. For this reason, it is hard to measure the value of a given data item.

On the other hand, data items in context do relate to cost, perhaps measurable by the cost to reconstruct or redevelop damaged or lost data. For example, confidential data leaked to a competitor may narrow a competitive edge. Data incorrectly modified can cost human lives. To see how, consider the flight coordinate data used by an airplane that is guided partly or fully by software, as many now are. Finally, inadequate security may lead to financial liability if certain personal data are made public. Thus, data have a definite value, even though that value is often difficult to measure.

Typically, both hardware and software have a relatively long life. No matter how they are valued initially, their value usually declines gradually over time. By contrast, the value of data over time is far less predictable or consistent. Initially, data may be valued highly. However, some data items are of interest for only a short period of time, after which their value declines precipitously.

To see why, consider the following example. In many countries, government analysts periodically generate data to describe the state of the national economy. The results are scheduled to be released to the public at a predetermined time and date. Before that time, access to the data could allow someone to profit from advance knowledge of the probable effect of the data on the stock market. For instance, suppose an analyst develops the data 24 hours before their release and then wishes to communicate the results to other analysts for independent verification before release. The data vulnerability here is clear, and, to the right people, the data are worth more before the scheduled release than afterward. However, we can protect the data and control the threat in simple ways. For example, we could devise a scheme that would take an outsider more than 24 hours to break; even though the scheme may be eminently breakable (that is, an intruder could eventually reveal the data), it is adequate for those data because confidentiality is not needed beyond the 24-hour period.

## DATA SECURITY SUGGESTS THE SECOND PRINCIPLE OF COMPUTER SECURITY

This principle says that things with a short life can be protected by security measures that are effective only for that short time. The notion of a small protection window applies primarily to data, but it can in some cases be relevant for software and hardware, too. The three goals of security apply to data. In particular, confidentiality prevents unauthorized disclosure of a data item, integrity prevents unauthorized modification, and availability prevents denial of authorized access.

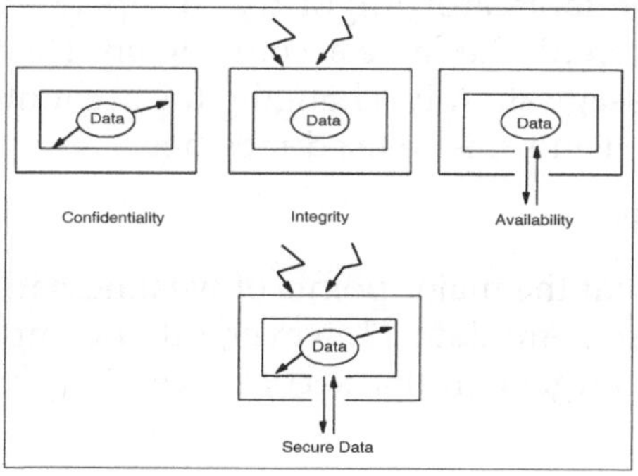


**Fig.** Security of Data.

### Data Confidentiality

Data can be gathered by many means, such as tapping wires, planting bugs in output devices, sifting through trash receptacles, monitoring electromagnetic radiation, bribing key employees, inferring one data point from other values, or simply requesting the data.

Because data are often available in a form people can read, the confidentiality of data is a major concern in computer security. Data are not just numbers on paper; computer data include digital recordings such as CDs and DVDs, digital signals such as network and telephone traffic, and broadband communications such as cable and satellite TV. Other forms of data are biometric identifiers embedded in passports, online activity preferences, and personal information such as financial records and votes. Protecting this range of data types requires many different approaches.

**Data Integrity**

Stealing, buying, finding, or hearing data requires no computer sophistication, whereas modifying or fabricating new data requires some understanding of the technology by which the data are transmitted or stored, as well as the format in which the data are maintained. Thus, a higher level of sophistication is needed to modify existing data or to fabricate new data than to intercept existing data. The most common sources of this kind of problem are malicious programmes, errant file system utilities, and flawed communication facilities. Data are especially vulnerable to modification. Small and skilfully done modifications may not be detected in ordinary ways. For instance, we saw in our truncated interest example that a criminal can perform what is known as a salami attack: The crook shaves a little from many accounts and puts these shavings together to form a valuable result, like the meat scraps joined in a salami.

A more complicated process is trying to reprocess used data items. With the proliferation of telecommunications among banks, a fabricator might intercept a message ordering one bank to credit a given amount to a certain person's account. The fabricator might try to replay that message, causing the receiving bank to credit the same account again. The fabricator might also try to modify the message slightly, changing the account to be credited or the amount, and then transmit this revised message.

**Other Exposed Assets**

We have noted that the major points of weakness in a computing system are hardware, software, and data. However, other components of the system may also be possible targets. In this section, we identify some of these other points of attack.

**Networks**

Networks are specialized collections of hardware, software, and data. Each network node is itself a computing system; as such, it experiences all the normal security problems. In addition, a network must confront communication problems that involve the interaction of system components and outside resources. The problems may be introduced by a very exposed storage medium or access from distant and potentially untrustworthy computing systems. Thus, networks can easily multiply the problems of computer security. The challenges are rooted in a network's lack of physical proximity, use of insecure shared media, and the inability of a network to identify remote users positively.

**Access**

Access to computing equipment leads to three types of vulnerabilities. In the first, an intruder may steal computer time to do general-purpose computing that does not attack the integrity of the system itself. This theft of computer services is analogous to the stealing of electricity, gas, or water. However, the value of the stolen computing services may be substantially higher than the value of the stolen utility products or services.

Moreover, the unpaid computing access spreads the true costs of maintaining the computing system to other legitimate users. In fact, the unauthorized access risks affecting legitimate computing, perhaps by changing data or programmes. A second vulnerability involves malicious access to a computing system, whereby an intruding person or system actually destroys software or data. Finally, unauthorized access may deny service to a legitimate user. For example, a user who has a time-critical task to perform may depend on the availability of the computing system. For all three of these reasons, unauthorized access to a computing system must be prevented.

**Key People**

People can be crucial weak points in security. If only one person knows how to use or maintain a particular programme, trouble can arise if that person is ill, suffers an accident, or leaves the organization (taking her knowledge with her). In particular, a disgruntled employee can cause serious damage by using inside knowledge of the system and the data that are manipulated. For this reason, trusted individuals, such as operators and systems programmers, are usually selected carefully because of their potential ability to affect all computer users.

# 8

# Network Security

Network security is a complicated subject, historically only tackled by well-trained and experienced experts. However, as more and more people become "wired", an increasing number of people need to understand the basics of security in a networked world. This document was written with the basic computer user and information systems manager in mind, explaining the concepts needed to read through the hype in the marketplace and understand risks and how to deal with them.

Some history of networking is included, as well as an introduction to TCP/IP and *internetworking*. We go on to consider risk management, network threats, firewalls, and more special-purpose secure networking devices. This is not intended to be a "frequently asked questions" reference, nor is it a "hands-on" document describing how to accomplish specific functionality. It is hoped that the reader will have a wider perspective on security in general, and better understand how to reduce and manage risk personally, at home, and in the workplace.

## COMPUTER NETWORK AND SECURITY

The networks are computer networks, both public and private, that are used every day to conduct transactions and communications among businesses, government agencies and individuals. The networks are comprised of "nodes", which are "client" terminals (individual user PCs) and one or more "servers" and/or "host" computers. They are linked by communication systems, some of which might be private, such as within a company, and others which might be open to public access.

The obvious example of a network system that is open to public access is the Internet, but many private networks also utilize publicly-accessible communications. Today, most companies' host computers can be accessed by their employees whether in their offices over a private communications network, or from their homes or hotel rooms while on the road through normal telephone lines.

Network security involves all activities that organizations, enterprises, and institutions undertake to protect the value and ongoing usability of assets and the integrity and continuity of operations. An effective network security strategy requires identifying threats and then choosing the most effective set of tools to combat them.

*Threats to network security include:*

- *Viruses*: Computer programmes written by devious programmers and designed to replicate themselves and infect computers when triggered by a specific event.
- *Trojan horse programmes*: Delivery vehicles for destructive code, which appear to be harmless or useful software programmes such as games.
- *Vandals*: Software applications or applets that cause destruction.
- *Attacks*: Including reconnaissance attacks (information-gathering activities to collect data that is later used to compromise networks); access attacks (which exploit network vulnerabilities in order to gain entry to e-mail, databases, or the corporate network); and denial-of-service attacks (which prevent access to part or all of a computer system).
- *Data interception*: Involves eavesdropping on communications or altering data packets being transmitted.
- *Social engineering*: Obtaining confidential network security information through nontechnical means, such as posing as a technical support person and asking for people's passwords.

*Network security tools include:*

- *Antivirus software packages*: These packages counter most virus threats if regularly updated and correctly maintained.
- *Secure network infrastructure*: Switches and routers have hardware and software features that support secure connectivity, perimeter security, intrusion protection, identity services, and security management.
- *Dedicated network security hardware and software*: Tools such as firewalls and intrusion detection systems provide protection for all areas of the network and enable secure connections.
- *Virtual private networks*: These networks provide access control and data encryption between two different computers on a network. This allows remote workers to connect to the network without the risk of a hacker or thief intercepting data.
- *Identity services*: These services help to identify users and control their activities and transactions on the network. Services include passwords, digital certificates, and digital authentication keys.
- *Encryption*: Encryption ensures that messages cannot be intercepted or read by anyone other than the authorized recipient.
- *Security management*: This is the glue that holds together the other building blocks of a strong security solution.

None of these approaches alone will be sufficient to protect a network, but when they are layered together, they can be highly effective in keeping a network safe from attacks and other threats to security. In addition, well-thought-out corporate policies are critical to determine and control access to various parts of the network.

## NETWORK SECURITY CONSULTING AND NETWORK MANAGEMENT SERVICES

Vulnerabilities in a network are exploited by both people inside the network and people outside the network. If your company is connected to the Internet or utilizes internal networking, a security evaluation is crucial to avoid compromises of valuable company resources and company information. We offer both on-site and off-site network testing, as well as evaluations and assessments for secure network architecture. Takniki also develops custom security software and provide educational and training classes on information security topics.

When we started business, breaking into computers wasn't even a crime. Since then, both major and small security problems have become a well-known and often looked as thorn in the side of almost every organization. You can contract Takniki to examine or build your existing network architecture and make recommendations to optimize security. Whether you are expanding, upgrading, or simply wanting to make improvements to the overall security of your network, this is a valuable service at any time. In particular, we look at third party connections, expanding and defining security parameters, identifying and securing critical systems.

We at Takniki not only have rich experience in dealing with network security but also have world-class expertise. Whether it is about explaining how to write a password policy to your technical staff or describing to developers why "save %sp, -96, %sp" causes a window overflow trap which can lead to a buffer overflow vulnerability, We're just as comfortable as we are in designing the network architecture.

Every Activity at Takniki is done by hands. While testing your network we don't take help of network security scan software. Our team of security experts examine the network manually for each protocol and security loop hole. While testing, we typically invent entirely new attacks, just like a "real" hacker would. While architecting or designing a new network, we start with a clean sheet design. This unique approach makes us completely different from any other security consulting company.

### TYPES OF NETWORK SECURITY SERVICES

#### Penetration Testing

A realistic assessment of security—creative by design and policy is absolutely invaluable. We have found vulnerabilities and security holes in everything from a Web Server to a Internet Instant Messenger or be it a Point of Sale Payment Terminal. We provide the most realistic and useful security analysis anywhere in any network system.

- *Network Testing*: We test everything from a single computer, servers and firewall to an entire enterprise.
- *Server Testing*: When you are deploying a new server, whether in-house or in a data centre, can result in significant security risks. We provide hard evidence of the risks, and then find a solution which doesn't reduce functionality and provides your the best working security model without compromising over functionality.
- *Application Review*: Many security lapses and vulnerabilities are caused by poorly written software applications. We can analyse source code to find inherent flaws. If source is not available, we can attack the application as an outsider, and suggest alternative mechanisms to ensure the applications meets the security criteria.
- *Embedded Devices*: We examine the devices to make sure that they comply with all security regulations. We also try to work closely with the device manufacturer to ensure its long-term security and necessary firmware updates are available.

*Our work focuses is always on:*

- *Functionality*: Normally when it comes to security the organization has to compromise over software or network functionality. But we have rarely foudn that to be the case. Despite security being typically viewed as the enemy of functionality, we always find a solution which doesn't reduce functionality and provides you the best working security model without compromising over functionality and information accessibility.
- *Scalability*: We at Takniki clearly understand that nothing is forever. An Network architecture is not a one-shot, rather it's a step by step methodology for implementing all new services, connectivity, and policies. The architecture and systems grow with the customer's needs and this is why all our solutions are typically canvassed with NO LIMITS.
- *Cost*: Despite our aggressive and extensive approach, significant capital expenditures are rarely recommended. In all most all of our suggested solutions time & materials costs are generally minimal.

Secure Architecture makes security easier to maintain, expand and understand. To create a custom EGS Secure Architecture Plan, we analyse your business structure through discussions of corporate security issues and reviews of documentation such as network maps, policies and business processes. We then advise you on the best implementation of the most appropriate solution, which would address policy, technology and administrative elements.

## SECURITY IN NETWORKS

Networks their design, development, and usage are critical to our style of computing. We interact with networks daily, when we perform banking transactions, make telephone calls, or ride trains and planes. The utility companies use networks to track electricity or water usage and bill for it. When we pay for groceries or gasoline, networks enable our credit or debit card transactions and billing. Life without networks would be considerably less convenient, and many activities would be impossible.

Not surprisingly, then, computing networks are attackers' targets of choice. Because of their actual and potential impact, network attacks attract the attention of journalists, managers, auditors, and the general public. For example, when you read the daily newspapers, you are likely to find a story about a network-based attack at least every month. The coverage itself evokes a sense of evil, using terms such as hijacking, distributed denial of service, and our familiar friends viruses, worms, and Trojan horses. Because any large-scale attack is likely to put thousands of computing systems at risk, with potential losses well into the millions of dollars, network attacks make good copy.

The media coverage is more than hype; network attacks are critical problems. Fortunately, your bank, your utility company, and even your Internet service provider take network security very seriously. Because they do, they are vigilant about applying the most current and most effective controls to their systems. Of equal importance, these organizations continually assess their risks and learn about the latest attack types and defence mechanisms so that they can maintain the protection of their networks.

In this chapter we describe what makes a network similar to and different from an application programme or an operating system. In investigating networks, you will learn how the concepts of confidentiality, integrity, and availability apply in networked settings. At the same time, you will see that the basic notions of identification and authentication, access control, accountability, and assurance are the basis for network security, just as they have been in other settings.

Networking is growing and changing perhaps even faster than other computing disciplines. Consequently, this chapter is unlikely to present you with the most current technology, the latest attack, or the newest defence mechanism; you can read about those in daily newspapers and at web sites. But the novelty and change build on what we know today: the fundamental concepts, threats, and controls for networks. By developing an understanding of the basics, you can absorb the most current news quickly and easily. More importantly, your understanding can assist you in building, protecting, and using networks.

### NETWORK CONCEPTS

To study network threats and controls, we first must review some of the relevant networking terms and concepts. This review does not attempt to provide the depth of a classic networking reference. Our study of security focused on the individual pieces of a computing system, such as a single application, an operating system, or a database. Networks involve not only the pieces but also importantly the connections among them.

Networks are both fragile and strong. To see why, think about the power, cable television, telephone, or water network that serves your home. If a falling tree branch breaks the power line to your home, you are without electricity until that line is repaired; you are vulnerable to what is called a single point of failure , because one cut to the network destroys electrical functionality for your entire home. Similarly, there may be one telephone trunk line or water main that serves your home and those nearby; a failure can leave your building, street, or neighbourhood without service.

But we have ways to keep the entire network from failing. If we trace back through the network from your home to the source of what flows through it, we are likely to see that several main distribution lines support an entire city or campus. That is, there is more than one way to get from the source to your neighbourhood, enabling engineers to redirect the flow along alternative paths. Redundancy makes it uncommon for an entire city to lose service from a single failure. For this reason, we say that such a network has resilience or fault tolerance.

Complex routing algorithms reroute the flow not just around failures but also around overloaded segments. The routing is usually done automatically; the control programme is often supplemented by human supervision or intervention. Many types of networks have very high reliability by design, not by accident. But because there often is less redundancy near a network's endpoints than elsewhere, we say that the network has great strength in the middle and fragility at the perimeter.

From the user's perspective, a network is sometimes designed so that it looks like two endpoints with a single connection in the middle. For example, the municipal water supply may appear to be little more than a reservoir (the source), the pipes (the transmission or communication medium), and your water faucet (the destination). Although this simplistic view is functionally correct, it ignores the complex design, implementation, and management of the "pipes." In a similar way, we describe computer networks in this chapter in ways that focus on the security concepts but present the networks themselves in a simplistic way, to highlight the role of security and prevent the complexity of the networks from distracting our attention. Please keep in mind that our network descriptions are often abstractions of a more complex actuality.

**The Network**

A network in its simplest form, as two devices connected across some medium by hardware and software that enable the communication. In some cases, one device is a computer (sometimes called a "server") and the other is a simpler device (sometimes called a "client") enabled only with some means of input (such as a keyboard) and some means of output (such as a screen). For example, a powerful computer can be a server, but a handheld personal digital assistant (PDA) or a cell phone might be a network client. In fact, because more consumer devices are becoming network-enabled, network security issues will continue to grow.

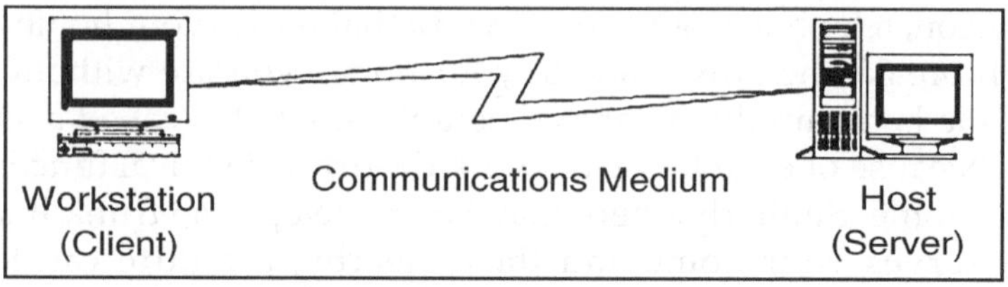


**Fig.** Simple View of Network.

*Although this model defines a basic network, the actual situation is frequently significantly more complicated.*

- The simpler client device, employed for user-to-computer communication, is often a PC or workstation, so the client has considerable storage and processing capability.
- A network can be configured as just a single client connected to a single server. But more typically, many clients interact with many servers.
- The network's services are often provided by many computers. As a single user's communication travels back and forth from client to server, it may merely pass through some computers but pause at others for significant interactions.
- The end user is usually unaware of many of the communications and computations taking place in the network on the user's behalf.

The user at one of the lettered client machines may send a message to System 3, unaware that communication is actually passing through the active Systems 1 and 2. In fact, the user may be unaware that System 3 sometimes passes work to System 4. A single computing system in a network is often called a node, and its processor (computer) is called a host . A connection between two hosts is known as a link . Network computing consists of users, communications media, visible hosts, and systems not generally visible to end users. Systems 1 through 4 are nodes. In our figure the users are at the lettered client machines, perhaps interacting with Server F.

Users communicate with networked systems by interacting directly with terminals, workstations, and computers. A workstation is an end-user computing device, usually designed for a single user at a time. Workstations often have powerful processors and good- sized memory and storage so that they can do sophisticated data manipulation (such as converting coded data to a graphical format and displaying the picture). A system is a collection of processors, perhaps including a mixture of workstations and independent processors, typically with more processing power and more storage capacity than a workstation.

## Environment of Use

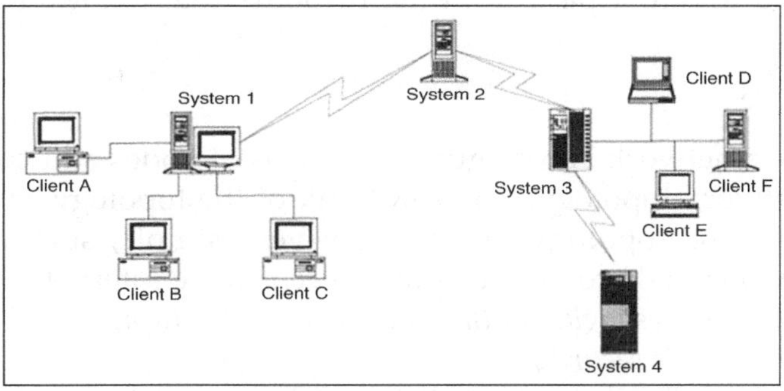


**Fig.** More Complex but More Typical View of Networks.

The biggest difference between a network and a stand-alone device is the environment in which each operates. Although some networks are located in protected spaces (for example, a local area network in a single laboratory or office), at least some portion of most networks is exposed, often to total strangers. The relatively simple network is a good example. Systems 2, 3, and 4 are remote from System 1, and they may be under different ownership or control.

*Networks can be described by several typical characteristics:*

- *Anonymity.* You may have seen the cartoon image that shows a dog typing at a workstation, and saying to another dog, "On the Internet, nobody knows you're a dog." A network removes most of the clues, such as appearance, voice, or context, by which we recognize acquaintances.
- *Automation.* In some networks, one or both endpoints, as well as all intermediate points, involved in a given communication may be machines with only minimal human supervision.
- *Distance.* Many networks connect endpoints that are physically far apart. Although not all network connections involve distance, the speed of communication is fast enough that humans usually cannot tell whether a remote site is near or far.
- *Opaqueness.* Because the dimension of distance is hidden, users cannot tell whether a remote host is in the room next door or in a different country. In the same way, users cannot distinguish whether they are connected to a node in an office, school, home, or warehouse, or whether the node's computing system is large or small, modest or powerful. In fact, users cannot tell if the current communication involves the same host with which they communicated the last time.
- *Routing diversity.* To maintain or improve reliability and performance, routings between two endpoints are usually dynamic. That is, the same interaction may follow one path through the network the first

time and a very different path the second time. In fact, a query may take a different path from the response that follows a few seconds later.

**Shape and Size**

The way a network is configured, in terms of nodes and connections, is called the network topology. You can think of the topology as the shape of the network. The topology ranges from very simple, such as two hosts connected by one path, to very complex, such as the Internet.

*These two extremes highlight three dimensions of networks that have particular bearing on a network's security*:

- *Boundary.* The boundary distinguishes an element of the network from an element outside it. For a simple network, we can easily list all the components and draw an imaginary line around it to separate what is in the network from what is outside. But listing all the hosts connected to the Internet is practically impossible. For example, a line surrounding the Internet would have to surround the entire globe today, and Internet connections also pass through satellites in orbit around the earth. Moreover, as people and organizations choose to be connected or not, the number and type of hosts change almost second by second, with the number generally increasing over time.
- *Ownership.* It is often difficult to know who owns each host in a network. The network administrator's organization may own the network infrastructure, including the cable and network devices. However, certain hosts may be connected to a network for convenience, not necessarily implying ownership.
- *Control.* Finally, if ownership is uncertain, control must be, too. To see how, pick an arbitrary host. Is it part of network A? If yes, is it under the control of network A's administrator? Does that administrator establish access control policies for the network, or determine when its software must be upgraded and to what version? Indeed, does the administrator even know what version of software that host runs?

The truth is that, for many networks, it is difficult and at times impossible to tell which hosts are part of that network, who owns the hosts, and who controls them. Even for networks significantly smaller than the Internet, major corporate, university, or government networks are hard to understand and are not even well known by their system administrators. Although it seems contrary to common sense, many corporations today have no accurate picture of how their networks are configured. To understand why, consider a network of automated teller machines for a multinational bank. The bank may have agreements with other banks to enable customers to withdraw money anywhere in the world. The multinational bank may understand its own bank's network, but it may have no conception of how the connecting banks' networks are configured; no "big picture" shows how the combined networks look or operate. Similarly, a given host may be part of more than one network. In such a situation, suppose a host has two network interfaces. Whose rules does that host (and that host's administrator) have to follow? Depicting, configuring, and administering networks are not easy tasks.

### Mode of Communication

A computer network implements communication between two endpoints. Data are communicated either in digital format (in which data items are expressed as discrete binary values) or analog (in which data items are expressed as points in a continuous range, using a medium like sound or electrical voltage). Computers typically store and process digital data, but some telephone and similar cable communications are in analog form (because telephones were originally designed to transmit voice). When the transmission medium expects to transfer analog data, the digital signals must be converted to analog for transmission and then back to digital for computation at the receiving end. Some mostly analog networks may even have some digital segments, so the analog signals are digitized more than once. These conversions are performed by a modem, which converts a digital data stream to tones and back again.

### Media

Communication is enabled by several kinds of media. We can choose among several types, such as along copper wires or optical fibre or through the air, as with cellular phones. Let us look at each type in turn.

### Cable

Because much of our computer communication has historically been done over telephone lines, the most common network communication medium today is wire. Inside our homes and offices, we use a pair of insulated copper wires, called a twisted pair or unshielded twisted pair (UTP). Copper has good transmission properties at a relatively low cost. The bandwidth of UTP is limited to under 10 megabits per second (Mbps), so engineers cannot transmit a large number of communications simultaneously on a single line. Moreover, the signal strength degrades as it travels through the copper wire, and it cannot travel long distances without a boost. Thus, for many networks, line lengths are limited to approximately 300 feet. Single twisted pair service is most often used locally, within a building or up to a local communications drop (that is, the point where the home or office service is connected to the larger network, such as the commercial telephone system). Although regular copper wire can transmit signals, the twisting reduces crossover (interference and signal transfer) between adjacent wires.

However, as speeds or capacities change, the basic ranking of two technologies tends to remain the same. Another choice for network communication is coaxial (coax) cable, the kind used for cable television. Coax cable is constructed with a single wire surrounded by an insulation jacket. The jacket is itself surrounded by a braided or spiral-wound wire. The inner wire carries the signal, and the outer braid acts as a ground. The most widely used computer communication coax cable is Ethernet, carrying up to 100 Mbps over distances of up to 1500 feet.

Coax cable also suffers from degradation of signal quality over distance. Repeaters (for digital signals) or amplifiers (for analog signals) can be spaced periodically along the cable to pick up the signal, amplify it, remove spurious signals called "noise," and retransmit it.

**Optical Fibre**

A newer form of cable is made of very thin strands of glass. Instead of carrying electrical energy, these fibres carry pulses of light. The bandwidth of optical fibre is up to 1000 Mbps, and the signal degrades less over fibre than over wire or coax; the fibre is good for a run of approximately 2.5 miles. Optical fibre involves less interference, less crossover between adjacent media, lower cost, and less weight than copper. Thus, optical fibre is generally a much better transmission medium than copper. Consequently, as copper ages, it is being replaced by optical fibre in most communication systems. In particular, most long distance communication lines are now fibre.

**Wireless**

Radio signals can also carry communications. Similar to pagers, wireless microphones, garage door openers, and portable telephones, wireless radio can be used in networks, following a protocol developed for short-range telecommunications, designated the 802.11 family of standards. The wireless medium is used for short distances; it is especially useful for networks in which the nodes are physically close together, such as in an office building or at home. Many 802.11 devices are becoming available for home and office wireless networks.

**Microwave**

Microwave is a form of radio transmission especially well suited for outdoor communication. Microwave has a channel capacity similar to coax cable; that is, it carries similar amounts of data. Its principal advantage is that the signal is strong from point of transmission to point of receipt. Therefore, microwave signals do not need to be regenerated with repeaters, as do signals on cable. However, a microwave signal travels in a straight line, presenting a problem because the earth curves. Microwave signals travel by line of sight: The transmitter and receiver must be in a straight line with one another, with no intervening obstacles, such as mountains. A straight microwave signal transmitted between towers of reasonable height can travel a distance of only about 30 miles because of the earth's curvature. Thus, microwave signals are "bounced" from receiver to receiver, spaced less than 30 miles apart, to cover a longer distance.

**Infrared**

Infrared communication carries signals for short distances (up to 9 miles) and also requires a clear line of sight. Because it does not require cabling, it is convenient for portable objects, such as laptop computers and connections to peripherals.

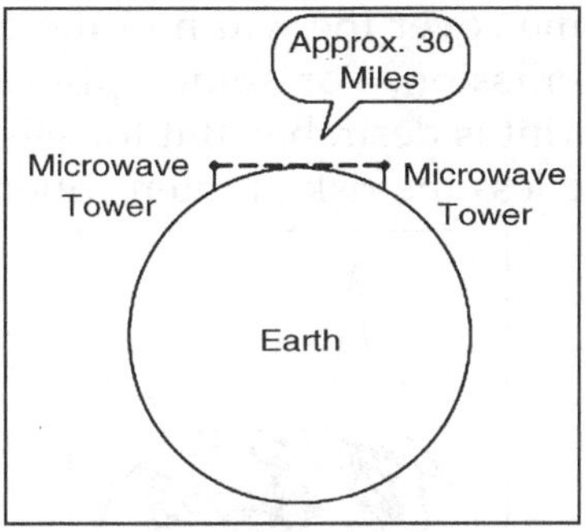


**Fig.** Microwave Transmission.

An infrared signal is difficult to intercept because it is a point-to-point signal. However, it is subject to "in the middle" attacks in which the interceptor functions like a repeater, receiving the signal, extracting any desired data, and retransmitting to the original destination the original signal or a modified version. Because of line-of-sight requirements and limited distance, infrared is typically used in a protected space, such as an office, in which in-the-middle attacks would be difficult to conceal.

**Satellite**

Many communications, such as international telephone calls, must travel around the earth. In the early days of telephone technology, telephone companies ran huge cables along the ocean's bottom, enabling calls to travel from one continent to another. Today, we have other alternatives. The communication companies place satellites in orbits that are synchronized with the rotation of the earth (called geosynchronous orbits), so the satellite appears to hover in a fixed position 22,300 miles above the earth. Although the satellite can be expensive to launch, once in space it is essentially maintenance free.

Furthermore, the quality of a satellite communication link is often better than an earthbound wire cable. Satellites act as nave transponders : Whatever they receive they broadcast out again. Thus, satellites are really sophisticated receivers, in that their sole function is to receive and repeat signals. From the user's point of view, the signal essentially "bounces" off the satellite and back to earth. For example, a signal from North America travels 22,300 miles into the sky and the same distance back to a point in Europe.

We can project a signal to a satellite with reasonable accuracy, but the satellite is not expected to have the same level of accuracy when it sends the signal back to earth. To reduce complexity and eliminate beam focusing, satellites typically spread their transmissions over a very wide area. A rather narrow angle of dispersion from the satellite's transmitter produces a fairly broad pattern (called the footprint) on the surface of the earth because of the 22,300-mile distance from the satellite to earth.

Thus, a typical satellite transmission can be received over a path several hundred miles wide; some cover the width of the entire continental United States in a single transmission. For some applications, such as satellite television, a broad footprint is desirable. But for secure communications, the smaller the footprint, the less the risk of interception.

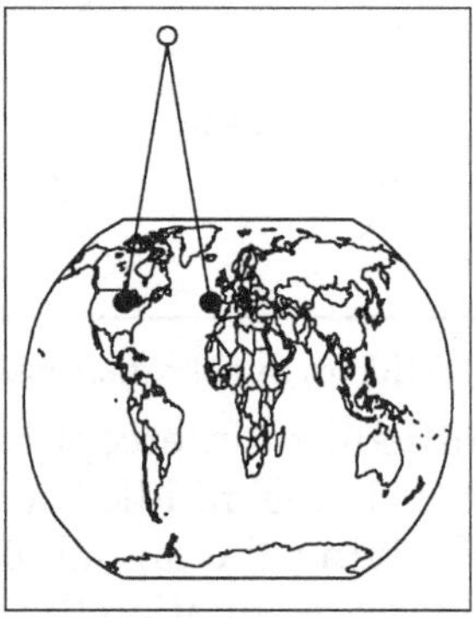

**Fig.** Satellite Communication.

## Protocols

When we use a network, the communication media are usually transparent to us. That is, most of us do not know whether our communication is carried over copper wire, optical fibre, satellite, microwave, or some combination. In fact, the communication medium may change from one transmission to the next. This ambiguity is actually a positive feature of a network: its independence. That is, the communication is separated from the actual medium of communication.

Independence is possible because we have defined protocols that allow a user to view the network at a high, abstract level of communication (viewing it in terms of user and data); the details of how the communication is accomplished are hidden within software and hardware at both ends. The software and hardware enable us to implement a network according to a protocol stack, a layered architecture for communications. Each layer in the stack is much like a language for communicating information relevant at that layer.

Two popular protocol stacks are used frequently for implementing networks: the Open Systems Interconnection (OSI) and the Transmission Control Protocol and Internet Protocol (TCP/IP) architecture. We examine each one in turn.

## ISO/OSI Reference Model

The International Standards Organization (ISO)/ Open Systems Interconnection model consists of layers by which a network communication occurs. How communication works across the different layers. We can think of the layers as creating an assembly line, in which each layer adds its own service to the communication. In concert, the layers represent the different activities that must be performed for actual transmission of a message. Separately, each layer serves a purpose; equivalent layers perform similar functions for the sender and receiver. For example, the sender's layer four affixes a header to a message, designating the sender, the receiver, and relevant sequence information. On the receiving end, layer four reads the header to verify that the message is for the intended recipient, and then removes this header.

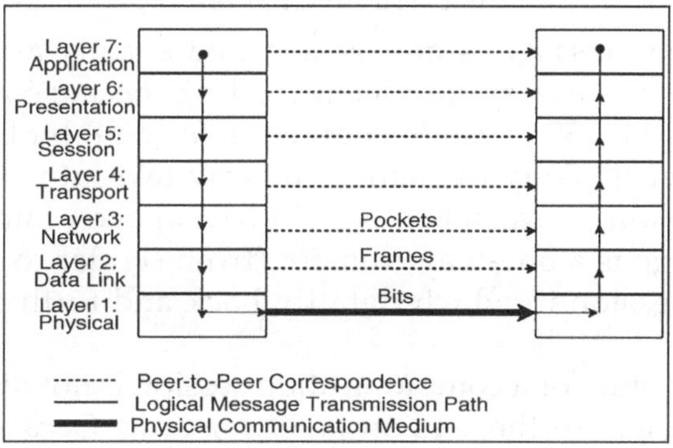


**Fig.** ISO/ OSI Network Model.

Each layer passes data in three directions: above with a layer communicating more abstractly, parallel or across to the same layer in another host, and below with a layer handling less abstract (that is, more fundamental) data items. The communications above and below are actual interactions, while the parallel one is a virtual communication path. Parallel layers are called "peers."

Let us look at a simple example of protocol transmission. Suppose that, to send e-mail to a friend, you run an application such as Eudora, Outlook, or Unix mail. You type a message, using the application's editor, and the application formats the message into two parts: a header that shows to whom the message is intended (as well as other things, such as sender and time sent), and a body that contains the text of your message. The application reformats your message into a standard format so that even if you and your friend use different mail applications, you can still exchange e-mail.

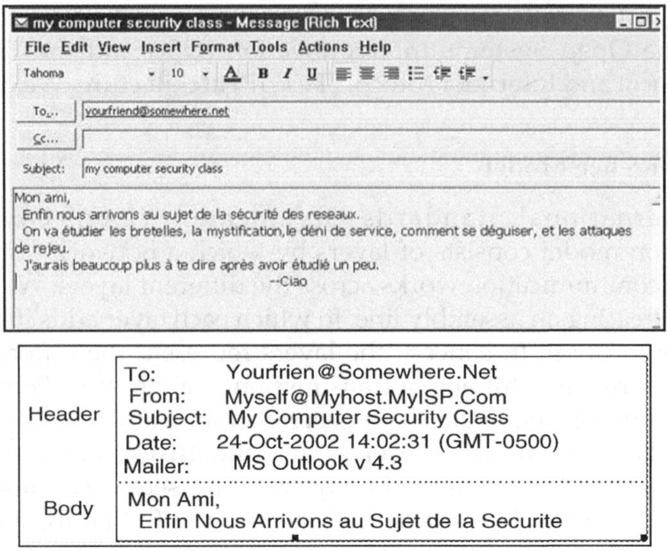


**Fig.** Transformation.

However, the message is not transmitted exactly as you typed it, as raw text. Raw text is a very inefficient coding, because an alphabet uses relatively few of the 255 possible characters for an 8-bit byte. Instead, the presentation layer is likely to change the raw text into something else. It may do compression, character conversions, and even some cryptography. An e-mail message is a one-way transfer (from sender to receiver), so it is not initiating a session in which data fly back and forth between the two endpoints.

Because the notion of a communication session is not directly relevant in this scenario, we ignore the session layer for now. Occasionally, spurious signals intrude in a communication channel, as when static rustles a telephone line or interference intrudes on a radio or television signal. To address this, the transport layer adds error detection and correction coding to filter out these spurious signals.

## Addressing

Suppose your message is addressed to yourfriend@somewhere.net. This notation means that "somewhere.net" is the name of a destination host (or more accurately, a destination network). At the network layer, a hardware device called a router actually sends the message from your network to a router on the network somewhere.net. The network layer adds two headers to show your computer's address as the source and somewhere.net's address as the destination.

Logically, your message is prepared to move from your machine to your router to your friend's router to your friend's computer. (In fact, between the two routers there may be many other routers in a path through the networks from you to your friend.) Together, the network layer structured with destination address, source address, and data is called a packet. The basic network layer protocol transformation is shown in Figure below.

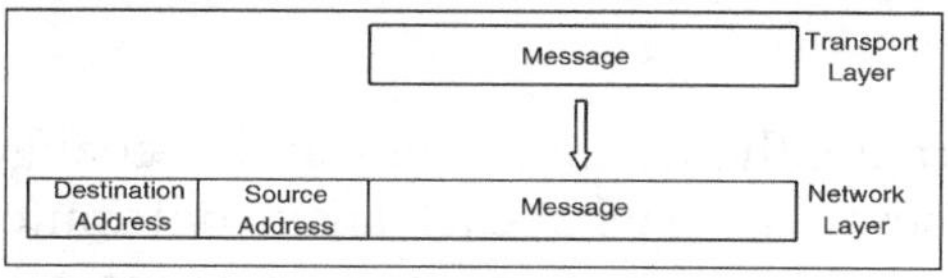


**Fig.** Network Layer Transformation.

The message must travel from your computer to your router. Every computer connected to a network has a network interface card (NIC) with a unique physical address, called a MAC address (for Media Access Control). At the data link level, two more headers are added, one for your computer's NIC address (the source MAC) and one for your router's NIC address. A data link layer structure with destination MAC, source MAC, and data is called a frame. Every NIC selects from the network those frames with its own address as a destination address. The data link layer adds the structure necessary for data to get from your computer to another computer (a router is just a dedicated computer) on your network.

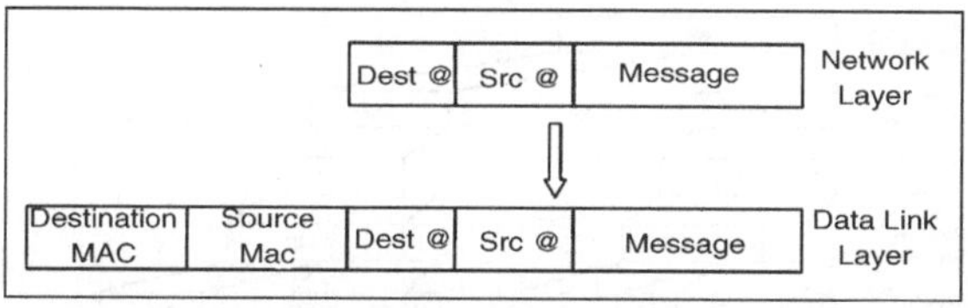


**Fig.** Data Link Layer Transformation.

Finally, the message is ready to be sent out as a string of bits. We noted earlier that analog transmissions communicate bits by using voltage or tone changes, and digital transmissions communicate them as discrete pulses. The physics and electronics of how bits are actually sent are handled at the physical layer.

On the receiving (destination) side, this process is exercised in reverse: Analog or digital signals are converted to digital data. The NIC card receives frames destined for it. The recipient network layer checks that the packet is really addressed to it. Packets may not arrive in the order in which they were sent (because of network delays or differences in paths through the network), so the session layer may have to reorder packets. The presentation layer removes compression and sets the appearance appropriate for the destination computer. Finally, the application layer formats and delivers the data as an e-mail message to your friend.

The layering and coordinating are a lot of work, and each protocol layer does its own part. But the work is worth the effort because the different layers are what enable Outlook running on an IBM PC on an Ethernet network in

Washington D.C. to communicate with a user running Eudora on an Apple computer via a dial-up connection in Prague. Moreover, the separation by layers helps the network staff troubleshoot when something goes awry.

## Layering

Each layer reformats the transmissions and exchanges information with its peer layer. Let us summarize what each layer contributes. A typical message that has been acted upon by the seven layers in preparation for transmission. Layer 6 breaks the original message data into blocks. At the session layer (5), a session header is added to show the sender, the receiver, and some sequencing information. Layer 4 adds information concerning the logical connection between the sender and receiver.

The network layer (3) adds routing information and divides the message into units called packets, the standard units of communication in a network. The data link layer (2) adds both a header and a trailer to ensure correct sequencing of the message blocks and to detect and correct transmission errors.

The individual bits of the message and the control information are transmitted on the physical medium by level 1. All additions to the message are checked and removed by the corresponding layer on the receiving side.

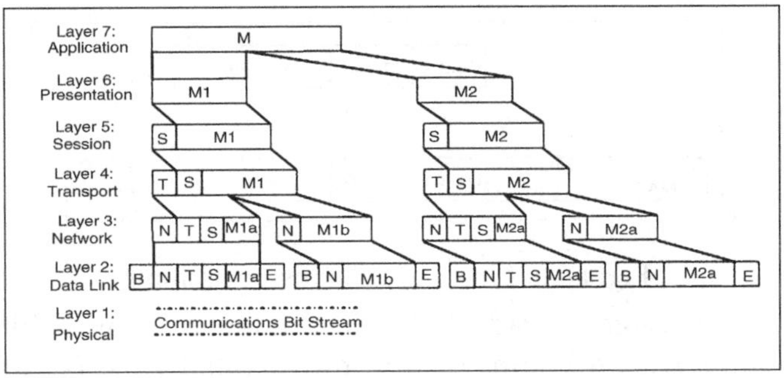


**Fig.** Message Prepared for Transmission.

The OSI model is one of several transmission models. Different network designers implement network activities in slightly different combinations, although there is always a clear delineation of responsibility. Some designers argue that the OSI model is overly complexit has too many levels and so other models are typically shorter.

## TCP/IP

The OSI model is a conceptual one; it shows the different activities required for sending a communication. However, full implementation of a seven-layer transmission carries too much overhead for megabit-per-second communications; the OSI protocol slows things down to unacceptable levels. For this reason, TCP/IP (Transmission Control Protocol/Internet Protocol) is the protocol stack used for most wide area network communications. TCP/IP was invented for what became the Internet. TCP/IP is defined by protocols, not layers, but we can think of it in terms of four layers: application, host-to-host (end-to-end) transport, Internet, and physical. In particular, an application programme deals only with abstract data items meaningful to the application user. Although TCP/IP is often used as a single acronym, it really denotes two different protocols: TCP implements a connected communications session on top of the more basic IP transport protocol. In fact, a third protocol, UDP (user datagram protocol) is also an essential part of the suite.

The transport layer receives variable-length messages from the application layer; the transport layer breaks them down into units of manageable size, transferred in packets. The Internet layer transmits application layer packets in datagrams, passing them to different physical connections based on the data's destination (provided in an address accompanying the data). The physical layer consists of device drivers to perform the actual bit-by-bit data communication. How each layer contributes to the complete interaction.

The TCP protocol must ensure the correct sequencing of packets as well as the integrity (correct transmission) of data within packets. The protocol will put out-of-sequence packets in proper order, call for retransmitting a missing packet, and obtain a fresh copy of a damaged packet. In this way, TCP hands a stream of correct data in proper order to the invoking application. But this service comes at a price. Recording and checking sequence numbers, verifying integrity checks, and requesting and waiting for retransmissions of faulty or missing packets take time and induce overhead. Most applications expect a flawless stream of bits, but some applications can tolerate a less accurate stream of data if speed or efficiency is critical.

A TCP packet is a data structure that includes a sequence number, an acknowledgment number for connecting the packets of a communication session, flags, and source and destination portnumbers. A port is a number designating a particular application running on a computer. For example, if Jose and Walter begin a communication, they establish a unique channel number by which their computers can route their respective packets to each of them. The channel number is called a port. Each service uses a well-known port, such as port 80 for HTTP (web pages), 23 for Telnet (remote terminal connection), 25 for SMTP (e-mail), or 161 for SNMP(network management). More precisely, each of these services has a waiting process that monitors the specified port number and tries to perform its service on any data passed to the port.

The UDP protocol does not provide the error-checking and correcting features of TCP, but it is a much smaller, faster protocol. For instance, a UDP datagram adds 8 bytes for control information, whereas the more complex TCP packet adds at least 24 bytes.

**Addressing**

Scheme for communication to occur, the bits have to be directed to somewhere. All networks use an addressing scheme so that data can be directed to the expected recipient. Because it is the most common, we use the

Internet addressing scheme known as IP addresses in our examples, since it is the addressing handled by the IP protocol. All network models implement an addressing scheme. An address is a unique identifier for a single point in the network. For obvious reasons, addressing in shared, wide area networks follows established rules, while addressing in local area networks is less constrained.

Starting at the local area network, each node has a unique address, defined in hardware on the network connector device (such as a network interface card) or its software driver. A network administrator may choose network addresses to be easy to work with, such as 1001, 1002, 1003 for nodes on one LAN, and 2001, 2002, and so forth on another.

A host on a TCP/IP wide area network has a 32-bit address, called an IP address. An IP address is expressed as four 8-bit groups in decimal notation, separated by periods, such as 100.24.48.6. People prefer speaking in words or pseudowords, so network addresses are also known by domain names, such as ATT.COM or CAM.AC.UK. Addressing tables convert domain names to IP addresses.

The world's networks are running out of unique addresses. This 32-bit standard address is being increased to 128 bits in a scheme called IPv6. But because 32-bit addresses will remain for some time, we focus on the older version.

A domain name is parsed from right to left. The rightmost portion, such as .COM, .EDU, .NET, .ORG, or .GOV, or one of the two-letter country specific codes, such as .UK, .FR, .JP, or .DE, is called a top-level domain. A small set of organizations called the Internet Registrars controls these top-level domains; the registrars also control the registration of second-level domains, such as ATT in ATT.COM. Essentially, the registrars publish addresses of hosts that maintain tables of the second-level domains contained in the top-level domain.

A host connected to the Internet queries one of these tables to find the numeric IP address of ATT in the .COM domain. AT&T, the company owning the ATT Internet site, must maintain its own host to resolve addresses within its own domain, such as MAIL.ATT.COM. You may find that the first time you try to resolve a fully qualified domain name to its IP address, your system performs a lookup starting at the top; for subsequent attempts, your system maintains a cache of domain name records that lets it resolve addresses locally. Finally, a domain name is translated into a 32-bit, four-octet address, and that address is included in the IP packets destined for that address. (We return to name resolution later in this chapter because it can be used in network attacks.)

**Routing Concepts**

A host needs to know how to direct a packet from its own IP address. Each host knows to what other hosts it is directly connected, and hosts communicate their connections to their neighbours. For the example network of Figure above, System 1 would inform System 2 that it was one hop away from Clients A, B, and C. In turn, System 2 would inform its other neighbour, System 3, that it (System 2) was two hops away from Clients A, B, and C. From System 3, System 2 would learn that System 3 was one hop away from Clients D and E, Server F, and System 4, which System 2 would then pass to System 1 as being a distance of two hops. The routing protocols are actually more complex than this description, but the concepts are the same; hosts advertise to their neighbours to describe to which hosts (addresses) they can route traffic and at what cost (number of hops). Each host routes traffic to a neighbour that offers a path at the cheapest cost.

# 9

# Advanced Security Technology in Networking

Networking security solutions provider Imperva has an impeccable pedigree for its specialty. Its founder and CEO Shlomo Kramer has been an integral part of the network security space since he co-founded Check Point Software Technologies back in 1993. After helping to create numerous network security solutions at Check Point, he went in his own direction and founded Imperva in 2002. Brian Contos, chief security strategist at Imperva (www.imperva.com), says that even though there were plenty of network security solutions available, Kramer noticed that none of these solutions specifically addressed application and data security. "He wanted to put a specific focus on data security for protecting Web applications and databases," Contos says.

Eight years later, Imperva now has customers from a wide range of verticals, including three of the top five U.S. commercial banks; more than 60 state, local, and federal government agencies or departments; and top healthcare providers, grocery stores, and utilities, in addition to more than 100 SMEs in various fields. Accor North America, GoDaddy.com, Agilent, and Vonage are among the many companies that have all deployed Imperva solutions. "We have a global reach right now with thousands of customers worldwide, and we want to continue growing that into both midsized businesses as well as large enterprises and service providers," Contos says.

## END-TO-END DATA-CENTRIC NETWORK SOLUTIONS

According to Contos, Imperva believes that network threats are for the most part targeting data security issues rather than the old paradigm of network security issues. "Because we look at Web applications and the database, we're the only company out there that covers any end-to-end solution for all things data-centric," Contos says. "We'd like to continue pushing that forward."

Contos explains that focusing on the network ultimately makes for a better solution than focusing only on the data itself. "If you asked anybody about security a few years ago, they would tell you they have a network firewall, antivirus protection, an IDS, VPN, and things like that. These are all important. But today's attacks, like SQL injections, cross-site scripting (XSS), [and] cross-site request forgery (CSRF), are focused on the applications and databases at the application/database layer. It doesn't matter whether the attacks are coming from an insider or an outsider [because] data is data," says Contos.

But too many organizations are trying to stop data-centric attacks with yesterday's technology. "It's a bit like stopping raindrops with a tennis racket. It's not going to do a really great job. But you can mitigate [attacks] with data-centric controls, such as Web application firewalls, database firewalls, and database activity monitoring [tools], and that's what we offer," says Contos.

## SECURESPHERE CENTRAL

Imperva's SecureSphere appliance is the central component around which all the company's solutions revolve. Imperva offers several different models, including those that have fault tolerance capabilities and those that can handle copper and different fibre interfaces. Imperva also offers a series of management servers called SecureSphere MX that integrates the configuration and monitoring of distributed SecureSphere gateway deployments.

SecureSphere Standard Edition offers affordable, effective data security for SMEs, with automated protection against data-centric attacks. It comes with Imperva's WAF (Web Application Firewall) and its DAS (Discovery and Assessment Server), which give users the ability to assess database vulnerabilities, as well as provide means to fix them. "It will go out and find all of your applications and databases and classify all the data, so essentially you know what you're trying to protect," Contos says. "You know what the bad guys are targeting, you know what type of data they can take, [and] you know where they reside, so you can apprise appropriate controls at that point."

### Next-Generation Advantages

Imperva considers its WAF a next-generation Web application firewall because of its ability to profile the ways in which users interact with applications and to track user activity from the application into the database and back so that administrators obtain an end-to-end stream of what users are doing. "Nobody else in the industry can do correlation at the data level because they don't have the second component, which is our Database Firewall and our DAS, which provides all those same things that our WAF provides with the addition of a full data audit for the database outside of the database," says Contos.

There are obvious advantages to auditing databases using an outside appliance solution like the one Imperva offers. First off, any substantive audit done on a database kills performance. "Nobody buys a database saying let's size it for running a full-blown audit," Contos says. In addition, if for whatever reason you have a malicious user inside your organization, Imperva's database solution lets IT administrators and data centre managers secure the system from them. "Since you're handling security outside of the database, there is nothing for [malicious users] to delete and no tracks to hide because they don't even know it's there," Contos says.

Contos presents a real-world example of how Imperva's database solutions can limit damage caused by malicious hackers. Most states have breach disclosure laws, which means that if a database storing a million customer records gets hacked, you need to be able to show evidence of what occurred. "If you don't know the specifics of the intrusion, you have to tell these million or so customers that their data was compromised," which Contos says could lead to having to buy the customers credit card monitoring services for a year, possibly losing them as customers, facing bad PR, and/or losing revenue. "Replay the same scenario where you're running our Database Firewall and DAS. You have empirical evidence that the hacker only accessed [a single] table that contains records for 100 customers," Contos says. "With hacking, it's not a question of if but of when. And when it happens, you want to make sure you're limiting your liability as much as possible."

### Using Attackers Against Themselves

ThreatRadar, Imperva's latest add-on security solution, provides automated defence against automated attacks leveraging the strengths that these sorts of attacks use. "It's an industry-changing solution [because] we take that automation and turn it on its ear," says Contos. "We track botnets, phishing sites, spammers, malicious IP addresses, hostile geographies, and other things of this nature, all of which change by the minute, and update our customers' solutions with these. It's like a real-time antivirus update that's constantly being pushed to our customers," he says. According to Contos, the big upside for ThreatRadar users is that they no longer have to waste time dealing with these automated attacks because ThreatRadar will automatically block or redirect that traffic. "Now, instead of looking at those 10,000 attacks, you know what's happening and can run reports, but you don't have to focus on these basic industrialized hackers," says Contos. "You can focus on advanced persistent threats, or APTs—the ones that are directly targeting your business—without getting inundated with all that noise."

## LIMITATIONS OF TRADITIONAL NETWORK SECURITY

As connectivity to the corporate network becomes ubiquitous, the task of distinguishing authorized users, devices and applications from unauthorized ones becomes more and more difficult. While strong password policies, firewalls, and other traditional security measures provide a layer in Defense in Depth – they do not address the full areas of risk.

- *Corporate firewalls*: Firewalls are extremely effective for blocking malicious scripts that take advantage of open ports and unmonitored network resources. However, when users need connectivity to resources that exist inside and outside the firewall, basic border security doesn't provide the flexibility needed to effectively defend against internal threats and unauthorized users. Firewalls are essential to networks protection, but more comprehensive methods of providing security for resources that exist inside and outside the network are necessary.

- *Computer security requirements*: Relying on end users to maintain security policies is fragile at best, uses when presented with a security choice will invariability select the choice that lets them complete their assigned task, which is not always the secure choice. For instance, users who have access to multiple network resources are often required to create different passwords to access each one. Often, this leads end users to choose passwords that are easy to remember—and easy to exploit.
- *Access for remote users*: For workers who connect from offsite locations, secure data transmission is essential. A traditional virtual private network (VPN) can provide a secure method of transmitting secure and reliable data. However, for organizations who want to take advantage of the increasing availability of broadband networking sources, a more secure option is desired—one that encompasses multiple levels of security and provides security settings equal to that of internal network sources.
- *Wireless connectivity*: The 802.11b wireless networks provide users the freedom of broadband networking without the limitations of wired connections. This can provide an organization large gains in user productivity, but must be implemented and managed in a way to reduce the risk to the network. In its most basic form, a wireless transmission is open to anyone who has the hardware and software to receive that information. Wireless security protocols and encryption methods, such as Wired Equivalent Privacy (WEP), encrypt wireless transmissions from unauthorized recipients. However, this simple encryption is not strong enough to deter hackers from breaking into static WEP keys on protected wireless networks.
- *Machine certificate technology and policies*: Through the Web or over an internal network connection, machine certificates provide a secure method of controlling access to a network for authorized devices and users. However, the administrative issues around the process of requesting, and installing certificates, tracking their expiration and renewal are barriers to their widespread adoption. If not monitored as certificates expire at the end of their lifetime access to trusted sites can be denied, authentication processes can fail causing increases in support desk calls and losses in productivity.

## SECURITY SOLUTION REQUIREMENTS

Today, a Defense in Depth approach to networks security is a best practice and one area to incorporate is a PKI that extends beyond user authentication and SSL. For networks with multiple resources types, a security infrastructure that efficiently protects all resources should be in place. The following list identifies elements of a successful network security solution that help reduce the risk to the network.

- *Multiple layers of security*. A secure network should encompass multiple levels of security to secure all network resources, including domain access and control, e-mail, extranets and Web sites, and remote and wireless connectivity.
- *Security for server and client computers*. Network security should be implemented at all levels of the network. Authentication to ensure users and computers are valid members of the network should occur at multiple levels of the log on process. After a user is properly authenticated, user privileges should propagate as that user accesses different parts of the network.
- *Secured lines of communication*. The Internet is a cost-effective way of transmitting data from point to point, but security on open lines is minimal. Open standards such as Internet Protocol Security (IPSec) and SSL certificates allow organizations to secure their networks from outside intrusion by encrypting data and securing the lines that carry the data.

For e-mail communication, rights-management and s/mime software in applications such as Microsoft Outlook allows e-mail messages and attachments to be protected against access by unauthorized users.

- Protection for remote and wireless connections. VPN connections can be made more secure by adding multi-layers of identification and authentication. For machines this would entail the issuance of machine certificates that allow for the identification of managed devices and for uses the incorporation of two factor identification and authentication. Two Factor authentication requires the end use to present something they have an something they know (the smart card and the pin).

Wireless connections can take advantage of the 802.1x security protocol, which enhances WEP.

Wireless access to network resources is vulnerable when WEP keys are not changed on a frequent basis because static WEP keys give hackers time to work on breaking the keys. Instead, WEP keys should be dynamic allocated to reduce this risk.

- Security that is easy to update and manage. With a centralized point of network management, network administrators would have greater control and visibility of threats to network resources.

Machine certificates should be renewed automatically, without the need for end-user or administrator intervention. When system administrators handle requests and renewals manually, the risk of unobserved machine certificate expiration increases dramatically. Leading to additional calls to the support desk.

## ESTABLISH AN ELECTRONIC INFORMATION, PRIVACY, AND SECURITY POLICY

Focus on managing this evolving risk by establishing an electronic privacy and security policy. Many camps already have some type of policy governing employee use of the Internet, e-mail, Facebook, and other social media. This is a good start. If these policies haven't been reviewed in a while, take some time to review these guidelines before summer. Expand on these to include some broader developing risks.

The following are some examples of issues to be addressed in your updated policy. This list is not exhaustive; consider including other risks – especially those which may be unique to your camp.

- Use of electronic communications systems; security and privacy of electronic information; use of passwords; structure for passwords; prohibitions on downloading personally identifiable information to notebook computers or flash drives; guidelines for camper contact outside of camp.
- Use of camp e-mail; no expectation of privacy for employee e-mail communications sent on camp e-mail systems; prohibition of offensive, hostile, discriminatory or intimidating content.
- Internet, Intranet, or Extranet to be used solely to facilitate the conduct of the camp's business.
- Establish guidelines for the use of social media (Facebook, LinkedIn, etc.), blogs, and other internet publications; identify prohibited conduct; emphasize the importance of using good judgment in postings; and clarify that employees have no permission to use the camp's name, etc.
- Consequences of violating the policies – disciplinary action, which may include termination of employment.

Enlist your insurance broker or insurance company loss control representatives in this process. Share your current policies on these topics with them and ask for their suggestions to improve and expand your guidelines. Your electronic privacy and security policy should be shared with every employee.

Require each employee to read the policies and acknowledge with a signature that the employee has received a copy of the policy, read it, and agrees to follow the guidelines set forth in the document. This acknowledgement should include a statement of consequences for failing to follow the company policy, such as disciplinary action up to and including termination of employment. A copy of the signed acknowledgment should be kept permanently with the employee's human resources records.

## SECURITY BREACHES AND FAILURE TO MANAGE PRIVACY

California was the first state to pass a data security breach law. Since then, forty-three other states, plus the District of Columbia, Puerto Rico, and the US Virgin Islands, have passed data security laws. The requirements of each state law are different, but the common thread is a requirement to notify the persons whose personally identifiable information was compromised.

Personally identifiable information includes name, address, social security number, gender, marital status, contact information, driver's license issue and expiry dates, credit card information, and medical history, among other things. This sounds like the very kind of information maintained in camp databases about their campers, camper families, and employees.

Notification costs have been quoted by various information technology industry experts to be in the $200 – $300 range per compromised data file. Not terrible, you say, but suppose your database had one thousand names, and all were compromised. That's an expense of $200,000 – $300,000 probably not covered by your camp insurance policies. If you store personally identifiable information in your camp databases, you need to be aware of your state's data security breach disclosure law. Other consequences will most likely include civil suits, depending on the extent of any financial damages.

## TYPES OF SITUATIONS CONTRIBUTING TO SECURITY BREACHES

Not all security breaches are major. In fact, some events are so minor you might not notice the event unless someone on your staff or an independent consultant is watching closely. A frequency of small events left unchecked may lead to a larger, more catastrophic event. Security breaches may occur when passwords are stolen because unprotected wireless networks were used.

Passwords should be complex and changed on a regular basis. Security may be compromised by failing to change employee login information when someone leaves. Not all former employees may be disgruntled and vindictive, but it only takes one. Sometimes employees are fooled into clicking on links that compromise their individual work stations and jeopardize network security.

Beware of clicking on a link in any e-mail that is from an unfamiliar source or that you didn't solicit. Don't click on ads that say you've "won," for example; they may download spyware that compromise security. If you allow employees to take notebook computers or flash drives out of the office with customer information stored on the devices, you are at risk of a security breach should the device be lost or stolen. Some smart phones are also capable of storing customer information with e-mail and text applications, posing a similar security and privacy breach risk if they are lost or stolen.

## My Information is in the Cloud

There are many internet service providers (ISPs) focused on the camp industry who offer directors the convenience of accessing software and storing customer information offsite on the Cloud. The Cloud in this instance is a metaphor for the Internet.

Your camp management information is accessed via the Internet from any computer, anywhere, at any time, usually through a Web browser. The experience is often the same as if the software applications and data were stored locally on the user's computer.

What about security in this situation? There are divergent views on this issue, but generally security is often as good as or better than other traditional network systems because the services are shared. As a result, these ISPs are able to devote greater resources to security than many businesses could afford on their own.

If you experience a security breach, don't expect the ISP to be responsible. Most Cloud computing contracts will contain comprehensive limitation of liability provisions, including both a financial cap on liability and an exclusion clause for indirect losses, and in most cases, a separate exclusion clause for data loss and data breaches.

Another common feature of Cloud computing contracts involves tying the financial cap in liability to the amount of fees paid by the Cloud customer under the contract, further limited to a specific time, such as the previous twelve months. This means you are most likely on your own to pay for breach notification costs and deal with any other legal consequences from a security breach.

It is recommended that directors read Cloud computing (ISP) agreements carefully and take the time to understand any limitation clauses or other provisions in the contracts that limit the ISP's liability for damages arising out of security breaches or other services.

## Defensive Strategy — Protect Your Computer Network

Whether your network is wired or wireless, whether you are Cloud computing or not, and regardless if you operate just one or twenty computers, protect them by using a network router. This electronic device allows a number of computers to share the same internet connection. It also provides security for the computer's access points or ports, as well as filtering communications and blocking unauthorized access. Wireless routers come with default administrator passwords. Unfortunately, these default passwords are not always changed before the wireless router is put into service. This increases the risk of unauthorized access and network security breaches. Be sure your camp computer network administrator is changing the default passwords in your wireless routers and using complicated passwords in their place. Also be sure that any transmitted wireless signal is encrypted.

*Other suggestions for protecting your computer network and keeping private information secure include:*

- Keep all operating systems up to date.
- Install and run a good antivirus and spyware scanner regularly.
- Use an external hard drive to store all information, including personally identifiable information, and disconnect it from your computer when not in use.
- Consider using Web-accessed e-mail.

As a practical matter, even the most savvy computer users can benefit from having an IT consultant. If you don't have such a person available to you, consider hiring one as part of your first line of defence against security breach risks and cyber thieves. This will be money well spent.

**Be Prepared**

In the final analysis, an effective strategy for managing the risk of computer network security involves constant vigilance. This vigilance needs to be backed up by a sophisticated information technology structure, as comprehensive as you can afford, with practical guidelines for people to follow. This approach will help to reduce the risks of privacy and security breaches. Once you've done all you can from a risk management perspective, consider buying some cyber liability insurance to protect against lawsuits alleging negligence and notification costs in the event a breach occurs in spite of your efforts.

## SHARING COMPUTER NETWORK LOGS FOR SECURITY AND PRIVACY

Log data is an essential resource to security teams at any organization large enough to hire full-time IT personnel. While IDSs can operate directly upon streaming network data, matching signatures and producing alerts, it is still necessary for human beings to examine logs to understand these alerts. Logs also form the core source of evidence for computer forensic investigations following security incidents. In addition to these very applied uses, logs are important to security researchers, for instance, those involved with research honeynets.

It is typical in the current security culture for each autonomous organization to use log data only to locally optimize network management and security protection. For example, when an organization notices an Internet attack (*e.g.*, an external reconnaissance scan) a typical reaction is to block the offending IP addresses at the organization's perimeter but not to alert others—

even administrators of the offending network— about this activity. Another example of this type of behaviour is reactively scanning for a vulnerability on all the organization's systems after noticing vulnerabilities being exploited, but not alerting others of this activity.

Although these examples are not universally true, as some security engineers have trusted channels for sharing security events, such sharing is the exception. There is a culture of pushing attackers away from oneself without any consideration of the poor overall security resulting from this lack of coordination between organizations. It is analogous to local policeman chasing criminals from one jurisdiction to another without crossing jurisdictional boundaries.

In these ways, administrators may miss the bigger picture and are unlikely to notice when they are just a piece of a larger target. Indeed, there are very few cross-sectional views of the Internet, and until recently there have been no mechanisms to enable such wider views. Furthermore, current examples of wide views, such as spam blacklists and worm signatures, are often focused on a specific characteristic even though signatures are gathered from events across the entire Internet. While security professionals are having problems sharing logs, sharing data is in fact quite common among attackers.

They trade zombies, publicly post information on vulnerable systems/ networks and coordinate attacks. Recent events at several U.S. supercomputing centres have demonstrated examples of coordinated attacks against organizations that do not have good mechanisms in place for data sharing and log correlation.

These problems highlight why it is no longer satisfactory to focus solely on the local picture; there is a need to look globally across the Internet. And while the data needed exists, tapping into thousands of data sources effectively and sharing critical information—intelligently and to the data owners' satisfaction—is an open problem.

The importance of solving this problem has even caught the government's attention as the Department of Homeland Security has recognized the importance of sharing information and established Information Sharing and Analysis Centers (ISACs) to facilitate the storage and sharing of information about security threats. The importance of log sharing has also gained industry recognition with investments in infrastructure dedicated solely for this purpose across multiple industry sectors.

The National Strategy to Secure Cyberspace (NSSC) explicitly lists sharing as one of its highest priorities—data sharing within the government, within industry sectors and between the government and industry. In fact, of the eight action items reached in the NSSC report, three of them are directly related to log data sharing: Item 2: "Provide for the development of tactical and strategic analysis of cyber attacks and vulnerability assessments"; Item 3: "Encourage the development of a private sector capability to share a synoptic view of the health of cyberspace"; and Item 8: "Improve and enhance public/ private information sharing involving cyber-attacks, threats, and vulnerabilities".

However, the reluctance to share logs—which has resulted in fewer entities sharing—is understandable due to the sensitivity of the information contained within logs. Logs may be accidently mishandled by friendly peers, or fall directly/indirectly into the hands of malicious crackers. Security engineers have enough concerns without worrying about being a contributor to a security compromise of their own organization, or even worse, creating third party liability to a security compromise of another organization.

The first phase of any digital attack is reconnaissance, and logs are like a treasure map for would-be attackers. Access to computer and network logs can provide intruders with special views of a network not visible from the outside, even with scanning tools. Information gleaned from these logs could indicate potential bottlenecks for DoS attacks or could even contain passwords—as often happens when a user accidentally types a password into the username field. Logs can even be used to identify machines infected by worms, which are most likely not well-maintained or monitored. Soft targets such as these can be used to get a foothold into a network.

While some would claim that the difficulties in sharing logs is social, we believe the problems are technical at the heart. To share logs and address these concerns about the sensitivity of the information within them, anonymization techniques must be employed.

However, the field of log anonymization is still immature. There are very few tools, and the ones that exist are deficient in many ways. Further, current anonymization tools are one-size-fits-all, or better put one-size-tries-to-fit-all. Ideally, they would support multiple levels of anonymization that trade-off between security—of the anonymization scheme— and utility—the amount of useful information retained in anonymized logs. Thus far, no log anonymizers—besides a tool we recently developed for NetFlow anonymization — support multiple levels of anonymization, even though there are typically multiple levels of trust between parties who might wish to share logs and those with whom they would share their logs.

We believe a new anonymization framework must be created that supports trade-offs between security and utility by providing multiple levels of anonymization. To achieve this goal two important research problems must be solved. *First,* a metric must be created for the utility of a log that is based on the fields or data types within that log. Utility should be measured by the types of attacks that can be detected with a log or set of logs. *Second,* a metric for the security of an anonymization scheme must be developed. This metric should be based upon the types of attacks that can be used against an anonymization scheme—a log and the anonymization algorithms used on it. The difficulty of the attack and the amount of information that can be obtained by reversing the anonymization will both affect this metric. This new framework should be based upon the data types and fields within logs rather than the specific log types and versions.

The prototype tools we are developing handle several log formats, but more importantly a framework that is extensible to handle almost any log is needed. Additionally, guidelines and standards must be developed to help organizations map trust levels to anonymization levels. In this way, organizations will be able to customize anonymization to fit their needs for the first time.

## SECURITY AND PRIVACY IN INFORMATION TECHNOLOGY

Computer networks have been around for several decades and evolved from interconnecting only a few computers in a single room, into integrating hundreds of millions of devices worldwide forming an entity we all know as the Internet. While in the past, computer networks usually consisted of classic hardware devices like terminals, servers and network accessories like storage systems or printers, networks nowadays cover a multitude of device classes, starting from the most powerful super computers going all the way via personal computers, laptops, household appliances to simple sensor nodes. With the demand for mobility, wireless communication means have been developed, allowing the appearance of ultra-portable computing devices such as notebooks, tablet computers and smart phones. Thanks to advanced miniaturization, wireless devices can be even smaller than a coin, allowing to connect virtually everything to a network following the imagination of Kristofer Pister.

He introduced the concept of smart dust in 2000, which is basically a hypothetical system of tiny wireless devices coping with a variety of tasks. Although it might take another ten years to come close to his vision of interconnecting everything, recent developments brought small, powerful mobile devices with outstanding connectivity to the mass market and therefore into our very homes and workplaces.

# 10

# Data Security

In simple terms, data security is the practice of keeping data protected from corruption and unauthorized access. The focus behind data security is to ensure privacy while protecting personal or corporate data. Data is the raw form of information stored as columns and rows in our databases, network servers and personal computers. This may be a wide range of information from personal files and intellectual property to market analytics and details intended to top secret. Data could be anything of interest that can be read or otherwise interpreted in human form. However, some of this information isn't intended to leave the system. The unauthorized access of this data could lead to numerous problems for the larger corporation or even the personal home user.

Having your bank account details stolen is just as damaging as the system administrator who was just robbed for the client information in their database. There has been a huge emphasis on data security as of late, largely because of the Internet. There are a number of options for locking down your data from software solutions to hardware mechanisms. Computer users are certainly more conscious these days, but is your data really secure? If you're not following the essential guidelines, your sensitive information just may be at risk.

## ENCRYPTION

Encryption has become a critical security feature for thriving networks and active home users alike. This security mechanism uses mathematical schemes and algorithms to scramble data into unreadable text. It can only by decoded or decrypted by the party that possesses the associated key. (FDE) Full-disk encryption offers some of the best protection available.

This technology enables you to encrypt every piece of data on a disk or hard disk drive. Full disk encryption is even more powerful when hardware solutions are used in conjunction with software components. This combination is often referred to as end-based or end-point full disk encryption.

## STRONG USER AUTHENTICATION

Authentication is another part of data security that we encounter with everyday computer usage. Just think about when you log into your e-mail or blog account. That single sign-on process is a form authentication that allows you to log into applications, files, folders and even an entire computer system. Once logged in, you have various given privileges until logging out. Some systems will cancel a session if your machine has been idle for a certain amount of time, requiring that you prove authentication once again to re-enter. The single sign-on scheme is also implemented into strong user authentication systems. However, it requires individuals to login using multiple factors of authentication. This may include a password, a one-time password, a smart card or even a fingerprint.

### Backup Solutions

Data security wouldn't be complete without a solution to backup your critical information. Though it may appear secure while confined away in a machine, there is always a chance that your data can be compromised. You could suddenly be hit with a malware infection where a virus destroys all of your files. Someone could enter your computer and thieve data by sliding through a security hole in the operating system. Perhaps it was an inside job that caused your business to lose those sensitive reports. If all else fails, a reliable backup solution will allow you to restore your data instead of starting completely from scratch.

## COMPUTER SECURITY BASICS

Making a computer secure requires a list of different actions for different reasons. There is a secondary rule that says security is an on going process. No matter how well a system is designed, if it is never changed that gives any potential infiltrator all the time in the world to examine the security for flaws. The information described here is neither detailed nor comprehensive. This should, however, serve as a good overview of the types of security measures sometimes taken. What measures are appropriate are best determined on a case by case basis.

### Physical Security

Theft is the physical threat of most concern and rightfully so. Keeping rooms locked is a good idea, but not always feasible. Keeping computers locked to a wall or table is a good deterrent against a casual, shoplifting style, theft but it will not deter a professional with a shopping list. We have seen a thief use a crow bar to remove a computer along with a portion of the formica table top (they were then foolish enough to take it to a repair shop with the table top still attached).

There are very loud alarms which sound when the power cable is unplugged. A combination of locks and alarms is an excellent theft prevention system for computer labs which must be publicly accessible, particularly at late hours.

Computer hardware is protected from fire damage by smoke detectors and sprinkler systems just like any other equipment. Computers are unique in that the most costly damage is the loss of data which can be prevented by storing back up tapes in remote locations.

Surge protectors and uninterruptable power supplies are a low cost investment that can save very costly equipment damage. These are particularly important if the computer must be used continuously or if your region is prone to severe thunder storms or frequent power outages. Some surge protectors have the ability to protect the phone line going to a modem also. The modem and mother board can be more readily damaged by lightning hitting a phone line than by lightning hitting the power lines because the computer power supply provides a minimal amount of protection.

**Data Integrity**

Backing up data is the single most important step in preventing data loss. Entire companies have gone out of business due to losing valuable information. An enormous amount of man hours are spent every year reproducing information which was lost in some manner. Back ups can be on removable disks, tapes, paper printouts or other computer systems. It is important to periodically put copies of these back ups in remote physical locations to prevent loosing the original and back up data through fire, etc.

In today's world, virus protection is a necessity for any PC or Macintosh and viruses are starting to appear on UNIX systems also. No system is completely safe from viruses since manufacturers have inadvertently shipped new computers with viruses on the hard drive and minted CDs with viruses.

For very important data, RAID systems are used. RAID stands for "Redundant Array of Inexpensive Disks". A RAID system is a computer with eight or more hard drives and software for storing data on those drives. Every byte of data is spread across all of these drives along with a parity bit that tells if it was an odd or even byte. In the event that a disk fails, it's contents can be completely reconstructed from the data on the other seven disks. This is a good way to store critical data which could not be reproduced, but the expense may not be justified otherwise.

**Data Security**

The primary threat to data security is illegal computer hackers. Studies show that the largest percentage of hackers are young men motivated by status with other hackers, malicious intent or the excitement of a challenging game. There have also been even more harmful cases of corporate spying and embezzlement of funds. Accounts on both multiuser machines and micro computers can be protected by passwords. Passwords can be very effective or not effective at all. Insecure password include ones that are easily guessed, never changed, shared or written down somewhere. Some systems, particularly UNIX, have password files which are encrypted but readable by all users. Hackers have developed automated programmes, such as "crack", to break the passwords in these files by raw brute force, trial & error techniques. Since it could take months to crack well chosen passwords, some systems use a password aging system that requires all users to set new passwords periodically. There are also programmes to prevent users from setting easily guessed passwords such as words in the dictionary, common names or permutations on the account name.

Systems holding data belonging to multiple users, such as UNIX or Windows NT, set an owner for each file and permissions defining who is allowed to read or write to it. Many hacker attacks are centered around finding flaws in the file permission system. There are ways to set default permissions and ways to control how much individual users can control their own file permissions.

Since most security attacks are now initiated from a remote location via the network, many organizations now separate their internal networks from the Internet with a firewall. A firewall is a piece of software running on a dedicated machine with two network boards. The software can filter which network traffic is allowed to pass between the internal and external networks. This is a very effective security measure, but there is an unfortunate tendency for organizations to make the firewall their only security measure making any breach of security across the firewall a breach for every machine in the whole organization. An even higher level of security can be achieved by not having any connection between the internal network and the internet or not even having an internal network.

Data encryption provides a second layer of security. Once someone gains access to data, that data is useless if it has been scrambled by an encryption programme which requires a second password to unscramble it. Passwords themselves should always be stored in an encrypted form.

Today's encryption systems are similar to military code systems but not as sophisticated as the systems used by the armed forces. Almost all encrypted data can be unencrypted without the password by the use of a very large amount of time on very powerful computers. Security is provided by making the encryption complex enough that no one would be likely to have enough computer power to break say a message about the merger next month in less than six months, at which time the message is no longer valuable.

There must always be someone able to fix a computer system by using a second password protected account called "system", "administrator", "root" or "superuser" which bypasses the file permission system. One of the most serious security attacks is one which gains the password to this account. As well as particularily stringent security for this account, the encryption systems, ensure that there is a second layer of protection against this type of attack. This also provides for a segmented internal security system, if such is necessary.

E-mail is particularly insecure. Mail messages are simple ascii files that travel across the network where no password is necessary to get to them. E-mail is easily forged and can be altered.

Of course, no one would have any particular reason for tampering with many personal messages, but people conducting sensitive business transactions over E-mail would be wise to use some sort of E-mail encryption system, such as PGP. These systems have several functions including encrypting the message itself, verifying who sent the message and verifying that it was not tampered with.

Audit trails are a means for the system administrators to find out if security has been breached and how much damage was done. Audit trails are records made by various pieces of software to log who logged into a system, from where and what files were accessed.

**How Hackers Get In**

*Here is the typical sequence of steps used to gain illegal entry into a computer system.*

- *Learn about the system.* Trying to connect to a system using networking utilities like telnet and ftp will be unsuccessful without a password, but even unsuccessful logins will often still display the machine manufacturer, and version of the operating system.
- *Look for openings.* Try known security flaws on that particular machine and operating system. Unless the system administrator is very diligent about installing security patches, many machines have openings in the security just waiting to be found.
- *Try sniffing to get a password.* Sniffing is when a machine has software to watch all of the network traffic and saves the messages corresponding to a valid user entering their password from a remote location.
- *Try spoofing.* Many machines share disks with other machines that are classified as "trusted hosts". In order to share the data on these disks the two machines must communicate without a password. Spoofing is when someone configures a third machine to use the network address of one of the trusted hosts to impersonate that machine. If the spoofing machine responds faster than the true trusted host, communications will be carried out with it unnoticed. Spoofing requires that the infiltrator have physical access to the network in a location that falls close to the target machine in the network topology, which usually means being physically close to the target machine.
- *Get into the system and cover tracks.* Once one of the above techniques is successful in gaining access to the system, the first order of business is to alter any records that would reveal the presence of an illegal entry to the system administrators.

- *Try to get superuser access.* Just as there are many ways to get into a user account, there are many ways to get into the root level account or get equivalent access to the machine.
- *Make back doors.* Once entry has been gained, that access can be used to intentionally install security breaches so that the hacker can still get back into the system if the original method of entry is cut off.
- *Use the system.* At this point, the hacker can steal data, destroy information, alter files, use CPU time, lock everyone else out of the system, etc.

**How to Combat Illegal Entry**

Here are a list of ways to make computers more secure and some minimal suggestions for when they should be used. For systems that are critical to operation, all of these and more may be warranted.

- *Physical security.* Keep doors locked if feasible. Install locks on accessible but attended machines. Install locks and alarms on machines left unattended.
- *Back up files.* This should be done on all computers.
- *Use a surge suppressor.* All computers.
- *Use an uninterruptable power supply.* Critical systems.
- *Periodic virus checking.* All PC and Macintosh computers. High volume or critical multiuser machines.
- *Continual memory resident virus checking.* PCs or Macs used by many people, such as in public labs. When data routinely comes from many sources.
- *Firewalls.* For organizations that can conduct business with limits on the internet services accessible from inside the organization. Where outside access to company data could do significant harm to the business.
- Having no internet connection or no internal network at all is done when data is particularly sensitive or reliability is of key importance. Bank record systems and air traffic control systems are some examples.
- Programmes to enforce the use of good passwords. Systems with a moderate to large number of users.
- *Password aging.* Systems which have a large number of users or are a likely target for illegal entry.
- *Remove old accounts.* Old, unused accounts are just that many more passwords for someone to find out. If it is not feasible to remove old accounts, the passwords can still be deleted. This is done by setting a null password for which no possible password will give acccess to the account.
- *Smart cards.* There are various varieties of smart cards to act as passwords electronically. One example is a card with a number that

changes every ten seconds and has its internal clock synchronized to one in the central computer. This way, even if someone get the password, it is only good for ten seconds. This expense is only warranted when someone would have a clear motive for trying to break into a system.

- *Install security patches to the operating system*. Invisible security patches should be installed anytime systems are being upgraded. On systems with many users or that are likely targets for illegal entry, the system administrator should install new patches frequently or perhaps instantly when available. Many break ins occur within 24 hours of when a security flaw and patch is announced. This occurs when someone has targeted a particular machine and hopes to figure out how to take advantage of the flaw before the system administrators upgrade the system. For this reason, many flaws are not announced until a patch or temporary work around can be announced with them. Networking patches and network software uprgrades are particularily important.
- *Security checking software*. There are programmes, like Satan, which will test a system for many known security flaws. These programmes were created so that administrators can test the integrity of the system, but they are also a favourite tool for the first step in infiltrating a system. It is a good idea to do this periodically. The software can be set to check many machines on a network without interrupting the people using those machines. There are programmes to check the system from the inside as well as checking network vulnerabilities.
- *Break in detection software*. There are also pieces of software to alert the system administrators when security is being tested by a known technique. This is a good way to know of an attack before they have gained entry.
- Some level of audit trail should be kept on any multiuser system and any system with sensitive data. Some level of auditing is built into many multiuser operating systems. An audit trail has to be maintained before a break in occurs in order to do any good.
- Use software to prevent sniffing, such as Kerberos or secure shell. These software packages allow remote logins to be authenticated, without sending an unencrypted password over the network. We have seen an increase in sites using these systems, particularily where many users login to machines remotely. The difficulty is setting up a system which is secure and reliable as well as not inconveniencing the users.
- *Encryption of disk files*. Disk files should be kept encrypted when the data is particularly important. Passwords, social security numbers

and credit card numbers should always be encrypted. Many accounting systems use encryption.

- Do not use your credit card over the web unless your browser (not their web page) identifies it as a secure server. Even at that it is advisable only to do so with reputable companies that you are familiar with. You should never need a credit card number to get something that is free.
- Encrypted E-mail software should be used when someone would have a reason to want to see, forge or alter E-mail messages.
- *Random manual monitoring*. For a few businesses that deal with very sensitive information and must use networks, the security administrators will occasionally manually look at the information being passed over the network, particularly through the firewall. This probably is not warranted unless security is important enough to be paying someone solely as a security manager.
- *Hiring tiger teams*. A tiger team is a group of honest expert hackers that are hired to break into your system in order to give you an analysis of your security. This is generally done by banks or others with extremely sensitive data.

## DATA SECURITY TECHNOLOGIES

### Disk Encryption

Disk encryption refers to encryption technology that encrypts data on a hard disk drive. Disk encryption typically takes form in either software or hardware. Disk encryption is often referred to as on-the-fly encryption ("OTFE") or transparent encryption.

### Hardware based Mechanisms for Protecting Data

Software based security solutions encrypt the data to prevent data from being stolen. However, a malicious programme or a hacker may corrupt the data in order to make it unrecoverable or unusable. Similarly, encrypted operating systems can be corrupted by a malicious programme or a hacker, making the system unusable. Hardware-based security solutions can prevent read and write access to data and hence offers very strong protection against tampering and unauthorized access.

Hardware based or assisted computer security offers an alternative to software-only computer security. Security tokens such as those using PKCS#11 may be more secure due to the physical access required in order to be compromised. Access is enabled only when the token is connected and correct PIN is entered.

However, dongles can be used by anyone who can gain physical access to it. Newer technologies in hardware based security solves this problem offering fool proof security for data. *Working of Hardware based security*: A hardware device allows a user to login, logout and to set different privilege levels by doing manual actions. The device uses biometric technology to prevent malicious users from logging in, logging out, and changing privilege levels. The current state of a user of the device is read by controllers in peripheral devices such as harddisks.

Illegal access by a malicious user or a malicious programme is interrupted based on the current state of a user by harddisk and DVD controllers making illegal access to data impossible. Hardware based access control is more secure than protection provided by the operating systems as operating systems are vulnerable to malicious attacks by viruses and hackers. The data on hard disks can be corrupted after a malicious access is obtained. With hardware based protection, software cannot manipulate the user privilege levels, it is impossible for a hacker or a malicious programme to gain access to secure data protected by hardware or perform unauthorized privileged operations.

The hardware protects the operating system image and file system privileges from being tampered. Therefore, a completely secure system can be created using a combination of hardware based security and secure system administration policies.

### Backups

Backups are used to ensure data which is lost can be recovered.

### Data Masking

Data Masking of structured data is the process of obscuring (masking) specific data within a database table or cell to ensure that data security is maintained and sensitive information is not exposed to unauthorized personnel. This may include masking the data from users (for example so banking customer representatives can only see the last 4 digits of a customers national identity number), developers (who need real production data to test new software releases but should not be able to see sensitive financial data), outsourcing vendors, etc.

### Data Erasure

Data erasure is a method of software-based overwriting that completely destroys all electronic data residing on a hard drive or other digital media to ensure that no sensitive data is leaked when an asset is retired or reused.

## DATA SECURITY: HOW TO SECURE A SMALL BUSINESS COMPUTER

Securing the small business computer systems is no trivial task, as there is a wide variety of threats to defend against. The majority of the threats we hear about are the flashy ones, such as a denial-of-service attack (DoS attack) against Amazon or eBay or a disastrous new virus wreaking havoc. Ironically, the most devastating issues we actually face aren't flashy at all. Most don't even originate from an external source; they come from within.

Have you ever had employees use USB flash drives to transfer files from their home computer to their office PC only to infect a company PC, or worse yet, your entire network? Or maybe an employee installed a favourite application on the office machine without admin approval. Renegade software installations can create system instabilities or introduce security vulnerabilities to the network. Plus, any application installed on a company PC needs to be legally licensed to the company.

An even greater danger is someone removing company data without authorization. Let's say an employee at a law firm copied a client's case files onto a USB flash drive to work on them at home. Should that flash drive be lost, all of the client's private information could be made public, and the company would be held liable. In addition to USB flash drives, workstation CD/DVD burners can also be potentially problematic. Data can be burned to disc just as easily as it can be copied to a flash drive. Employees can even use these drives to create duplicates of company-owned software.

You can minimize these risks by simply preventing employees from accessing the CD/DVD-ROM drive or from using USB flash drives on their workstations. Larger companies with dedicated IT departments typically use Windows Group Policy Editor to disable these devices. Group Policies are a great approach when you're dealing with hundreds of PCs, but for small business owners with only a handful of systems to manage and limited technical expertise, a more straightforward approach is available.

## WELCOME TO WINDOWS REGISTRY

By making a simple modification to the Windows Registry, you can easily prevent people from accessing the computer's CD/DVD-ROM drive, or connecting a USB flash drive. Even if the employees have administrator rights to their local PCs, they won't be able to re-enable these devices using Window's Device Manager. They can only be re-enabled via Windows Registry. Best of all, disabling the USB Flash drive in this fashion will not prevent other USB devices like USB keyboards and mice from working. This modification should work with most versions of Windows and will affect any person who logs into this system.

To modify the Registry we need to launch the *Registry Editor*. To do this just click on the Start button, type REGEDIT and press Enter. You should now be looking at the Registry, which is laid out like Windows Explorer with a left and right pane view. The left pane shows you Hives, similar to folders, while the right side shows you Keys and their Values, similar to files. To make any modifications to the Registry you'll need to have administrative rights to the local PC. Windows Registry is basically a centralized database that stores and manages all of the configuration settings for all the hardware, software, users and preferences for the PC. Think of it as the DNA of Windows. The Registry is very important to the proper functioning of Windows, and modifications to it could result in Windows becoming unstable or unusable. Therefore, we'll create a Registry backup before we continue, just to be safe.

Click on the Computer at the top of the left pane. Now on the Menu bar, click FileExport... and select a location to save the Registry to. Give it a name and press Save. The Registry will now be exported, and we're ready to proceed. Should you need to restore the Registry, simply select FileImport..., and navigate to the file you exported. Select it and press Open to begin the Registry restoration.

## SECURITY AND DATA INTEGRITY THREATS

*The range of means by which the security and integrity of computing resources can be threatened is very broad, and encompasses:*

- Operator error (for example a user inadvertently deleting the wrong file).
- Hardware or media failure (either as a result of wear-and-tear, old age or accidental damage).
- Theft or sabotage (of hardware and/or data or its media).
- Hackers (who obtain unauthorised online access via the Internet).
- Malware (any form of virus, and including "Trojan" e-mail attachments that users are encouraged to open).
- Power surges and/or outages (which are one of the most common means of hard disk corruption and hardware damage).
- Flood, fire, storm or other natural disasters.
- Fraud or embezzlement.
- Industrial espionage.
- Terrorism.

### Physical Security Measures

Given the breadth of the human reliance on computer technology, physical security arrangements to try and ensure that hardware and storage media are not compromised by theft or unauthorised access are more important today than ever before. And yet surprisingly they still often not taken seriously enough. Indeed, the number of high-profile instances of CDs, DVDs, hard disks and laptops going missing from government offices in the United Kingdom over the past year is quite staggering. Not least due to advances in mobile and cloud computing, computing resources are more vulnerable to theft than ever before. Twenty or more years ago, most computer equipment and data lived in a secure IT "glass house" well out of the reach of the casual thief, and with the hardware involved of little or no street value anyway. However, this is obviously no longer the case.

Personal and business data is now stored across a wide range of organisational, cloud vendor and personal locations, more work is conducted at home than since the rise of the modern city, and IT departments therefore have a right to be nervous. At the very least, physical computing security measures—such as external building safeguards and the control of access to areas of a building where computers are located—should be subject to regular formal updating and review.

Most large organizations—particularly in the public sector—have a horror story or several to tell of computer equipment that has "walked". Many such stories suggest that people who walk out of buildings with computer equipment under their arm are rarely challenged (and sometimes even assisted!). Locking-down computer equipment and/or ensuring adequate door and window security at all computer locations should today just be pure common sense.

Physical security also needs to be particularly carefully considered in semi-public locations (such as many open plan offices). For example, it needs to be considered how easy it would be for somebody to gain access to a PC, insert a USB memory stick, and walk away with valuable or sensitive data. Large corporate data centres in which the computer equipment is located in an air conditioned room typically have fire control systems that will hermetically seal the location and put out a fire using an inert gas.

In smaller companies and domestically this clearly is not an option. However, whilst computers themselves may be at risk from fire (and indeed the cause of a fire!), back-up media can be protected in a fire safe, and/or via off-site storage. The physical security ofstorage media against the threats of fire, flood and other forms of damage.

Alongside theft, fire and flood, the other most significant threat that can damage computer equipment and/or the data held on it comes from power surges (voltage spikes) or power outages (brown-outs or black-outs). Many hard disk failures in particular are thought to be linked to power surge or outage issues of which users are often unaware. To protect against this very real but often ignored threat to computer equipment and data, a power surge protector and/or uninteruptable power supply (UPS) unit can be employed. Surge protectors are relatively cheap and protect against voltage spikes. They are today often built into multi-socket outlets with an insurance guarantee included for the connected equipment.

For even greater protection, a UPS unit includes a rechargeable battery that will continue to power a computer and key peripherals during a mains power brown-out or black-out. Software is usually also used to permit a controlled shut-down of equipment when a power black-out occurs. UPS units are more expensive than surge protectors, somewhat bulky, and often very heavy. However, for a server or key personal computer (such as one used to run a business or key part thereof) they are also a very good investment.

## Minimising the Impact of Error, Failure or Loss

Whilst physical threats need to be protected against, most data is lost or corrupted following user error or hardware failure. The best defence against this is an appropriate back-up strategy, triggered on both a time and event basis and with appropriate physical resilience. In other words, users need to ensure that they take regular backs-ups at regular intervals and before and after making key data changes. They also need to store multiple back-ups on different media in different locations. There is no such thing as a permanent store of any form of computer data.

Nor is any storage location entirely safe (although the cloud data centres run by Google, Amazon, IBM, Microsoft and other computing industry giants are pretty well protected these days!). Whilst any back-up strategy does require the selection of appropriate storage media, user education is often an equally key a consideration. Taking regular back-ups is at best only half of the story. Far too many individuals and businesses keep their back-up media—be they removable hard drives, optical disks and even USB memory sticks, in an entirely insecure manner in the same physical location as their computer. Even in corporate IT departments this has been known. Such practice has to significantly reduce the value of back-ups.

When making their disaster recovery plans and addressing the key computer security questions, the location of back-up media needs careful consideration. Even on a domestic level, most households could keep a few writable CD or DVD disks (or even SD cards) of key back-ups (including photographs and their music collection) in a secure location (in the roof or under a floorboard or with family and friends or wherever), and which would provide significantly increased data storage resilience. However, unfortunately most people still only ever think of this kind of simple strategy after it is too late.

## Passwords and Appropriate User Authentication

Physically protecting computer equipment and data against damage or loss is a large element of computer security. However, another large element is limiting access to all or part of a system or data store to authorised users only.

*In the broadest of terms, user authorisation within any security system can be verified via one three means:*

- Something known by the individual (a piece of information such as a password)
- Something possessed by the individual (a physical token such a credit, security or ID card), or
- A biometric characteristic of the individual (for example their signature, finger print, retinal scan or DNA).

For good security, two of the above measures should be employed for what is known as "two-factor security". For example, to obtain money from a bank cash machine both a card and a PIN (personal identification number password) are required. Where computer security is concerned, one measure of user verification will almost always be a password given the relative technical ease with which this can be implemented.

Computer keyboards, mobile computers and dedicated input devices that include finger print readers are also becoming more common, and can be combined with passwording to achieve two-factor security. ID cards and even retinal scans are also used in conjunction with passwords on high-end security systems. However, any system that requires a token or biometric to be read has proved difficult to rollout en-mass. This said, recently some banks have started to provide each customer with a reader device into which their bank card is inserted. This allows for two-factor security, as the unit displays a number for each transaction that is uniquely in sequence with their bank.

Today at least, and probably in practice for many years to come, one-factor security based on passwords is all that is available for identifying authorised users in the majority of computing situations. This in turn means that users must be educated to use strong passwording—or in other words, to choose and use passwords in a manner that makes the password difficult to either fathom or otherwise obtain by an unauthorised party.

*To be classed as "strong", passwords,*

- Should be at least six and preferably eight or more characters in length.
- Should be mixed case alphanumeric (a mix of apparently random upper and lower case letters and numbers is best).
- Should be changed regularly (at least every three months is a common rule).
- Should be known only to the user.
- Should not be obviously related to the user.
- Should be different for each application used.
- Should not be based on data (such as a favourite place) listed publically on Facebook or another social networking site, and
- Should not be written down (let alone stuck on a post-it note on the side of a computer!)

Users should also try and ensure password security by following the measures as outlined below under "Internet Security".

**Maintaining Confidentiality**

In part the confidentiality of data is protected via physical security measures and appropriate user authentication precautions as already outlined above. However, effective security should plan for what happens if these measures fail, and how data confidentiality can be protected even if computer equipment or media fall into the wrong hands. This is particularly important when it comes to the protection of sensitive information such as financial data. The confidentiality of the data on stolen hardware or of data accessed by unauthorised users can be protected via encryption. For example, software such as the open-source TrueCrypt (available from www.truecrypt.org) can be used to encrypt the data on any storage device (for example a USB key carried in your pocket). Office documents can also or alternatively be protected by securing them with a password. This can be a particularly sensible thing to do when e-mailing sensitive documents, or posting them by snail mail on removable media. In an office package such as the freely downloadable OpenOffice, password protecting a file is as simple as ticking the "save with password" option when selecting "Save As".

Data confidentiality also needs to be protected on output and disposal. In the case of the former, in an open plan office environment precautions should be taken when sending documents containing confidential information to a communal network printer. In the case of the latter, printed output containing sensitive data needs to be disposed of securely (eg via shredding and/or incineration), as do waste media (such as discarded optical disks). At the end of a computer's life or when components are being upgraded, care also needs to be taken to ensure that discarded hard disk drives (including those located in external hard drive units) are appropriately erased before disposal.

**Internet Security**

The connection of most computers in the world to the Internet, coupled with the growth of cloud computing, has inevitably broadened significantly the scope of computer security and control vulnerabilities. Before the widespread adoption of personal computers, rogue programmers with malicious or criminal intent would try to "hack" into big computing facilities via the phone network. Then, once personal computing really took told, the focus for many such malicious programmers shifted to writing computer viruses that could be unknowingly distributed on floppy disks, and which could hence disrupt the operation of those millions of computers not connected to the telephone network.

Today, this situation has evolved again, with many personal computers having an "always on" broadband connection which makes them potentially prone to unauthorised access via a computer network. And on top of this, the virus writers are still at work, the fruits of their corruptive programming labours now distributed both online and via physical storage media. Whilst there are very real security risks associated with both the consumer and business use of the Internet, it is also the case than many such security concerns are perceptual. To an extent, all that has really changed over the past few years has been the willingness of people and organizations to conduct their affairs over the world-wide web.

The sensible use of a credit card over the web is not that much more secure that it was five years ago. The fact that it has become the norm is therefore due to the fact that the risk/benefit ratio of doing e-business has shifted significantly in favour of the "benefit" side in the eyes of the value-seeking majority. Care, of course, does need to be taken. For a start these days it is foolish in the absolute extreme to run any computer with an Internet connection without antivirus software.

Such software—such as the range of Norton security software available from www.symantec.com—is most usually commercially purchased with a yearly subscription for regular updates to its virus definition database. However, it is possible to obtain antivirus software for free. Indeed, my own current recommendation for PC owners is to install Microsoft Security Essentials. For most people this is a very good option, does not hog resources, comes from a reputable organization—and is free!

In addition (though often bundled with) antivirus software, all computers with a potentially always-on Internet connection should be protected via a firewall. Whilst antivirus software is intended to detect and prevent infestation with malicious software (including viruses and other "malware"), the job of a firewall is to regulate the network communications a computer receives, permitting or denying such communications based on how trusted the communications source is considered to be.

Firewalls can be implemented via either hardware or software. A personal computer firewall will almost certainly be software based, although increasingly some form of hardware firewall is being incorporated into wireless ADSL routers (wireless access points). Like antivirus software, a firewall needs to be regularly updated with the latest threat information to be most effective. Windows XP, Vista and Windows 7 all include a software firewall, although many people choose to adopt third party firewall software as an alternative to this.

In addition to antivirus software and a firewall, user vigilance and even plain common sense provide one of the most effective defences against potential Internet-related security vulnerabilities. For example, users should be educated never to open unsolicited (spam) emails, and doubly-so never to open any e-mail attachments included with such e-mails (and as may be automatically opened by some configurations of e-mail software). Viruses and other malware (such as "sniffer" software intended to record and communicate usernames and passwords) can be attached as "Trojan" (horses) to e-mails. However, it is only when the user opens such messages and executes their attachments that corruption or security risks can occur.

Users also need to ensure that they use strong passwording when setting up accounts for web transactions. They should also never permit their browser software to remember their login details for a website unless they are absolutely certain of who else may have access to the computer they are using. Indeed, it is still potentially unwise to let even a single-user PC remember passwords for activities such as online shopping or online banking. This is because the theft of the PC would permit direct access to the user's bank and other online accounts. Talking of online transactions, users should also be careful only to conduct business online with trusted websites and over secure (encrypted) connections.

Trusted websites are those that are well known, have an established trading history, and which advertise contact points for both online and off-line customer support. Secure connections can be identified by looking for the letters "HTTPS" (a secure version of the hypertext transfer protocol that facilitates web communications) at the start of the web address seen at the top of a web browser window. HTTPS connections exchange digital certificates to encrypt communications via what is known as a "secure socket layer" (SSL). As a basic rule, never enter your credit card details into a web page without first checking that the address of the page starts "HTTPS".

For users of cloud computing services such as SaaS applications, all of the above points relating to good Internet security clearly apply. Computing in the cloud is still deemed by many to be risky. However, it can also bring security advantages as user data is protected off-site in large vendor data centres. For example users of Google Docs are always safe in the knowledge that their files are always securely stored on two different servers in two different data centres. For private individauls and small companies, such a high level of off-site data protection and replication is hard to achieve by other means.

In addition to using antivirus software, a firewall, strong passwords, and uploading regular operating system and browser updates, it is doubly important for users of the cloud to ensure the security of the computer they use to access their chosen online services. In particular care needs to be taken to make certain that they never leave active accounts on a device that may be stolen or otherwise accessed by inappropriate users. For example, files held in Google Docs or indeed another other SaaS application are not at all secure if a user leaves their netbook or smartphone in a public place and all anybody has to do to gain access is to boot up the machine and visit the appropriate web address. SaaS users who share desktop PCs—or who for example use public desktop computers in cyber cafes—ought also to be very careful indeed to ensure that they log-out from cloud services whenever they finish using them.

**Disaster Recovery Planning**

Both individuals and in particular businesses should have plans in place to cover the eventuality of hardware failure or loss and/or data loss or corruption. Such disaster recovery or "business continuity" plans need to address how data would be recovered, what hardware would be used to run critical applications, and by whom. Such plans particularly need to take into account any current use of out-of-date software applications that may not be able to be replaced and/or run on replacement hardware and operating systems. To recover back-ups of data that cannot be run on any available hardware and software will not in any way ensure business continuity!

Depending on the types of threat they are intended to cover, disaster recover plans may rely on one of a mix of strategies (and a mix is arguably often best). One option is on-site standby, where duplicate systems exist that can be used to run critical operations (provided that data is still available or can be recovered). Such duplicate systems need not necessarily be standing idle waiting for disaster (as they would be in a nuclear power station), but may be everyday systems used in one part of the business that are prepared to run key applications from other parts of a business if the need arises. As an alternative to on-site standby, some sort of off-site standby is very common. If a company has multiple buildings or premises, then it makes sense both to hold off-site back-ups across these locations, and to ensure that key system functionality can be duplicated across sites.

Some businesses also have "reciprocal agreements" with other companies to make use of their computers to run key operations in the event of a disaster (such as a fire that destroys their premises). Often small and medium-sized companies make such reciprocal agreements with nearby schools who have suitable computer suites which they are prepared to offer as an off-site standby provision for a reasonable cost. For larger organizations, or those highly dependent on computing continuity, "hot-site agreements" can be made with firms that offer commercial disaster recovery as a service, and who can deliver (for a price) portable working computer rooms at very short notice.

As a final element of disaster recovery planning, replacement purchase plans should be in place. In the event of fire or theft, the last thing most individual users or companies would want to be thinking about is where to purchase new computer equipment from, and what specification to choose. Not least this is an issue because direct-specification let alone exact-model replacements for any items of computer hardware or software more than a year old are incredibly unlikely to be available.

## Data Protection Legislation

We live in a world where data is held on everybody and used and inter-linked for a very wide range of purposes. In an attempt to provide some redress against inappropriate data use, in the United Kingdom the Data Protection Act (DPA) 1998 protects data held on living individuals. Any individual can submit a subject action request to any party that holds data on them. This allows them to obtain a copy of all data held on them within 40 days of the subject action request being received. Following a subject action request, individuals can challenge the validity of the data held on them, and if appropriate can claim compensation relating to any inaccuracy or misuse.

The Data Protection Commissioner is charged with ensuring that all data in the UK "shall be obtained and subsequently processed in a fair and lawful manner". All organizations have to have a "data controller" who, with a few limited exceptions, must register all data stored with the Data Protection Commissioner. They must also be open about the data's purpose, and ensure its accuracy and security. Whilst the Data Protection Act protects individuals on whom data it held, it does not protect data itself or computer systems. Such protection is provided in the United Kingdom by the Computer Misuse Act (CMA) 1990. This created three levels of offence, and which make it illegal to gain unauthorised access to computer material; to gain unauthorised access with intent to commit or facilitate further offences; and to make an authorised modification of computer material. The last of these offences in theory at least makes it illegal to write and distribute computer viruses.

## HOW TO SECURE A COMPUTER

The confidentiality, availability and the integrity of the data is the most important aspect of the computer security. Computer security refers to securing your computer from the unauthorized access and from internal and external threats like virus, spyware, Trojan horses, phishing attacks, hackers and intruders. There are a large number of techniques that can be used to protect your computer from all these threats. In this chapter you will learn that how to secure your computer from the most common security threats. Security can be implemented from the operating system to computer hardware level. Following is an overview of some of the common PC threats and the solutions from preventing them.

### Computer Viruses

Computer viruses are the one of the most common threats to a computer. Any online computer can be attacked by the viruses and other online threats in less than 20 minutes if it has not been using a proper security mechanism. A virus infected computer can transmitted the viruses to the other connected computers in a network. Viruses can harm your computer in a variety of ways such as they can corrupt data, corrupt the hard disk, delete the operating system files and can crash the system. Install an up-to-dated antivirus software and regularly scan your computer to get rid of the potentially dangerous computer viruses.

### Spyware

Spyware is another big threat for the online computers. Spyware enter in your computer through the numbers of ways such as when you visit a spyware infected website, install spyware infected software and access online spyware infected online application. To get rid of the spyware, install an up-to-date anti spyware software and regularly scan your computer with it.

### Phishing

Phishing attack is another growing threat for the online computers. Phishing is a type of online deception techniques that is designed to steal your confidential information, passwords, credit card information and important login and password through the fraudulent emails. The best solution to avoid this treat is to not open the E-mail attachments from the unknown and unreliable sources. Secondly, never give your personal information to anyone even the emails claim to be delivered from big sources. Companies like LifeLock.com offer protection for your identity and personal information if your computer is attacked.

**Firewall and System Probing**

If you haven't implemented a firewall system on your computer then chances are that your computer can be accessed by the unauthorized users and hackers. The best solution to avoid this problem and keep your privacy intact is to install and configure a software or hardware firewall into your system.

**Physical Threats**

The physical threats to a computer involves the physically damage to the computer components with the fire, water and destructions. The best solution to avoid the physical threats to your important computer system and data is to set an off-site replication. Replicate your data regularly at some remote location.

**Employee's Sabotage**

An organization's employees are most familiar with the computers inside an organization. There are a lot of examples where the annoyed employees of a company are involved in sabotaging the computer system. Employee's sabotage include entering data incorrectly, destroying system hardware, deleting data, changing data, changing the passwords and entering the data incorrectly. The best way to avoid the situations like these is to delete the employees' account after they leaves the company so that they can't no more access company's systems. Secondly, regularly monitor the activities of the employees and restrict their access to the sensitive resources in the overall IT infrastructure.

**Vendor's Default Password Attack**

Vendors of the computer systems have the default passwords at many different hardware and software components like the router, system BIOS and others. It is very important to change the default password of the computer devices and applications.

**Human Error**

Errors and the omissions are the great threats to the integrity of the data and the computer system. Data entry operators, programmers, system administrators often make errors that can compromise the system's security. The effect of the various security threats caused by the human errors varies. Employee's training and awareness training should be given to the employees to avoid such kinds of errors that can lead to the financial losses for a company.

## OPTIONS FOR SECURING CONFIDENTIAL ELECTRONIC DATA

Confidential data, including personal information, must be secured against theft, loss, and inadvertent sharing. This page is designed to provide you with information about how to secure confidential electronic data.

*The options are especially important if you are using:*

- A computer to access confidential data, including personal information.
- Mobile devices such as laptops, USB keys, smartphones, tablet devices, portable hard drives, flash drives, etc.
- Any computing device that is used by other people.

## CURRENTLY AVAILABLE OPTIONS

Consider the sensitivity of the information you are using, where you are accessing, using or sending it, and choose the appropriate option. Portable devices are a great convenience but also increase the risk that confidential information will be lost, stolen, or inadvertently shared.

- One way to limit security risks for confidential electronic data is not to store it on your own devices. Computing and Communications Services (CCS) and some departments provide servers that are designed to provide secure locations to save confidential data. This has security advantages over saving confidential data directly on your computer, particularly in the event your computer is lost or stolen. CCS provides personal and shared-access folders on file servers free of charge for faculty and staff. Click here to request access to the Central File and Print Services (CFAPS). Some other academic and administrative departments offer similar services.
- If you need to access data stored on the server from a remote location, you can do so securely using RU-VPN- a virtual private network system that encrypts data in transit between Ryerson's servers and your computer. Clickhere to request access to RU-VPN
- For very sensitive data, you can set up encrypted folders containing private or confidential data on devices like laptops or shared workstations. The folders can be stored on the server (recommended) or on your hard-drive. Current operating systems such as the most recent releases of Windows and Mac OS support folder-level encryption.
- If you must use portable devices like USB keys and Flash drives, purchase devices that support password protection and encryption. For example Ryerson's bookstore sells the Kingston Data Traveler Vault - Privacy.

### Password Protection of Workstations, Laptops, Phones, and Tablets

All computers, including mobile devices, should be password protected. Information on choosing a strong password is available here. Whenever screen savers are used, they should be configured so that a password is required to exit screen saver mode.

### Permission to Take Data Off Campus

In some cases Ryerson departments may have policies in place that restrict the transport of data off campus. If you are unsure, check with your Chair, Director or Manager first.

### New Security Tools

CCS has purchased the Sophos Endpoint Security and Data Protection system. The system provides malware and virus protection. It also includes the ability to encrypt data and recover lost encryption keys. The new system with encryption enabled will be available at the end of October 2011.

# 11

# The Protection of Information in Computer Systems

## BASIC PRINCIPLES OF INFORMATION PROTECTION

### CONSIDERATIONS SURROUNDING THE STUDY OF PROTECTION

*General Observations:* As computers become better understood and more economical, every day brings new applications. Many of these new applications involve both storing information and simultaneous use by several individuals. The key concern in this paper is multiple use. For those applications in which all users should not have identical authority, some scheme is needed to ensure that the computer system implements the desired authority structure.

For example, in an airline seat reservation system, a reservation agent might have authority to make reservations and to cancel reservations for people whose names he can supply. A flight boarding agent might have the additional authority to print out the list of all passengers who hold reservations on the flights for which he is responsible. The airline might wish to withhold from the reservation agent the authority to print out a list of reservations, so as to be sure that a request for a passenger list from a law enforcement agency is reviewed by the correct level of management.

The airline example is one of protection of corporate information for corporate self-protection (or public interest, depending on one's view). A different kind of example is an online warehouse inventory management system that generates reports about the current status of the inventory. These reports not only represent corporate information that must be protected from release outside the company, but also may indicate the quality of the job being done by the warehouse manager.

In order to preserve his personal privacy, it may be appropriate to restrict the access to such reports, even within the company, to those who have a legitimate reason to be judging the quality of the warehouse manager's work.

Many other examples of systems requiring protection of information are encountered every day: credit bureau data banks; law enforcement information systems; time-sharing service bureaus; on-line medical information systems; and government social service data processing systems. These examples span a wide range of needs for organizational and personal privacy. All have in common controlled sharing of information among multiple users.

All, therefore, require some plan to ensure that the computer system helps implement the correct authority structure. Of course, in some applications no special provisions in the computer system are necessary. It may be, for instance, that an externally administered code of ethics or a lack of knowledge about computers adequately protects the stored information. Although there are situations in which the computer need provide no aids to ensure protection of information, often it is appropriate to have the computer enforce a desired authority structure.

The words "privacy," "security," and "protection" are frequently used in connection with information-storing systems. Not all authors use these terms in the same way. This chapter uses definitions commonly encountered in computer science literature.

*The term "privacy" denotes a socially defined ability of an individual (or organization) to determine whether, when, and to whom personal (or organizational) information is to be released.*

This chapter will not be explicitly concerned with privacy, but instead with the mechanisms used to help achieve it.

*The term "security" describes techniques that control who may use or modify the computer or the information contained in it.*

Security specialists have found it useful to place potential security violations in three categories.

- Unauthorized information release: an unauthorized person is able to read and take advantage of information stored in the computer. This category of concern sometimes extends to "traffic analysis," in which the intruder observes only the patterns of information use and from those patterns can infer some information content. It also includes unauthorized use of a proprietary programme.
- Unauthorized information modification: an unauthorized person is able to make changes in stored information—a form of sabotage. Note that this kind of violation does not require that the intruder see the information he has changed.
- Unauthorized denial of use: an intruder can prevent an authorized user from referring to or modifying information, even though the intruder may not be able to refer to or modify the information. Causing a system "crash," disrupting a scheduling algorithm, or firing a bullet into a computer are examples of denial of use. This is another form of sabotage.

The term "unauthorized" in the three categories listed above means that release, modification, or denial of use occurs contrary to the desire of the person who controls the information, possibly even contrary to the constraints supposedly enforced by the system. The biggest complication in a general-purpose remote-accessed computer system is that the "intruder" in these definitions may be an otherwise legitimate user of the computer system.

*Examples of security techniques sometimes applied to computer systems are the following:*

1. Labelling files with lists of authorized users,
2. Verifying the identity of a prospective user by demanding a password,
3. Shielding the computer to prevent interception and subsequent interpretation of electromagnetic radiation,
4. Enciphering information sent over telephone lines,
5. Locking the room containing the computer,
6. Controlling who is allowed to make changes to the computer system (both its hardware and software),
7. Using redundant circuits or programmed cross-checks that maintain security in the face of hardware or software failures,
8. Certifying that the hardware and software are actually implemented as intended.

It is apparent that a wide range of considerations are pertinent to the engineering of security of information. Historically, the literature of computer systems has more narrowly defined the term *protection* to be just those security techniques that control the access of executing programmes to stored information.

An example of a protection technique is labelling of computer-stored files with lists of authorized users. Similarly, the term *authentication* is used for those security techniques that verify the identity of a person (or other external agent) making a request of a computer system. An example of an authentication technique is demanding a password. This chapter concentrates on protection and authentication mechanisms, with only occasional reference to the other equally necessary security mechanisms.

One should recognize that concentration on protection and authentication mechanisms provides a narrow view of information security, and that a narrow view is dangerous. The objective of a secure system is to prevent all unauthorized use of information, a negative kind of requirement. It is hard to prove that this negative requirement has been achieved, for one must demonstrate that every possible threat has been anticipated. Thus an expansive view of the problem is most appropriate to help ensure that no gaps appear in the strategy. In contrast, a narrow concentration on protection mechanisms, especially those logically impossible to defeat, may lead to false confidence in the system as a whole.

## Functional Levels of Information Protection

Many different designs have been proposed and mechanisms implemented for protecting information in computer systems. One reason for differences among protection schemes is their different functional properties—the kinds of access control that can be expressed naturally and enforced. It is convenient to divide protection schemes according to their functional properties. A rough categorization is the following.

### *Unprotected Systems*

Some systems have no provision for preventing a determined user from having access to every piece of information stored in the system. Although these systems are not directly of interest here, they are worth mentioning since, as of 1975, many of the most widely used, commercially available batch data processing systems fall into this category—for example, the Disk Operating System for the IBM System 370.

Our definition of protection, which excludes features usable only for mistake prevention, is important here since it is common for unprotected systems to contain a variety of mistake-prevention features. These may provide just enough control that any breach of control is likely to be the result of a deliberate act rather than an accident. Nevertheless, it would be a mistake to claim that such systems provide any security.

### *All-or-nothing Systems*

These are systems that provide isolation of users, sometimes moderated by total sharing of some pieces of information. If only isolation is provided, the user of such a system might just as well be using his own private computer, as far as protection and sharing of information are concerned. More commonly, such systems also have public libraries to which every user may have access. In some cases the public library mechanism may be extended to accept user contributions, but still on the basis that all users have equal access.

Most of the first generation of commercial timesharing systems provide a protection scheme with this level of function. Examples include the Dartmouth Time-Sharing System (DTSS) and IBM's VM/370 system. There are innumerable others.

### *Controlled Sharing*

Significantly more complex machinery is required to control explicitly who may access each data item stored in the system. For example, such a system might provide each file with a list of authorized users and allow an owner to distinguish several common patterns of use, such as reading, writing, or executing the contents of the file as a programme. Although conceptually straightforward, actual implementation is surprisingly intricate, and only a few complete examples exist. These include M.I.T.'s Compatible Time-Sharing

System (CTSS), Digital Equipment Corporation's DECsystem/10, System Development Corporation's Advanced Development Prototype (ADEPT) System, and Bolt, Beranek, and Newman's TENEX

***User-programmed Sharing Controls***

A user may want to restrict access to a file in a way not provided in the standard facilities for controlling sharing. For example, he may wish to permit access only on weekdays between 9:00 A.M. and 4:00 P.M. Possibly, he may wish to permit access to only the average value of the data in a file. Maybe he wishes to require that a file be modified only if two users agree. For such cases, and a myriad of others, a general escape is to provide for user-defined *protected objects* and *subsystems.*

A *protected subsystem* is a collection of programmes and data with the property that only the programmes of the subsystem have direct access to the data (that is, the protected objects). Access to those programmes is limited to calling specified entry points. Thus the programmes of the subsystem completely control the operations performed on the data. By constructing a protected subsystem, a user can develop any programmable form of access control to the objects he creates. Only a few of the most advanced system designs have tried to permit user-specified protected subsystems.

These include Honeywell's Multics, the University of California's CAL system, Bell Laboratories' UNIX system, the Berkeley Computer Corporation BCC-500, and two systems currently under construction: the CAP system of Cambridge University, and the HYDRA system of Carnegie-Mellon University. Exploring alternative mechanisms for implementing protected subsystems is a current research topic. A specialized use of protected subsystems is the implementation of protection controls based on data content.

For example, in a file of salaries, one may wish to permit access to all salaries under $15 000. Another example is permitting access to certain statistical aggregations of data but not to any individual data item. This area of protection raises questions about the possibility of discerning information by statistical tests and by examining indexes, without ever having direct access to the data itself. Protection based on content is the subject of a variety of recent or current research projects and will not be explored in this tutorial.

***Putting Strings on Information***

The foregoing three levels have been concerned with establishing conditions for the release of information to an executing programme. The fourth level of capability is to maintain some control over the user of the information even *after* it has been released. Such control is desired, for example, in releasing income information to a tax advisor; constraints should prevent him from passing the information on to a firm which prepares mailing lists.

The printed labels on classified military information declaring a document to be "Top Secret" are another example of a constraint on information after its release to a person authorized to receive it. One may not (without risking severe penalties) release such information to others, and the label serves as a notice of the restriction. Computer systems that implement such strings on information are rare and the mechanisms are incomplete. For example, the ADEPT system keeps track of the classification level of all input data used to create a file; all output data are automatically labelled with the highest classification encountered during execution.

There is a consideration that cuts across all levels of functional capability: the *dynamics of use*. This term refers to how one establishes and changes the specification of who may access what. At any of the levels it is relatively easy to envision (and design) systems that statically express a particular protection intent. But the need to change access authorization dynamically and the need for such changes to be requested by executing programmes introduces much complexity into protection systems. For a given functional level, most existing protection systems differ primarily in the way they handle protection dynamics.

To gain some insight into the complexity introduced by programme-directed changes to access authorization, consider the question "Is there any way that O'Hara could access file X?" One should check to see not only if O'Hara has access to file X, but also whether or not O'Hara may change the specification of file X's accessibility. The next step is to see if O'Hara can change the specification of who may change the specification of file X's accessibility, etc. Another problem of dynamics arises when the owner revokes a user's access to a file while that file is being used. Letting the previously authorized user continue until he is "finished" with the information may not be acceptable, if the owner has suddenly realised that the file contains sensitive data. On the other hand, immediate withdrawal of authorization may severely disrupt the user. It should be apparent that provisions for the dynamics of use are at least as important as those for static specification of protection intent.

In many cases, it is not necessary to meet the protection needs of the person responsible for the information stored in the computer entirely through computer-aided enforcement. External mechanisms such as contracts, ignorance, or barbed wire fences may provide some of the required functional capability. However, is focused on the internal mechanisms.

**Design Principles**

Whatever the level of functionality provided, the usefulness of a set of protection mechanisms depends upon the ability of a system to prevent security violations. In practice, producing a system at any level of functionality (except level one) that actually does prevent all such unauthorized acts has proved to be extremely difficult. Sophisticated users of most systems are aware of at least one way to crash the system, denying other users authorized access to stored information. Penetration exercises involving a large number of different general-purpose systems all have shown that users can construct programmes that can obtain unauthorized access to information stored within.

Even in systems designed and implemented with security as an important objective, design and implementation flaws provide paths that circumvent the intended access constraints. Design and construction techniques that systematically exclude flaws are the topic of much research activity, but no complete method applicable to the construction of large general-purpose systems exists yet. This difficulty is related to the negative quality of the requirement to prevent *all* unauthorized actions.

In the absence of such methodical techniques, experience has provided some useful principles that can guide the design and contribute to an implementation without security flaws. Here are eight examples of design principles that apply particularly to protection mechanisms.

### *Economy of Mechanism*

Keep the design as simple and small as possible. This well-known principle applies to any aspect of a system, but it deserves emphasis for protection mechanisms for this reason: design and implementation errors that result in unwanted access paths will not be noticed during normal use (since normal use usually does not include attempts to exercise improper access paths). As a result, techniques such as line-by-line inspection of software and physical examination of hardware that implements protection mechanisms are necessary. For such techniques to be successful, a small and simple design is essential.

### *Fail-safe Defaults*

Base access decisions on permission rather than exclusion. This principle, suggested by E. Glaser in 1965, means that the default situation is lack of access, and the protection scheme identifies conditions under which access is permitted. The alternative, in which mechanisms attempt to identify conditions under which access should be refused, presents the wrong psychological base for secure system design. A conservative design must be based on arguments why objects should be accessible, rather than why they should not. In a large system some objects will be inadequately considered, so a default of lack of permission is safer. A design or implementation mistake in a mechanism that gives explicit permission tends to fail by refusing permission, a safe situation, since it will be quickly detected. On the other hand, a design or implementation mistake in a mechanism that explicitly excludes access tends to fail by allowing access, a failure which may go unnoticed in normal use. This principle applies both to the outward appearance of the protection mechanism and to its underlying implementation.

### *Complete Mediation*

Every access to every object must be checked for authority. This principle, when systematically applied, is the primary underpinning of the protection system. It forces a system-wide view of access control, which in addition to normal operation includes initialization, recovery, shutdown, and maintenance. It implies that a foolproof method of identifying the source of every request must be devised. It also requires that proposals to gain performance by remembering the result of an authority check be examined skeptically. If a change in authority occurs, such remembered results must be systematically updated.

### *Open Design*

The design should not be secret. The mechanisms should not depend on the ignorance of potential attackers, but rather on the possession of specific, more easily protected, keys or passwords. This decoupling of protection mechanisms from protection keys permits the mechanisms to be examined by many reviewers without concern that the review may itself compromise the safeguards. In addition, any skeptical user may be allowed to convince himself that the system he is about to use is adequate for his purpose. Finally, it is simply not realistic to attempt to maintain secrecy for any system which receives wide distribution.

### *Separation of Privilege*

Where feasible, a protection mechanism that requires two keys to unlock it is more robust and flexible than one that allows access to the presenter of only a single key. The relevance of this observation to computer systems was pointed out by R. Needham in 1973. The reason is that, once the mechanism is locked, the two keys can be physically separated and distinct programmes, organizations, or individuals made responsible for them. From then on, no single accident, deception, or breach of trust is sufficient to compromise the protected information.

This principle is often used in bank safe-deposit boxes. It is also at work in the defence system that fires a nuclear weapon only if two different people both give the correct command. In a computer system, separated keys apply to any situation in which two or more conditions must be met before access should be permitted. For example, systems providing user-extendible protected data types usually depend on separation of privilege for their implementation.

### *Least Privilege*

Every programme and every user of the system should operate using the least set of privileges necessary to complete the job. Primarily, this principle limits the damage that can result from an accident or error. It also reduces the number of potential interactions among privileged programmes to the minimum for correct operation, so that unintentional, unwanted, or improper uses of privilege are less likely to occur. Thus, if a question arises related to misuse of a privilege, the number of programmes that must be audited is minimized. Put another way, if a mechanism can provide "firewalls," the principle of least privilege provides a rationale for where to install the firewalls. The military security rule of "need-to-know" is an example of this principle.

***Least Common Mechanism***

Minimize the amount of mechanism common to more than one user and depended on by all users. Every shared mechanism (especially one involving shared variables) represents a potential information path between users and must be designed with great care to be sure it does not unintentionally compromise security. Further, any mechanism serving all users must be certified to the satisfaction of every user, a job presumably harder than satisfying only one or a few users.

For example, given the choice of implementing a new function as a supervisor procedure shared by all users or as a library procedure that can be handled as though it were the user's own, choose the latter course. Then, if one or a few users are not satisfied with the level of certification of the function, they can provide a substitute or not use it at all. Either way, they can avoid being harmed by a mistake in it.

***Psychological Acceptability***

It is essential that the human interface be designed for ease of use, so that users routinely and automatically apply the protection mechanisms correctly. Also, to the extent that the user's mental image of his protection goals matches the mechanisms he must use, mistakes will be minimized. If he must translate his image of his protection needs into a radically different specification language, he will make errors.

**Analysts of Traditional Physical Security Systems**

Analysts of traditional physical security systems have suggested two further design principles which, unfortunately, apply only imperfectly to computer systems.

***Work Factor***

Compare the cost of circumventing the mechanism with the resources of a potential attacker. The cost of circumventing, commonly known as the "work factor," in some cases can be easily calculated. For example, the number of experiments needed to try all possible four letter alphabetic passwords is $26^4 = 456976$. If the potential attacker must enter each experimental password at a terminal, one might consider a four-letter password to be adequate. On the other hand, if the attacker could use a large computer capable of trying a million passwords per second, as might be the case where industrial espionage or military security is being considered, a four-letter password would be a minor barrier for a potential intruder.

The trouble with the work factor principle is that many computer protection mechanisms are *not* susceptible to direct work factor calculation, since defeating them by systematic attack may be logically impossible. Defeat can be accomplished only by indirect strategies, such as waiting for an accidental hardware failure or searching for an error in implementation. Reliable estimates of the length of such a wait or search are very difficult to make.

### *Compromise Recording*

It is sometimes suggested that mechanisms that reliably record that a compromise of information has occurred can be used in place of more elaborate mechanisms that completely prevent loss. For example, if a tactical plan is known to have been compromised, it may be possible to construct a different one, rendering the compromised version worthless. An unbreakable padlock on a flimsy file cabinet is an example of such a mechanism. Although the information stored inside may be easy to obtain, the cabinet will inevitably be damaged in the process and the next legitimate user will detect the loss. For another example, many computer systems record the date and time of the most recent use of each file. If this record is tamperproof and reported to the owner, it may help discover unauthorized use. In computer systems, this approach is used rarely, since it is difficult to guarantee discovery once security is broken. Physical damage usually is not involved, and logical damage (and internally stored records of tampering) can be undone by a clever attacker. As is apparent, these principles do not represent absolute rules—they serve best as warnings. If some part of a design violates a principle, the violation is a symptom of potential trouble, and the design should be carefully reviewed to be sure that the trouble has been accounted for or is unimportant.

## Considerations Surrounding Protection

Briefly, then, we may outline our discussion to this point. The application of computers to information handling problems produces a need for a variety of security mechanisms. We are focusing on one aspect, computer protection mechanisms—the mechanisms that control access to information by executing programmes. At least four levels of functional goals for a protection system can be identified: all-or-nothing systems, controlled sharing, user-programmed sharing controls, and putting strings on information. But at all levels, the provisions for dynamic changes to authorization for access are a severe complication.

Since no one knows how to build a system without flaws, the alternative is to rely on eight design principles, which tend to reduce both the number and the seriousness of any flaws: Economy of mechanism, fail-safe defaults, complete mediation, open design, separation of privilege, least privilege, least common mechanism, and psychological acceptability. Finally, some protection designs can be evaluated by comparing the resources of a potential attacker with the work factor required to defeat the system, and compromise recording may be a useful strategy.

## TECHNICAL UNDERPINNINGS

### The Development Plan

At this point we begin a development of the technical basis of information protection in modern computer systems. There are two ways to approach the subject: from the top down, emphasizing the abstract concepts involved, or from the bottom up, identifying insights by, studying example systems. We shall follow the bottom-up approach, introducing a series of models of systems as they are, (or could be) built in real life.

The reader should understand that on this point the authors' judgment differs from that of some of their colleagues. The top-down approach can be very satisfactory when a subject is coherent and self-contained, but for a topic still containing *ad hoc* strategies and competing world views, the bottom-up approach seems safer.

Our first model is of a multiuser system that completely isolates its users from one another. We shall then see how the logically perfect walls of that system can be lowered in a controlled way to allow limited sharing of information between users. The mechanics of sharing using two different models: the capability system and the access control list system. It then extends these two models to handle the dynamic situation in which authorizations can change under control of the programmes running inside the system.

Further extensions to the models control the dynamics. The final model (only superficially explored) is of protected objects and protected subsystems, which allow arbitrary modes of sharing that are unanticipated by the system designer. These models are not intended so much to explain the particular systems as they are to explain the underlying concepts of information protection.

Our emphasis throughout the development is on direct access to information (for example, using LOAD and STORE instructions) rather than acquiring information indirectly (as when calling a data base management system to request the average value of a set of numbers supposedly not directly accessible). Control of such access is the function of the protected subsystems developed near the end of the paper. Herein lies perhaps the chief defect of the bottom-up approach, since conceptually there seems to be no reason to distinguish direct and indirect access, yet the detailed mechanics are typically quite different. The beginnings of a top-down approach based on a message model that avoids distinguishing between direct and indirect information access may be found in a paper by Lampson.

**The Essentials of Information Protection**

For purposes of discussing protection, the information stored in a computer system is not a single object. When one is considering direct access, the information is divided into mutually exclusive partitions, as specified by its various creators. Each partition contains a collection of information, all of which is intended to be protected uniformly. The uniformity of protection is the same kind of uniformity that applies to all of the diamonds stored in the same vault: any person who has a copy of the combination can obtain any of the diamonds. Thus the collections of information in the partitions are the fundamental objects to be protected.

Conceptually, then, it is necessary to build an impenetrable wall around each distinct object that warrants separate protection, construct a door in the wall through which access can be obtained, and post a guard at the door to control its use. Control of use, however, requires that the guard have some way of knowing which users are authorized to have access, and that each user have some reliable way of identifying himself to the guard. This authority check is usually implemented by having the guard demand a match between something he knows and something the prospective user possesses. Both protection and authentication mechanisms can be viewed in terms of this general model.

Before extending this model, we pause to consider two concrete examples, the multiplexing of a single computer system among several users and the authentication of a user's claimed identity. These initial examples are complete isolation systems—no sharing of information can happen. Later we will extend our model of guards and walls in the discussion of shared information.

**An Isolated Virtual Machine**

A typical computer consists of a processor, a linearly addressed memory system, and some collection of input/output devices associated with the processor. It is relatively easy to use a single computer to simulate several, each of which is completely unaware of the existence of the others, except that each runs more slowly than usual.

Such a simulation is of interest, since during the intervals when one of the simulated (commonly called *virtual*) processors is waiting for an input or output operation to finish, another virtual processor may be able to progress at its normal rate. Thus a single processor may be able to take the place of several. Such a scheme is the essence of a multiprogramming system.

To allow each virtual processor to be unaware of the existence of the others, it is essential that some isolation mechanism be provided. One such mechanism is a special hardware register called a *descriptor register*. In this figure, all memory references by the processor are checked by an extra piece of hardware that is interposed in the path to the memory. The descriptor register controls exactly which part of memory is accessible. The descriptor register contains two components: a *base* value and a *bound* value.

The base is the lowest numbered address the programme may use, and the bound is the number of locations beyond the base that may be used. We will call the value in the descriptor register a *descriptor*, as it describes an object (in this case, one programme) stored in memory. The programme controlling the processor has full access to everything in the base-bound range, by virtue of possession of its one descriptor. As we go on, we shall embellish the concept of a descriptor: it is central to most implementations of protection and of sharing of information.

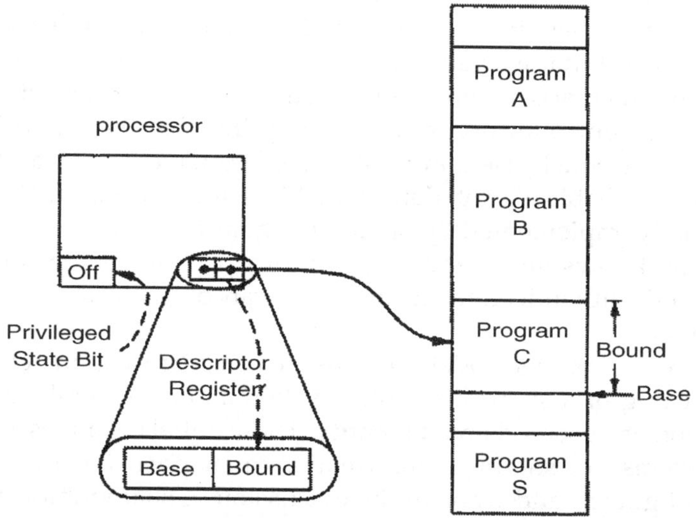


**Fig.** Use of a Descriptor Register to Simulate Multiple Virtual Machines. Programme C is in Control of the Processor. The Privileged State bit has Value OFF, indicating that Programme C is a User Programme. When Programme S is Running, the Privileged State bit has Value ON.

So far, we have not provided for the dynamics of a complete protection scheme: we have not discussed who loads the descriptor register. If any running programme could load it with any arbitrary value, there would be no protection. The instruction that loads the descriptor register with a new descriptor must have some special controls—either on the values it will load or on who may use it. It is easier to control who may use the descriptor, and a common scheme is to introduce an additional bit in the processor state. This bit is called the *privileged state* bit. All attempts to load the descriptor register are checked against the value of the privileged state bit; the privileged state bit must be ON for the register to be changed. One programme runs with the privileged state bit ON, and controls the simulation of the virtual processors for the other programmes.

All that is needed to make the scheme complete is to ensure that the privileged state bit cannot be changed by the user programmes except, perhaps, by an instruction that simultaneously transfers control to the supervisor programme at a planned entry location. (In most implementations, the descriptor register is not used in the privileged state.)

One might expect the supervisor programme to maintain a table of values of descriptors, one for each virtual processor. When the privileged state bit is OFF, the index in this table of the programme currently in control identifies exactly which programme—and thus which virtual processor—is accountable for the activity of the real processor. For protection to be complete, a virtual processor must not be able to change arbitrarily the values in the table of descriptors. If we suppose the table to be stored inside the supervisor programme, it will be inaccessible to the virtual processors. We have here an example of a common strategy and sometime cause of confusion: the protection mechanisms not only protect one user from another, *they may also protect their own implementation.* We shall encounter this strategy again.

So far, this virtual processor implementation contains three protection mechanisms that we can associate with our abstractions. For the first, the information being protected is the distinct programmes. The guard is represented by the extra piece of hardware that enforces the descriptor restriction. The impenetrable wall with a door is the hardware that forces all references to memory through the descriptor mechanism. The authority check on a request to access memory is very simple. The requesting virtual processor is identified by the base and bound values in the descriptor register, and the guard checks that the memory location to which access is requested lies within the indicated area of memory.

The second mechanism protects the contents of the descriptor register. The wall, door, and guard are implemented in hardware, as with the first mechanism. An executing programme requesting to load the descriptor register is identified by the privileged state bit. If this bit is OFF, indicating that the requester is a user programme, then the guard does not allow the register to be loaded. If this bit is ON, indicating that the requester is the supervisor programme, then the guard does allow it.

The third mechanism protects the privileged state bit. It allows an executing programme identified by the privileged state bit being OFF (a user programme) to perform the single operation "turn privileged state bit ON and transfer to the supervisor programme." An executing programme identified by the privileged state bit being ON is allowed to turn the bit OFF. This third mechanism is an embryonic form of the sophisticated protection mechanisms required to implement protected subsystems. The supervisor programme is an example of a protected subsystem, of which more will be said later. The supervisor programme is part of all three protection mechanisms, for it is responsible for maintaining the integrity of the identifications manifest in the descriptor register and the privileged state bit. If the supervisor does not do its job correctly, virtual processors could become labelled with the wrong base and bound values, or user programmes could become labelled with a privileged state bit that is ON, The supervisor protects itself from the user programmes with the same isolation hardware that separates users, an example of the "economy of mechanism" design principle.

With an appropriately sophisticated and careful supervisor programme, we now have an example of a system that completely isolates its users from one another. Similarly isolated permanent storage can be added to such a system by attaching some longterm storage device (*e.g.*, magnetic disk) and developing a similar descriptor scheme for its use. Since long-term storage is accessed less frequently than primary memory, it is common to implement its descriptor scheme with the supervisor programmes rather than hardware, but the principle is the same. Data streams to input or output devices can be controlled similarly. The combination of a virtual processor, a memory area, some data streams, and an isolated region of long-term storage is known as a virtual machine.

Long-term storage does, however, force us to face one further issue. Suppose that the virtual machine communicates with its user through a typewriter terminal. If a new user approaches a previously unused terminal and requests to use a virtual machine, which virtual machine (and, therefore, which set of long-term stored information) should he be allowed to use? We may solve this problem outside the system, by having the supervisor permanently associate a single virtual machine and its long-term storage area with a single terminal. Then, for example, padlocks can control access to the terminal. If, on the other hand, a more flexible system is desired, the supervisor programme must be prepared to associate any terminal with any virtual machine and, as a result, must be able to verify the identity of the user at a terminal. Schemes for performing this authentication are the subject of our next example.

**Authentication Mechanisms**

Our second example is of an authentication mechanism: a system that verifies a user's claimed identity. The mechanics of this authentication mechanism differ from those of the protection mechanisms for implementing virtual machines mainly because not all of the components of the system are under uniform physical control. In particular, the user himself and the communication system connecting his terminal to the computer are components to be viewed with suspicion. Conversely, the user needs to verify that he is in communication with the expected computer system and the intended virtual machine. Such systems follow our abstract model of a guard who demands a match between something he knows and something the requester possesses. The objects being protected by the authentication mechanism are the virtual machines. In this case, however, the requester is a computer system user rather than an executing programme, and because of the lack of physical control over the user and the communication system, the security of the computer system must depend on either the secrecy or the unforgeability of the user's identification. In time-sharing systems, the most common scheme depends on secrecy. The user begins by typing the name of the person he claims to be, and then the system demands that the user type a password, presumably known only to that person.

There are, of course, many possible elaborations and embellishments of this basic strategy. In cases where the typing of the password may be observed, passwords may be good for only one use, and the user carries a list of passwords, crossing each one off the list as he uses it. Passwords may have an expiration date, or usage count, to limit the length of usefulness of a compromised one. The list of acceptable passwords is a piece of information that must be carefully guarded by the system. In some systems, all passwords are passed through a hard-to-invert transformation before being stored, an idea suggested by R. Needham. When the user types his password, the system transforms it also and compares the transformed versions.

Since the transform is supposed to be hard to invert (even if the transform itself is well known), if the stored version of a password is compromised, it may be very difficult to determine what original password is involved. It should be noted, however, that "hardness of inversion" is difficult to measure. The attacker of such a system does not need to discern the general inversion, only the particular one applying to some transformed password he has available. Passwords as a general technique have some notorious defects. The most often mentioned defect lies in choice of password—if a person chooses his own password, he may choose something easily guessed by someone else who knows his habits. In one recent study of some 300 self-chosen passwords on a typical time-sharing system, more than 50 percent were found to be short enough to guess by exhaustion, derived from the owner's name, or something closely associated with the owner, such as his telephone number or birth date. For this reason, some systems have programmes that generate random sequences of letters for use as passwords.

They may even require that all passwords be system-generated and changed frequently. On the other hand, frequently changed random sequences of letters are hard to memorize, so such systems tend to cause users to make written copies of their passwords, inviting compromise. One solution to this problem is to provide a generator of "pronounceable" random passwords based on digraph or higher order frequency statistics to make memorization easier. A second significant defect is that the password must be exposed to be used. In systems where the terminal is distant from the computer, the password must be sent through some communication system, during which passage a wiretapper may be able to intercept it. An alternative approach to secrecy is unforgeability. The user is given a key, or magnetically striped plastic card, or some other unique and relatively difficult-to-fabricate object. The terminal has an input device that examines the object and transmits its unique identifying code to the computer system, which treats the code as a password that need not be kept secret. Proposals have been made for fingerprint readers and dynamic signature readers in order to increase the effort required for forgery.

The primary weakness of such schemes is that the hard-to-fabricate object, after being examined by the specialized input device, is reduced to a stream of bits to be transmitted to the computer. Unless the terminal, its object reader, and its communication lines to the computer are physically secured against tampering, it is relatively easy for an intruder to modify the terminal to transmit any sequence of bits he chooses. It may be necessary to make the acceptable bit sequences a secret after all. On the other hand, the scheme is convenient, resists casual misuse, and provides a conventional form of accountability through the physical objects used as keys.

A problem common to both the password and the unforgeable object approach is that they are "one-way" authentication schemes. They authenticate the user to the computer system, but not *vice-versa*. An easy way for an intruder to penetrate a password system, for example, is to intercept all communications to and from the terminal and direct them to another computer—one that is under the interceptor's control. This computer can be programmed to "masquerade," that is, to act just like the system the caller intended to use, up to the point of requesting him to type his password. After receiving the password, the masquerader gracefully terminates the communication with some unsurprising error message, and the caller may be unaware that his password has been stolen. The same attack can be used on the unforgeable object system as well.

A more powerful authentication technique is sometimes used to protect against masquerading. Suppose that a remote terminal is equipped with enciphering circuitry, such as the LUCIFER system, that scrambles all signals from that terminal. Such devices normally are designed so that the exact encipherment is determined by the value of a key, known as the *encryption* or *transformation* key.

For example, the transformation key may consist of a sequence of 1000 binary digits read from a magnetically striped plastic card. In order that a recipient of such an enciphered signal may comprehend it, he must have a deciphering circuit primed with an exact copy of the transformation key, or else he must cryptanalyse the scrambled stream to try to discover the key. The strategy of encipherment/decipherment is usually invoked for the purpose of providing communications security on an otherwise unprotected communications system. However, it can simultaneously be used for authentication, using the following technique, first published in the unclassified literature by Feistel.

The user, at a terminal, begins bypassing the enciphering equipment. He types his name. This name passes, unenciphered, through the communication system to the computer. The computer looks up the name, just as with the password system. Associated with each name, instead of a secret password, is a secret transformation key. The computer loads this transformation key into its enciphering mechanism, turns it on, and attempts to communicate with the user. Meanwhile, the user has loaded his copy of the transformation key into his enciphering mechanism and turned it on.

Now, if the keys are identical, exchange of some standard hand-shaking sequence will succeed. If they are not identical, the exchange will fail, and both the user and the computer system will encounter unintelligible streams of bits. If the exchange succeeds, the computer system is certain of the identity of the user, and the user is certain of the identity of the computer. The secret used for authentication—the transformation key—has not been transmitted through the communication system. If communication fails (because the user is unauthorized, the system has been replaced by a masquerader, or an error occurred), each party to the transaction has immediate warning of a problem.

Relatively complex elaborations of these various strategies have been implemented, differing both in economics and in assumptions about the psychology of the prospective user. For example, Branstad explored in detail strategies of authentication in multinode computer networks. Such elaborations, though fascinating to study and analyse, are diversionary to our main topic of protection mechanisms.

**Shared Information**

The virtual machines are totally independent, as far as information accessibility was concerned. Each user might just as well have his own private computer system. With the steadily declining costs of computer manufacture there are few technical reasons not to use a private computer. On the other hand, for many applications some sharing of information among users is useful, or even essential. For example, there may be a library of commonly used, reliable programmes. Some users may create new programmes that other users would like to use.

Users may wish to be able to update a common data base, such as a file of airline seat reservations or a collection of programmes that implement a biomedical statistics system. In all these cases, virtual machines are inadequate, because of the total isolation of their users from one another. Before extending the virtual machine example any further, let us return to our abstract discussion of guards and walls.

*Implementations of protection mechanisms that permit sharing fall into the two general categories described by Wilkes:*

- "List-oriented" implementations, in which the guard holds a list of identifiers of authorized users, and the user carries a unique unforgeable identifier that must appear on the guard's list for access to be permitted. A store clerk checking a list of credit customers is an example of a list-oriented implementation in practice. The individual might use his driver's license as a unique unforgeable identifier.
- "Ticket-oriented" implementations, in which the guard holds the description of a single identifier, and each user has a collection of unforgeable identifiers, or tickets, corresponding to the objects to which he has been authorized access. A locked door that opens with a key is probably the most common example of a ticket-oriented mechanism; the guard is implemented as the hardware of the lock, and the matching key is the (presumably) unforgeable authorizing identifier.

*Authorization*, defined as giving a user access to some object, is different in these two schemes. In a list-oriented system, a user is authorized to use an object by having his name placed on the guard's list for that object. In a ticket-oriented system, a user is authorized by giving him a ticket for the object.

We can also note a crucial mechanical difference between the two kinds of implementations. The list-oriented mechanism requires that the guard examine his list at the time access is requested, which means that some kind of associative search must accompany the access. On the other hand, the ticket-oriented mechanism places on the user the burden of choosing which ticket to present, a task he can combine with deciding which information to access. The guard only need compare the presented ticket with his own expectation before allowing the physical memory access.

Because associative matching tends to be either slower or more costly than simple comparison, list-oriented mechanisms are not often used in applications where traffic is high. On the other hand, ticket-oriented mechanisms typically require considerable technology to control forgery of tickets and to control passing tickets around from one user to another. As a rule, most real systems contain both kinds of sharing implementations—a list-oriented system at the human interface and a ticket-oriented system in the underlying hardware implementation.

This kind of arrangement is accomplished by providing, at the higher level, a list-oriented guard whose only purpose is to hand out temporary tickets which the lower level (ticket-oriented) guards will honor. Some added complexity arises from the need to keep authorizations, as represented in the two systems, synchronized with each other. Computer protection systems differ mostly in the extent to which the architecture of the underlying ticket-oriented system is visible to the user.

Finally, let us consider the degenerate cases of list- and ticket-oriented systems. In a list-oriented system, if each guard's list of authorized users can contain only one entry, we have a "complete isolation" kind of protection system, in which no sharing of information among users can take place. Similarly, in a ticket-oriented system, if there can be only one ticket for each object in the system, we again have a "complete isolation" kind of protection system. Thus the "complete isolation" protection system turns out to be a particular degenerate case of both the list-oriented and the ticket-oriented protection implementations.

These observations are important in examining real systems, which usually consist of interacting protection mechanisms, some of which are list-oriented, some of which are ticket-oriented, and some of which provide complete isolation and therefore may happen to be implemented as degenerate examples of either of the other two, depending on local circumstances.

We should understand the relationship of a user to these transactions. We are concerned with protection of information from programmes that are executing. The user is the individual who assumes accountability for the actions of an executing programme. Inside the computer system, a programme is executed by a virtual processor, so one or more virtual processors can be identified with the activities directed by the user.

In a list-oriented system it is the guard's business to know whose virtual processor is attempting to make an access. The virtual processor has been marked with an unforgeable label identifying the user accountable for its actions, and the guard inspects this label when making access decisions. In a ticket-oriented system, however, the guard cares only that a virtual processor present the appropriate unforgeable ticket when attempting an access. The connection to an accountable user is more diffuse, since the guard does not know or care how the virtual processor acquired the tickets.

In either case, we conclude that in addition to the information inside the impenetrable wall, there are two other things that must be protected: the guard's authorization information, and the association between a user and the unforgeable label or set of tickets associated with his virtual processors. Since an association with some user is essential for establishing accountability for the actions of a virtual processor, it is useful to introduce an abstraction for that accountability—the *principal*. A principal is, by definition, the entity accountable for the activities of a virtual processor. In the situations discussed so far, the principal corresponds to the user outside the system. However, there are situations in which a one-to-one correspondence of individuals with principals is not adequate.

For example, a user may be accountable for some very valuable information and authorized to use it. On the other hand, on some occasion he may wish to use the computer for some purpose unrelated to the valuable information. To prevent accidents, he may wish to identify himself with a different principal, one that does not have access to the valuable information—following the principle of least privilege. In this case there is a need for two different principals corresponding to the same user.

Similarly, one can envision a data base that is to be modified only if a committee agrees. Thus there might be an authorized principal that cannot be used by any single individual; all of the committee members must agree upon its use simultaneously. Because the principal represents accountability, that authorizing access is done in terms of principals. That is, if one wishes a friend to have access to some file, the authorization is done by naming a principal only that friend can use.

For each principal we may identify all the objects in the system which the principal has been authorized to use. We will name that set of objects the *domain* of that principal. Summarizing, then, a principal is the unforgeable identifier attached to a virtual processor in a list-oriented system.

When a user first approaches the computer system, that user must identify the principal to be used. Some authentication mechanism, such as a request for a secret password, establishes the user's right to use that principal.

The authentication mechanism itself may be either list- or ticket-oriented or of the complete isolation type. Then a computation is begun in which all the virtual processors of the computation are labelled with the identifier of that principal, which is considered accountable for all further actions of these virtual processors.

The authentication mechanism has allowed the virtual processor to enter the domain of that principal. That description makes apparent the importance of the authentication mechanism. Clearly, one must carefully control the conditions under which a virtual processor enters a domain.

Finally, we should note that in a ticket-oriented system there is no mechanical need to associate an unforgeable identifier with a virtual processor, since the tickets themselves are presumed unforgeable. Nevertheless, a collection of tickets can be considered to be a domain, and therefore correspond to some principal, even though there may be no obvious identifier for that principal.

Thus accountability in ticket-oriented systems can be difficult to pinpoint. Now we shall return to our example system and extend it to include sharing. Consider for a moment the problem of sharing a library programme—say, a mathematical function subroutine. We could place a copy of the math routine in the long-term storage area of each virtual machine that had a use for it. This scheme, although workable, has several defects. Most obvious, the multiple copies require multiple storage spaces.

More subtly, the scheme does not respond well to changes. If a newer, better math routine is written, upgrading the multiple copies requires effort proportional to the number of users. These two observations suggest that one would like to have some scheme to allow different users access to a single *master copy* of the programme. The storage space will be smaller and the communication of updated versions will be easier.

In terms of the virtual machine model of our earlier example, we can share a single copy of the math routine by adding to the real processor a second descriptor register, placing the math routine somewhere in memory by itself and placing a descriptor for it in the second descriptor register. Following the previous strategy, we assume that the privileged state bit assures that the supervisor programme is the only one permitted to load either descriptor register.

In addition, some scheme must be provided in the architecture of the processor to permit a choice of which descriptor register is to be used for each address generated by the processor. A simple scheme would be to let the high-order address bit select the descriptor register.

Thus, all addresses in the lower half of the address range would be interpreted relative to descriptor register 1, and addresses in the upper half of the address range would be relative to descriptor register 2. An alternate scheme, suggested by Dennis, is to add explicitly to the format of instruction words a field that selects the descriptor register intended to be used with the address in that instruction.

The use of descriptors for sharing information is intimately related to the addressing architecture of the processor, a relation that can cause considerable confusion. The reason why descriptors are of interest for sharing becomes apparent by comparing parts a and b. When programme A is in control, it can have access only to itself and the math routine; similarly, when programme B is in control, it can have access only to itself and the math routine.

Since neither programme has the power to change the descriptor register, sharing of the math routine has been accomplished while maintaining isolation of programme A from programme B.

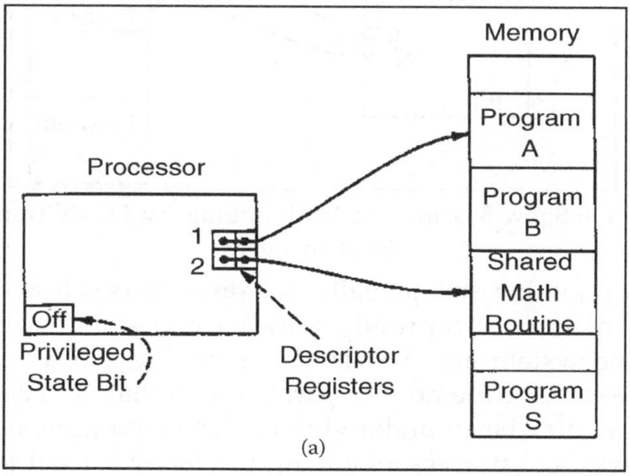


(a)

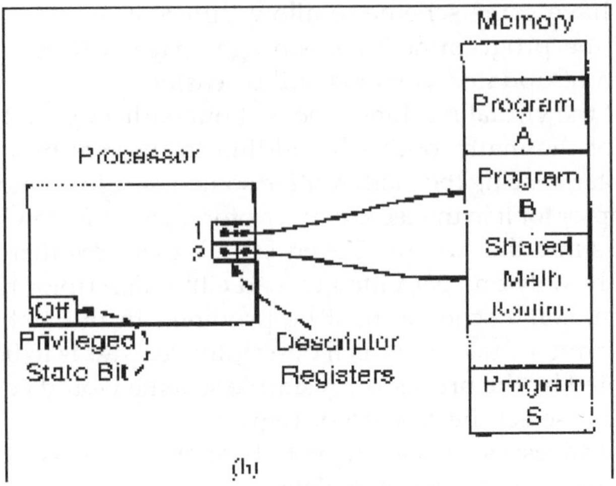


**Fig.** Sharing of a Math Routine by use of Two Descriptor Registors. (a) Programme A in Control of Processor. (b) Programme B in Control of Processor.

The effect of sharing is shown even more graphically redrawn with two virtual processors, one executing programme A and the other executing programme B.

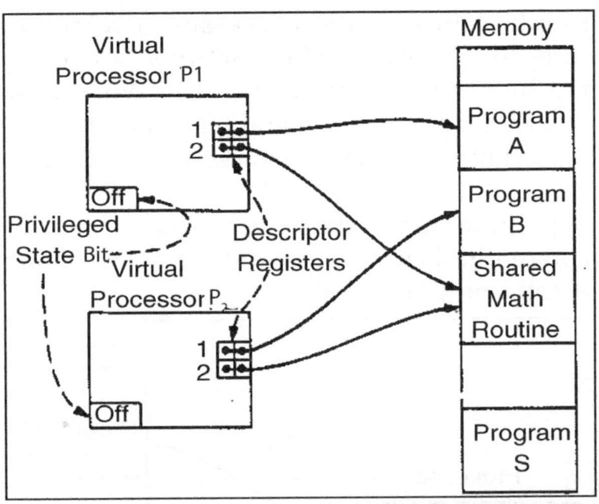


**Fig.** Redrawn to Show Sharing of a Math Routine by Two Virtual Processors Simultaneously.

Whether or not there are actually two processors is less important than the existence of the conceptually parallel access paths. Every virtual processor of the system may be viewed as having its own real processor, capable of access to the memory in parallel with that of every other virtual processor. There may be an underlying processor multiplexing facility that distributes a few real processors among the many virtual processors, but such a multiplexing facility is essentially unrelated to protection. Recall that a virtual processor is not permitted to load its own protection descriptor registers. Instead, it must call or trap to the supervisor programme S which call or trap causes the privileged state bit to go ON and thereby permits the supervisor programme to control the extent of sharing among virtual processors.

The processor multiplexing facility must be prepared to switch the entire state of the real processor from one virtual processor to another, including the values of the protection descriptor registers.

Although the basic mechanism to permit information sharing is now in place, a remarkable variety of implications that follow from its introduction require further mechanisms.

*These implications include the following.*

- If virtual processor $P_1$ can overwrite the shared math routine, then it could disrupt the work of virtual processor $P_2$.
- The shared math routine must be careful about making modifications to itself and about where in memory it writes temporary results, since it is to be used by independent computations, perhaps simultaneously.
- The scheme needs to be expanded and generalized to cover the possibility that more than one programme or data base is to be shared.
- The supervisor needs to be informed about which principals are authorized to use the shared math routine (unless it happens to be completely public with no restrictions).

Let us consider these four implications in order. If the shared area of memory is a procedure, then to avoid the possibility that virtual processor $P_1$ will maliciously overwrite it, we can restrict the methods of access. Virtual processor $P_1$ needs to retrieve instructions from the area of the shared procedure, and may need to read out the values of constants embedded in the programme, but it has no need to write into any part of the shared procedure.

We may accomplish this restriction by extending the descriptor registers and the descriptors themselves to include *accessing permission,* an idea introduced for different reasons in the original Burroughs B5000 design. For example, we may add two bits, one controlling permission to read and the other permission to write in the storage area defined by each descriptor.

In virtual processor $P_1$, descriptor 1 would have both permissions granted, while descriptor 2 would permit only reading of data and execution of instructions.

An alternative scheme would be to attach the permission bits directly to the storage areas containing the shared programme or data. Such a scheme is less satisfactory because, unlike the descriptors so far outlined, permission bits attached to the data would provide identical access to all processors that had a descriptor. Although identical access for all users of the shared math routine might be acceptable, a data base could not be set up with several users having permission to read but a few also having permission to write.

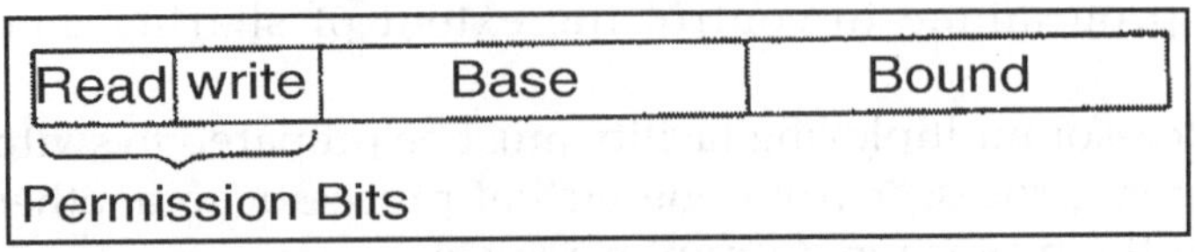


**Fig.** A Descriptor Containing READ and WRITE Permission Bits

The second implication of a shared procedure, mentioned before, is that the shared procedure must be careful about where it stores temporary results, since it may be used simultaneously by several virtual processors. In particular, it should avoid modifying itself. The enforcement of access permission by descriptor bits further constrains the situation.

To prevent programme A from writing into the shared math routine, we have also prohibited the shared math routine from writing into itself, since the descriptors do not change when, for example, programme A transfers control to the math routine. The math routine will find that it can read but not write into itself, but that it can both read and write into the area of programme A.

Thus programme A might allocate an area of its own address range for the math routine to use as temporary storage. As for the third implication, the need for expansion, we could generalize our example to permit several distinct shared items merely by increasing the number of descriptor registers and informing the supervisor which shared objects should be addressable by each virtual processor.

However, there are two substantially different forms of this generalization—*capability systems* and *access control list systems*. The capability systems are ticket-oriented, while access control list systems are list-oriented. Most real systems use a combination of these two forms, the capability system for speed and an access control list system for the human interface. Before we can pursue these generalizations, and the fourth implication, authorization, more groundwork must be laid.

The development of protection continues with a series of successively more sophisticated models. The initial model, of a capability system, explores the use of encapsulated but copyable descriptors as tickets to provide a flexible authorization scheme. In this context we establish the general rule that communication external to the computer must precede dynamic authorization of sharing.

The limitations of copyable descriptors—primarily lack of accountability for their use—lead to analysis of revocation and the observation that revocation requires indirection. That observation in turn leads to the model of access control lists embedded in indirect objects so as to provide detailed control of authorization.

The use of access control lists leads to a discussion of controlling changes to authorizations, there being at least two models of control methods which differ in their susceptibility to abuse. Additional control of authorization changes is needed when releasing sensitive data to a borrowed programme, and this additional control implies a nonintuitive constraint on where data may be written by the borrowed programme. The concept of implementing arbitrary abstractions, such as extended types of objects, as programmes in separate domains.

# 12

# System Programming

## DEFINITION

System programming is the activity of programming system software. The primary distinguishing characteristic of systems programming when compared to application programming is that application programming aims to produce software which provides services to the user (e.g. word processor), whereas systems programming aims to produce software which provides services to the computer hardware. It also requires a greater degree of hardware awareness.

The architects of the earliest computer systems gave little thought to software. (The very word was still a decade in the future.) Building the machine itself was the serious intellectual challenge; converting mathematical formulas into programme statements looked like a routine clerical task. The awful truth came out soon enough.

Maurice V.Wilkes, who wrote what may have been the first working computer programme, had his personal epiphany in 1949, when "the realization came over me with full force that a good part of the remainder of my life was going to be spent in finding errors in my own programmes." Half a century later, we're still debugging.

The very first programmes were written in pure binary notation: Both data and instructions had to be encoded in long, featureless strings of 1s and 0s. Moreover, it was up to the programmer to keep track of where everything was stored in the machine's memory. Before you could call a subroutine, you had to calculate its address. The technology that lifted these burdens from the programmer was assembly language, in which raw binary codes were replaced by symbols such as load, store, add, sub.

The symbols were translated into binary by a programme called an assembler, which also calculated addresses. This was the first of many instances in which the computer was recruited to help with its own programming. Assembly language was a crucial early advance, but still the programmer had to keep in mind all the minutiae in the instruction set of a specific computer.

Evaluating a short mathematical expression such as x2+y2 might require dozens of assembly-language instructions. Higher-level languages freed the programmer to think in terms of variables and equations rather than registers and addresses. In Fortran, for example, x2+y2 would be written simply as X** 2+Y**2. Expressions of this kind are translated into binary form by a programme called a compiler. With Fortran and the languages that followed, programmers finally had the tools they needed to get into really serious trouble.

By the 1960s large software projects were notorious for being late, overbudget and buggy; soon came the appalling news that the cost of software was overtaking that of hardware. Frederick P. Brooks, Jr., who managed the OS/360 software programme at IBM, called large- system programming a "tar pit" and remarked,"Everyone seems to have been surprised by the stickiness of the problem."

One response to this crisis was structured programming, a reform movement whose manifesto was Edsger W. Dijkstra's brief letter to the editor titled "Go to statement considered harmful." Structured programmes were to be built out of subunits that have a single entrance point and a single exit (eschewing the goto command,which allows jumps into or out of the middle of a routine).

Three such constructs were recommended: sequencing (do A, then B, then C), alternation (either do A or do B) and iteration (repeat A until some condition is satisfied). Corrado Böhm and Giuseppe Jacopini proved that these three idioms are sufficient to express essentially all programmes. Structured programming came packaged with a number of related principles and imperatives. Top-down design and stepwise refinement urged the programmer to set forth the broad outlines of a procedure first and only later fill in the details.

Modularity called for self-contained units with simple interfaces between them. Encapsulation, or data hiding,required that the internal workings of a module be kept private, so that later changes to the module would not affect other areas of the programme. All of these ideas have proved their worth and remain a part of software practice today. But they did not rescue programmers from the tar pit.

## SYSTEM PROGRAMMING LANGUAGE

System programming languages are higher level and they are strongly typed languages. The term "higher level" means that many details are handled automatically so that programmers can write less code to get the same job done. System programming languages are well suited to building components where the complexity is in the data structures and algorithms.

*System programming support following features*:

- Register allocation is handled by the compiler so that programmers need not write code to move information between registers and memory.

- Programmers can use simple keywords such as while and if for control structures; the compiler generates all the detailed instructions to implement the control structures.
- Procedure calling sequences are generated automatically: programmers need not worry about moving arguments to and from the call stack.

## EMBEDDED SYSTEM PROGRAMMING

Embedded System Programming was first used in Apollo guidance computer to guide Apollo. Technological advancement brought the price of embedded system (ICs) lower making it possible to use them for commercial purpose. Today embedded systems are widely used in various devices performing specific functions with drastic improvement in processing power.

Embedded system programming has been derived from the word embedded system. An embedded system is nothing but a special purpose system in which the computer is fully encapsulated by the device it controls. Embedded software designs have advanced enough to produce widely used devices performing specific function devices such as ATM, PDA, mobile phones etc.

This widely used technological term in the field of Information Technology, is the combination of computer hardware and software which is either fixed in facility or programmable. In short it is purposely designed for a meticulous kind of application device. Systems that hosts this embedded systems are various industrial machines, automobiles, medical equipment, cameras, household appliances, and airplanes, vending machines, toys, cellular phone and PDA.

Seeing its importance and worth embedded systems programming has gained lot popularity and people are looking for companies providing this service. If you are looking for a company providing embedded systems programming then your search is over as Softage is there for you.

Softage is Russia's leading IT service provider providing best and advanced embedded systems programming. Embedded systems programming is specially dedicated to unequivocal tasks so that design engineers can optimize it by reducing the magnitude and cost of the product. In fact nowadays, embedded systems are frequently mass-produced. This has resulted in the cost savings that may be multiplied by millions of items. Apart from the other devices embedded systems also range from portable devices such as MP3 players, to large stationary installations like traffic lights or factory controllers.

According to the experts embedded systems are easily programmable and are provided with a programming interface. Embedded system programming is a tough and professional work which is efficiently handled by Softage. Backed by years of experience Softage hosts some of the best and professional programmers those are experts in embedded system software programming.

Embedded systems programm-ing is basically done in various languages such as J2e, C/C++, x86 assembler, ADSP assembler, and SQL accessing appropriate language for specific devices. All these languages are supported and provided by Softage and that too easily affordable. Thus, what you are waiting for if you are looking for embedded systems programming then Softage is there for you.

## WINDOWS SYSTEM PROGRAMMING

In old days, the operating system programme executes the program's instructions in sequence one instruction after another as they arranged by the programmer. When the programme calls a function or interacts with the Operating System (OS) by calling one of the OS's service functions, the function's instructions executed in similar way and the execution continue sequentially until the end of the last instruction of the main programme.

In this traditional way of programming the programme only need one main function to start the execution. Nowadays, in event driven programming environment such as Windows, the interaction between the programme and the OS is a message-based interaction. In this interaction the programme start in a wait mode until the user create an event like for example, press a key or click a mouse button.

The OS generates appropriate message and inserts it in application's message queue. The programme, when it ready, should dispatch the messages (read a message from the queue and send it back to the OS) one message after another for time scheduling purpose. After that, the OS then send the message again to the programme and the programme respond by taking appropriate actions. In this kind of interaction, a simple programme need at least two functions, the main function that start the message loop (WinMain ()) and the other called by the OS (Windows Function())and respond to the passed message.

## UNIX SYSTEMS PROGRAMMING

The Unix systems programming API has been standardised by a large number of POSIX standards documents from the IEEE. For the majority of programmers the most important of these is POSIX 1003.1 which covers process primitives and environments, directories and files, I/O primitives and device specific functions. Later standards cover other issues, such as Shells and Utilities (POSIX 1003.2) and Administration (POSIX 1387.2).

One of the unusual characteristics of POSIX 1003.1 is its use of the C language throughout. Whereas IEEE standards would normally be expected to be language independent, the history of Unix is so bound up with C that this was the only feasible route. The document claims that it will be the basis for definitions that are independent of particular programming languages. In fact, new language dependent versions have arisen, such as Ada (POSIX 1003.5) and Fortran. Irrespective of the formal standards mechanisms, designers of libraries for other languages have used POSIX 1003.1 as the specification for their own libraries.

For example, tcl [Ousterhout] and Perl [Wall] have well-developed Unix bindings that copy the syntax, and rely on the semantics, of POSIX 1003.1. Java [Arnold] is the latest flavour in programming languages for all sorts of excellent reasons, despite some serious shortcomings. It is a full O/O language (although not as pure as SmallTalk or Eiffel); it is based on C/C++, but avoids the worst of both languages (not completely, though); by use of a virtual machine it is cross-platform (although some vendors have variant versions); it has a rich set set of libraries that deal with, for example, graphics and networking.

These are combining to produce the "Web programming" environment where applications or applets are written once to run on any platform. Java extends the open authoring environment of HTML to an open programming environment.

How do Unix and Java co-exist? Very well in general terms. A Java application can do exactly the same things in a Unix environment that it can do in a Mac or Windows environment. With care, applications can even be written that transparently handle such issues as forward- versus back-slashes for directory separators. Java currently lacks the depth of hooks into the POSIX API that tcl and Perl have.

The standard must continue to have this lack or it will lose its universal applicability. However, *extensions* by *non-standard* libraries can supply this depth, as long as they are done in an appropriate manner. This paper reports on a project to make the POSIX API available to Java applications or applets using a non-standard library. It encapulates POSIX calls within Java methods for a new set of classes in the posix package.

This project must be contrasted in aims and methods to the Microsoft policy with J++: their attempt is to make J++ the best environment for doing Windows programming in Java J++, and this implicitly rejects the notion of a cross-platform environment. It may even turn out to be difficult for the programmer using J++ to be certain of how general their code is. The statements from Microsoft do not seem to dispel any uncertainty.

This project, on the other hand, makes it explicit about the introduction of non-standard features, by placing all the new classes in a package that is non-standard. No application using the posix package will ever pass the "Java Pure" tests. On the other hand, this package will develop by an open process method: the source code will be freely available to all, and can be freely modified. If interest is high enough, it can be divorced from individual control and given to a suitable co-ordinating authority.

# LINKERS

## DEFINITION

In computer science, a linker is a programme that takes one or more objects generated by a compiler and assembles them into a single executable programme. In IBM mainframe environments such as OS/360 this programme is known as a "linkage editor". On Unix variants the term loader is often used as a synonym for linker.

Because this usage blurs the distinction between the compile-time process and the run-time process, this article will use "linking" for the former and "loading" for the latter. However, in some operating systems the same programme handles both the jobs of linking and loading a programme; see "dynamic linking".

Computer programmes are typically comprised of several parts or modules; these parts, if not all contained within a single object file, refer to each other by means of symbols.

*Typically, an object file can contain three kinds of symbols*:

- Defined symbols, which allow it to be called by other modules.
- Undefined symbols, which call the other modules where these symbols are defined.
- Local symbols, used internally within the object file to facilitate relocation.

When a programme comprises multiple object files, the linker combines these files into a unified executable programme, resolving the symbols as it goes along. Linkers can take objects from a collection called a "library". Some linkers do not include the whole library in the output; they only include its symbols that are referenced from other object files or libraries. Libraries exist for diverse purposes, and one or more system libraries are usually linked in by default. The linker also takes care of arranging the objects in a program's address space.

This may involve "relocating" code that assumes a specific base address to another base. Since a compiler seldom knows where an object will reside, it often assumes a fixed base location (for example, zero). Relocating machine code may involve re-targeting of absolute jumps, loads and stores. The executable output by the linker may need another relocation pass when it is finally loaded into memory (just before execution). This pass is usually omitted on hardware offering virtual memory — every programme is put into its own address space, so there is no conflict even if all programmes load at the same base address. This pass may also be omitted if the executable is a position independent executable.

## CONCEPT

The basic job of any linker is simple: it binds more abstract names to more concrete names, which permits programmers to write code using the more abstract names. That is, it takes a name written by a programmer such as get line and binds it to "the location 612 bytes from the beginning of the executable code in module iosys." Or it may take a more abstract numeric address such as "the location 450 bytes beyond the beginning of the static data for this module" and bind it to a numeric address. A linkers is used in the development of computer programming in systems.

The earliest computers were programmed entirely in machine language. Programmers would write out the symbolic programmes on sheets of paper, hand assemble them into machine code and then toggle the machine code into the computer, or perhaps punch it on paper tape or cards. If the programmer used symbolic addresses at all, the symbols were bound to addresses as the programmer did his or her hand translation.

If it turned out that an instruction had to be added or deleted, the entire programme had to be hand-inspected and any addresses affected by the added or deleted instruction adjusted. The problem was that the names were bound to addresses too early. Assemblers solved that problem by letting programmers write programmes in terms of symbolic names, with the assembler binding the names to machine addresses. If the programme changed, the programmer had to reassemble it, but the work of assigning the addresses is pushed off from the programmer to the computer.

Libraries of code compound the address assignment problem. Since the basic operations that computers can perform are so simple, useful programmes are composed of subprograms that perform higher level and more complex operations. Computer installations keep a library of pre-written and debugged subprograms that programmers can draw upon to use in new programmes they write, rather than requiring programmers to write all their own subprograms.

The programmer then loads the subprograms in with the main programme to form a complete working programme. Programmers were using libraries of subprograms even before they used assemblers. By 1947, John Mauchly, who led the ENIAC project, wrote about loading programmes along with subprograms selected from a catalog of programmes stored on tapes, and of the need to relocate the subprograms' code to reflect the addresses at which they were loaded.

Perhaps surprisingly, these two basic linker functions, relocation and library search, appear to predate even assemblers, as Mauchly expected both the programme and subprograms to be written in machine language. The relocating loader allowed the authors and users of the subprograms to write each subprogram as though it would start at location zero, and to defer the actual address binding until the subprograms were linked with a particular main programme.

With the advent of operating systems, relocating loaders separate from linkers and libraries became necessary. Before operating systems, each programme had the machine's entire memory at its disposal, so the programme could be assembled and linked for fixed memory addresses, knowing that all addresses in the computer would be available.

But with operating systems, the programme had to share the computer's memory with the operating system and perhaps even with other programmes, This means that the actual addresses at which the programme would be running weren't known until the operating system loaded the programme into memory, deferring final address binding past link time to load time.

Linkers and loaders now divided up the work, with linkers doing part of the address binding, assigning relative addresses within each programme, and the loader doing a final relocation step to assign actual addresses. As systems became more complex, they called upon linkers to do more and more complex name management and address binding.

Fortran programmes used multiple subprograms and common blocks, areas of data shared by multiple subprograms, and it was up to the linker to lay out storage and assign the addresses both for the subprograms and the common blocks. Linkers increasingly had to deal with object code libraries.

Including both application libraries written in Fortran and other languages, and compiler support libraries called implicitly from compiled code to handle I/O and other high-level operations. Programmes quickly became larger than available memory, so linkers provided overlays, a technique that let programmers arrange for different parts of a programme to share the same memory, with each overlay loaded on demand when another part of the programme called into it.

Overlays were widely used on mainframes from the advent of disks around 1960 until the spread of virtual memory in the mid-1970s, then reappeared on microcomputers in the early 1980s in exactly the same form, and faded as virtual memory appeared on PCs in the 1990s.

They're still used in memory limited embedded environments, and may yet reappear in other places where precise programmer or compiler control of memory usage improves performance. With the advent of hardware relocation and virtual memory, linkers and loaders actually got less complex, since each programme could again have an entire address space.

Programmes could be linked to be loaded at fixed addresses, with hardware rather than software relocation taking care of any load-time relocation. But computers with hardware relocation invariably run more than one programme, frequently multiple copies of the same programme.

When a computer runs multiple instances of one programme, some parts of the programme are the same among all running instance (the executable code, in particular), while other parts are unique to each instance. If the parts that don't change can be separated out from the parts that do change, the operating system can use a single copy of the unchanging part, saving considerable storage. Compilers and assemblers were modified to create object code in multiple sections, with one section for read only code and another section for writable data, the linker had to be able to combine all of sections of each type so that the linked programme would have all the code in one place and all of the data in another. This didn't delay address binding any more than it already was, since addresses were still assigned at link time, but more work was deferred to the linker to assign addresses for all the sections.

## LINKER ACTION

### Programme Loading

Copy a programme from secondary storage (which since about 1968 invariably means a disk) into main memory so it's ready to run. In some cases loading just involves copying the data from disk to memory, in others it involves allocating storage, setting protection bits, or arranging for virtual memory to map virtual addresses to disk pages.

### Relocation

Compilers and assemblers generally create each file of object code with the programme addresses starting at zero, but few computers let you load your programme at location zero. If a programme is created from multiple subprograms, all the subprograms have to be loaded at non-overlapping addresses. Relocation is the process of assigning load addresses to the various parts of the programme, adjusting the code and data in the programme to reflect the assigned addresses.

In many systems, relocation happens more than once. It's quite common for a linker to create a programme from multiple subprograms, and create one linked output progra-mme that starts at zero, with the various subprograms relocated to locations within the big programme. Then when the programme is loaded, the system picks the actual load address and the linked programme is relocated as a whole to the load address.

### Symbol Resolution

When a programme is built from multiple subprograms, the references from one subprogram to another are made using symbols; a main programme might use a square root routine called sqrt, and the math library defines sqrt. A linker resolves the symbol by noting the location assigned to sqrt in the library, and patching the caller's object code to so the call instruction refers to that location.

Although there's considerable overlap between linking and loading, it's reasonable to define a programme that does programme loading as a loader, and one that does symbol resolution as a linker. Either can do relocation, and there have been all-in-one linking loaders that do all three functions. The line between relocation and symbol resolution can be fuzzy. Since linkers already can resolve references to symbols, one way to handle code relocation is to assign a symbol to the base address of each part of the programme, and treat relocatable addresses as references to the base address symbols.

## TWO-PASS LINKING PROCESS

Now we turn to the general structure of linkers. Linking, like compiling or assembling, is fundamentally a two pass process. A linker takes as its input a set of input object files, libraries, and perhaps command files, and produces as its result an output object file, and perhaps ancillary information such as a load map or a file containing debugger symbols.

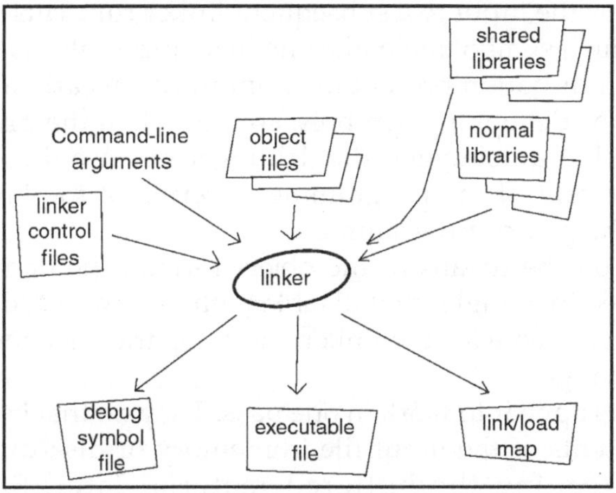


Each input file contains a set of *segments*, contiguous chunks of code or data to be placed in the output file. Each input file also contains at least one *symbol table*. Some symbols are exported, defined within the file for use in other files, generally the names of routines within the file that can be called from elsewhere. Other symbols are imported, used in the file but not defined, generally the names of routines called from but not present in the file.

When a linker runs, it first has to scan the input files to find the sizes of the segments and to collect the definitions and references of all of the symbols It creates a segment table listing all of the segments defined in the input files, and a symbol table with all of the symbols imported or exported.

Using the data from the first pass, the linker assigns numeric locations to symbols, determines the sizes and location of the segments in the output address space, and figures out where everything goes in the output file. The second pass uses the information collected in the first pass to control the actual linking process. It reads and relocates the object code, substituting numeric addresses for symbol references, and adjusting memory addresses in code and data to reflect relocated segment addresses, and writes the relocated code to the output file. It then writes the output file, generally with header information, the relocated segments, and symbol table information. If the programme uses dynamic linking, the symbol table contains the info the runtime linker will need to resolve dynamic symbols.

In many cases, the linker itself will generate small amounts of code or data in the output file, such as "glue code" used to call routines in overlays or dynamically linked libraries, or an array of pointers to initialization routines that need to be called at programme startup time. Whether or not the programme uses dynamic linking, the file may also contain a symbol table for relinking or debugging that isn't used by the programme itself, but may be used by other programmes that deal with the output file.

Some object formats are relinkable, that is, the output file from one linker run can be used as the input to a subsequent linker run. This requires that the output file contain a symbol table like one in an input file, as well as all of the other auxiliary information present in an input file. Nearly all object formats have provision for debugging symbols, so that when the programme is run under the control of a debugger, the debugger can use those symbols to let the programmer control the programme in terms of the line numbers and names used in the source programme.

Depending on the details of the object format, the debugging symbols may be intermixed in a single symbol table with symbols needed by the linker, or there may be one table for the linker and a separate, somewhat redundant table for the debugger.

A few linkers appear to work in one pass. They do that by buffering some or all of the contents of the input file in memory or disk during the linking process, then reading the buffered material later. Since this is an implementation trick that doesn't fundamentally affect the two-pass nature of linking, we don't address it further here.

## RELOCATION AND CODE MODIFICATION

The heart of a linker or loader's actions is relocation and code modification. When a compiler or assembler generates and object file, it generates the code using the unrelocated addresses of code and data defined within the file, and usually zeros for code and data defined elsewhere. As part of the linking process, the linker modifies the object code to reflect the actual addresses assigned. For example, consider this snippet of x86 code that moves the contents of variable a to variable b using the eax register.

If a is defined in the same file at location 1234 hex and b is imported from somewhere else, the generated object code will be: A1 34 12 00 00 mov a,%eax A3 00 00 00 00 mov %eax,b Each instruction contains a one-byte operation code followed by a fourbyte address.

The first instruction has a reference to 1234 (byte reversed, since the x86 uses a right to left byte order) and the second a reference to zero since the location of b is unknown. Now assume that the linker links this code so that the section in which a is located is relocated by hex 10000 bytes, and b turns out to be at hex 9A12.

*The linker modifies the code to be*:

- A1 34 12 01 00 mov a,%eax
- A3 12 9A 00 00 mov %eax,b

That is, it adds 10000 to the address in the first instruction so now it refers to a's relocated address which is 11234, and it patches in the address for b. These adjustments affect instructions, but any pointers in the data part of an object file have to be adjusted as well. On older computers with small address spaces and direct addressing, the modification process is fairly simple, since there are only only one or two address formats that a linker has to handle.

Modern computers, including all RISCs, require considerably more complex code modification. No single instruction contains enough bits to hold a direct address, so the compiler and linker have to use complicated addressing tricks to handle data at arbitrary addresses. In some cases, it's possible to concoct an address using two or three instructions, each of which contains part of the address, and use bit manipulation to combine the parts into a full address.

In this case, the linker has to be prepared to modify each of the instructions appropriately, inserting some of the bits of the address into each instruction. In other cases, all of the addresses used by a routine or group of routines are placed in an array used as an "address pool", initialization code sets one of the machine registers to point to that array, and code loads pointers out of the address pool as needed using that register as a base register. The linker may have to create the array from all of the addresses used in a programme, then modify instructions that so that they refer to the appropriate address pool entry.

## LINKER COMMAND LANGUAGES

Every linker has some sort of command language to control the linking process. At the very least the linker needs the list of object files and libraries to link. Generally there is a long list of possible options: whether to keep debugging symbols, whether to use shared or unshared libraries, which of several possible output formats to use.

Most linkers permit some way to specify the address at which the linked code is to be bound, which comes in handy when using a linker to link a system kernel or other programme that doesn't run under control of an operating system. In linkers that support multiple code and data segments, a linker command language can specify the order in which segments are to be linked, special treatment for certain kinds of segments, and other application-specific options.

- *Command line:* Most systems have a command line or the equivalent, via which one can pass a mixture of file names and switches. This is the usual approach for Unix and Windows linkers. On systems with limited length command lines, there's usually a way to direct the linker to read commands from a file and treat them as though they were on the command line.

### Intermixed with Object Files

Some linkers, such as IBM mainframe linkers, accept alternating object files and linker commands in a single input file. This dates from the era of card decks, when one would pile up object decks and hand-punched command cards in a card reader.

### Embedded in Object Files

Some object formats, notably Microsoft's, permit linker commands to be embedded inside object files. This permits a compiler to pass any options needed to link an object file in the file itself. For example, the C compiler passes commands to search the standard C library.

### Separate Configuration Language

A few linkers have a full fledged configuration language to control linking. The GNU linker, which can handle an enormous range of object file formats, machine architectures, and address space conventions, has a complex control language that lets a programmer specify the order in which segments should be linked, rules for combining similar segments, segment addresses, and a wide range of other options. Other linkers have less complex languages to handle specific features such as programmer-defined overlays.

## LOADER

It is the Loader's function to fix absolute addresses for the relocated values in a relocatable module, thereby converting a relocatable module into an "executable" output file. The Loader is usually called automatically by the Linker but it may also be called separately by the user. As indicated below, several different Loaders are (optionally) available for use with Introl-C and, if the user has elected to obtain such optional Loaders, a variety of executable output file formats can be generated, depending on the Loader being used.

Each resident Introl-C compiler package, and each Introl-C cross-compiler package, nominally includes a single, specific type of Introl Loader which is considered as being the "standard" Loader for that compiler's particular host system configuration. For resident Introl-C Compiler packages, the 'standard' Loader that is furnished is an "operating system dependent" type of Loader which generates an output file that is executable on that particular Compiler's host system.

For cross-compiler versions of Introl-C, the "standard" Loader furnished is typically a "hex" type Loader that generates a file of output load records, which can be either Motorola S-Records, intel Hex, Tektronix Hex, or Tektronix Extended Hex at user option. Besides the "standard" Loader that accompanies any given Compiler type, it is also possible for the user to optionally obtain and use other compatible "cross-Loaders" which generate output formats unrelated to the Compiler's host operating system. For example, "hex-type" Loaders are optionally available for use with resident versions of Introl-C; "operating system dependent" type Loaders are optionally available for use with cross-compiler versions; etc.

There are, therefore, several different species of Loaders, (as well as several different types of related Standard Libraries) that may potentially be used under Introl-C. The "standard" Loader supplied with your Introl-C package, as well as any other Loaders that may have been optionally ordered, are described in detail in the Loader Appendix of this Linker Reference Manual. This Loader section describes the general features that are common to all Loader types. Normally the input to the Loader is expected to be a relocatable file which has no unresolved external references; if unresolved references do exist in its input, loading will normally not be successful.

A Loader option is provided, however, to force a file to be loaded even if it contains unresolved references. Usually a relocatable file has to be linked before it can be used as input to the Loader. It is also possible, of course, to assemble a file which makes no external references and then use the relocatable output file produced by the Assembler directly as input to the Loader (ie without having actually linked it)

## LOADER COMMAND LINE

The "standard" Loader supplied with your Introl-C package is normally automatically called by the Linker when the Linker pass finishes. However, linker command line options exist (see Linker Section of this manual) that mav be used to alternatively force the Linker to automatically call other optional Loaders. Situations also arise when it is desirable to explicitly call the Loader alone, without first executing the Linker. When such situations arise, the Loader may be independently called by the user with a loader command line of the general form:

```
<c>ld <file> {<option>}
```

where <c>ld represents the Introl filename of the specific Loader being called, <file> is the name of the (linked) relocatable module which is to be loaded, and (<option>) represents zero or more Loader option specifiers.

Each of the potentially usable Introl Loaders is uniquely identified by a 3-letter Loader filename, the last two letters of which are always "ld". The <c> designator indicated in the "<c>ld" loader call on the command line therefore represents the first letter in the three-letter Loader name.

For example, to call the Introl hex type of Loader, which has the filename "hld", the "<c>ld" entry on the command line would actually become "hld". For further specifics on the names of the loaders which can be legally accessed. The relocatable file that is input to the Loader is expected to have a filenarne extension; if none is specified, the default filename extension ".RL" is assumed.

Normally the name of the executable output file will be identical to the name of the input file, but with a filename extension typically added by the Loader. The filename extensions each Loader appends are discussed in the Loader Appendices to this manual.

**LOADER OPTIONS**

Each type of Loader available for use with the Introl-C has its own, generally unique set of options. When the Loader is being called separately, Loader options are specified directly on the loader command line when the Loader is being automatically called by the Linker, Loader options are specified on the link command line, together with the Linker options.

If Loader options are specified on the link command line, any such options (ie those that do not apply to the Linker) will be automatically sent on to the Loader. For the most part Linker and Loader option specifiers tend to be distinct, so that there is little ambiguity when Loader options are specified on the link command line.

**LIBRARY FILES**

A library file is a file which contains one or more linkable object modules of the type produced by the Introl Assembler. When a file is compiled and assembled, the result is exactly one linkable module which is placed into a file. This file is actually a library which happens to contain only a single module. When the user links a programme, one or more of these "libraries" are specified on the link command line. Usually the "libraries" are those produced as a result of a compilation and contain only a single module, however, they may also contain several modules.

The Library Manager, "libman", is a programme which allows the user to place several modules into a single library file. When the user has a large set of modules which are commonly used in programmes, it is usually convenient to place them all in one library and then simply specify the library once on the link command line. The Linker will extract only those modules it requires in order to satisfy the external references of the programme.

The Linker is designed to automatically search the "Standard Library", libc.R, if it still has external references to satisfy after it has exhausted all the alternatives provided by the modules specified an the link command line. For many C programmes, the Standard Library is usually where most of the external references are satisfied. Many users find it useful to add to, or modify routines in, the Standard Library. The Library Manager is the utility programme which allows the user to create new libraries and also to maintain existing ones.

## MODES OF OPERATION

The Library Manager has three modes of operation: Direct Mode, Interactive Mode, and Command File Mode. The most convenient to use for simple additions and deletions to the library is the Direct Mode. For more extensive modifications the user may instead wish to use Interactive mode. The third mode is the Command File mode which causes the Library Manager to read its commands from a file rather than getting them from the user terminal.

*Direct Mode*: In Direct Mode the user is permitted to specify a single command on the library manager command line. When the Library Manager is called, it executes this single command function and then immediately exits from the Library Manager.

When modifying libraries, however, a single command function is often all that is necessary to accomplish the change desired by the user. When Direct Mode is being used, the desired command is specified right on the command line, following the <lib> library specification. Any Library Manager command may be used in the Direct Mode. Interactive Mode: if no command is specified on the Library Manager call line, the Library Manager will enter its Interactive Mode of operation.

In Interactive Mode the Library Manager will print a colon (".") as a promet and will accept a succession of commands directly from the user terminal.

Interactive Mode is useful when the user must make extensive changes to a library, or when the user wishes to step through the library checking and/or changing modules in an "interactive" manner. Once selected, the Interactive Mode will remain in effect until the user enters a "quit" or "omit" command.

Command File Mode: One of the commands which the user can specify as an Interactive code or a Direct Mode command entry is the "Comfile" command. This command instructs the Library Manager to read subsequent instructions from a command file.

When a "Comfile command is entered, the Library Manager will read from the file specified until it reads a "quit" or "omit" command or, alternatively, until it reaches the end of the file. when exiting the Command File Mode, the Library Manager will return to whatever mode it was in before the Command File Mode was entered. If the Command File Mode was entered as the result of a Direct Mode command, then the Library Manager will terminate when Command File Mode is exited. If entered from the Interactive Mode, it will return to the Interactive Mode.

# ASSEMBLER

## DEFINITION

An assembler is a programme that converts simple commands into machine code. The simple commands, written in an assembly language, are used in groups to perform more complicated tasks.

## FUNCTION

The function of the assembler is to translate programmes written in the assembler language into object modules. The code will then be in a suitable form for processing by the Linkage Editor. The assembler language is a symbolic representation of machine language.

The correspondence between the two can be best understood by examining the listings produced by an assembler. The assembler, like the linkage editor, is supplied as part of VSE, CMS, and MVS, and executes under control of the appropriate control programme. It accepts, as input, a source programme written in the Assembler Language.

*This consists of three types of instructions*:

- C Machine instructions.
- C Assembler instructions.
- C Macro instructions.

As expected with an IBM language, code can also be copied in from a source statement library (VSE) or a pds (MVS) or MACLIB (CMS).

## SEGMENTS AND OFFSETS IN ASSEMBLER

The original designers of the 8088, decided that nobody will every need to use more that one megabyte of memory. So they built the machine so it couldn't access above that. The problem is to access a whole megabyte 20 bits are needed (one bit being either a one or a zero).

Registers only have 16 bits, and they didn't want to use two because that would be 32 bits and that was too much for anyone. They decided to do the addressing with two registers but not 32 bits. Is this confusing? Blame the designers of the 8088.

```
OFFSET = SEGMENT * 16
SEGMENT = OFFSET / 16 (the lower 4 bits are lost)
SEGMENT * 16 |0010010000010000—-| range (0 to 65535) * 16
+OFFSET |—-0100100000100010| range (0 to 65535)
=20 bit address |00101000100100100010| range 0 to 1048575 (1
MEG)
 ====== DS ======
 ====== SI ======
```

(note DS and SI overlap). This is how DS:SI is used to make a 20 bit address. The segment is in DS and the offset is in SI.

*Segment registers are*: CS, DS, ES, SS. On the 386+ there are also FS & GS. *Offset registers are*: BX, DI, SI, BP, SP, IP. In 386+ protected mode, ANY general register (not a segment register) can be used as an Offset register. (Except IP, which you can't access.)

**REGISTERS**

- *AX*: This is split into half - into AL and AH (for low and high). They store the high part and the low part of the number in ax.
- *BX (BH/BL)*: Same as AX
- *CX (CH/CL)*: Same as AX (used for loops)
- *DX (DH/DL)*: Same as AX (used for multiplication/division)
- *DI and SI*: Are index registers and can be used as offset registers.
- *SP*: Stack Pointer. Does just that. Points to the current position in the stack. *Don't* alter unless you REALLY know what you are doing.

## INTERPRETER

**DEFINITION**

- An interpreter runs programme code by converting it to machine code on the fly. You save some time in the front by avoiding the compiling and linking steps, but interpreters generally run slower because they have to convert the same code (in a loop, say) again and again. An example of a common interpreter is the one that executes, bat files.
- An *interpreter* is also a programme that translates a high-level language into a low-level one, but it does it at the moment the programme is run. You write the programme using a text editor or something similar, and then instruct the interpreter to run the programme. It takes the programme, one line at a time, and translates each line before running it: It translates the first line and runs it, then translates the second line and runs it etc. The interpreter has no "memory" for the translated lines, so if it comes across lines of the programme within a loop, it must translate them afresh every time that particular line runs.
  *Consider this simple Basic programme*:
- 10 FOR COUNT = 1 TO 1000
- 20 PRINT COUNT * COUNT
- 30 NEXT COUNT
- Line 20 of the programme displays the square of the value stored in COUNT and this line has to be carried out 1000 times. The interpreter must also translate that line 1000 times, which is clearly an inefficient process. However, interpreted languages do have their uses, as we will see in a later section.

- Examples of interpreted languages are Basic, JavaScript and LISP
- The Interpreter pattern discusses: defining a domain language (i.e. problem characterization) as a simple language grammar, representing domain rules as language sentences, and interpreting these sentences to solve the problem. The pattern uses a class to represent each grammar rule. And since grammars are usually hierarchical in structure, an inheritance hierarchy of rule classes maps nicely.
- An abstract base class specifies the method interpret(). Each concrete subclass implements interpret() by accepting (as an argument) the current state of the language stream, and adding its contribution to the problem solving process.

## STRUCTURE

- Interpreter suggests modeling the domain with a recursive grammar. Each rule in the grammar is either a "composite" (a rule that references other rules) or a terminal (a leaf node in a tree structure). Interpreter relies on the recursive traversal of the Composite pattern to interpret the "sentences" it is asked to process.

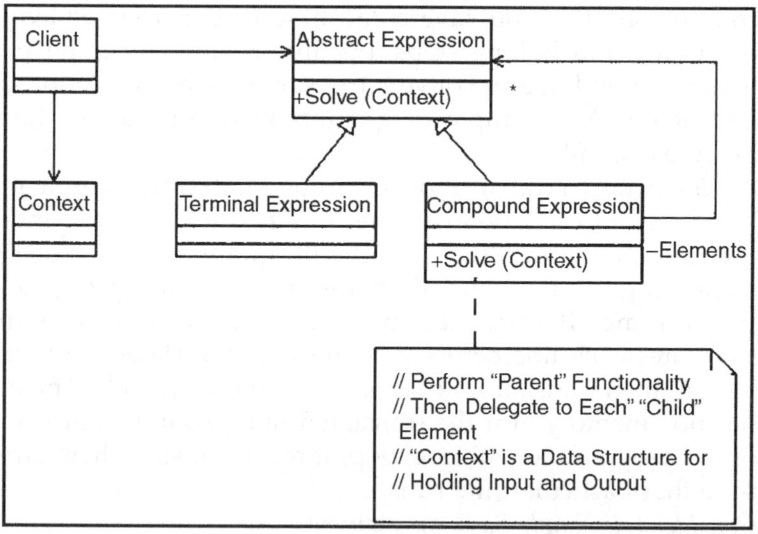


## Example

- The Interpreter pattern defines a grammatical representation for a language and an interpreter to interpret the grammar. Musicians are examples of Interpreters. The pitch of a sound and its duration can be represented in musical notation on a staff. This notation provides the language of music. Musicians playing the music from the score are able to reproduce the original pitch and duration of each sound represented.

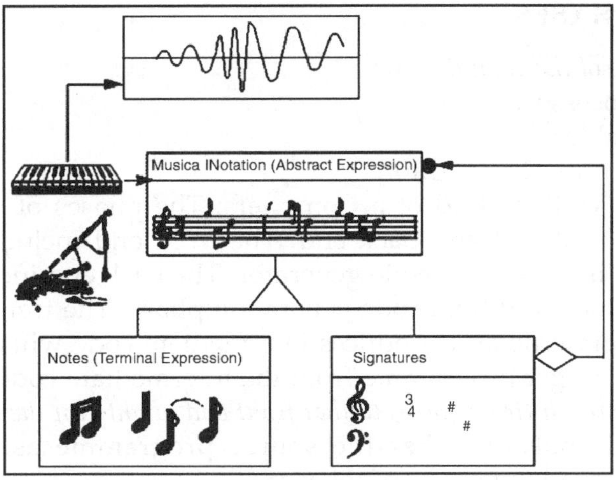


**COMPILER**

## DEFINITION

A compiler completely converts programme code to machine code once. The computer user runs the machine code in the form of an executable command, ending in .exe say. Because the translation is complete before execution, compiled code is much faster. The translation process should also report the presence of errors in the source programme.

Source Programme → Compiler → Target Programme
↓
Error Messages

There are two parts of compilation. The analysis part breaks up the source programme into constant piece and creates an intermediate representation of the source programme. The synthesis part constructs the desired target programme from the intermediate representation. *Compilers* were the first sort of translator programme to be written. The idea is simple: You write the programme, then hand it to the compiler which translates it. Then run the result.

The compiler takes the file that you have written and produces another file from it. In the case of Pascal programmes, for instance, you might write a programme called my Prog.pas and the Pascal compiler would translate it into the file myProg.exe which you could then run. If you tried to examine the contents of myProg.exe using, say, a text editor, then it would just appear as gobbledy-gook.

The compiler has another task apart from translating your programme. It also checks it to make sure that it is grammatically correct. Only when it is sure that there are no grammatical errors does it do the translation. Any errors that the compiler detects are called compile-time errors or syntax errors. If it finds so much as one syntax error, it stops compiling and reports the error to you. Here is an example of the C++ compiler reporting a whole list of errors:

## COMPILER PHASES

*The cousins of the compiler are*:

- Preprocessor.
- Assembler.
- Loader and Link-editor.

Front End vs Back End of a Compilers. The phases of a compiler are collected into front end and back end. The front end includes all analysis phases end the intermediate code generator. The back end includes the code optimization phase and final code generation phase. The front end analyzes the source programme and produces intermediate code while the back end synthesizes the target programme from the intermediate code.

*A naive approach (front force) to that front end might run the phases serially*:

- Lexical analyzer takes the source programme as an input and produces a long string of tokens.
- Syntax Analyzer takes an out of lexical analyzer and produces a large tree.
- Semantic analyzer takes the output of syntax analyzer and produces another tree.
- Similarly, intermediate code generator takes a tree as an input produced by semantic analyzer and produces intermediate code.

### Minus Points

- Requires enormous amount of space to store tokens and trees.
- Very slow since each phase would have to input and output to and from temporary disk

### Remedy

- use syntax directed translation to inter leaves the actions of phases.
- Compiler construction tools.

### Parser Generators

The specification of input based on regular expression. The organization is based on finite automation.

### Scanner Generator

The specification of input based on regular expression. The organization is based on finite automation.

### Syntax-Directed Translation

It walks the parse tee and as a result generate intermediate code.

### Automatic Code Generators

Translates intermediate rampage into machine language.

### Data-Flow Engines

It does code optimization using data-flow analysis.

## WORKING OF COMPILER

Compiling a programme takes several stages of processing, which outlined as shown. The principles which are explained below also apply to interpreters, with the exception that the interpreters translate each programme one line at a time before running it, and then moving on to the next line.

### Tokenising

This part of the process is also sometimes called *Lexical Analysis*. It involves turning the programme from a series of characters into a series of *tokens* that represent the building blocks of a programme. The tokens are keywords of the language i.e. important words such as *if, print* or *repeat*), variable names and mathematical operators (+, *, brackets etc.). The tokeniser takes each of the characters in turn, and as soon as it recognises a legitimate token, it reports it to the next stage of the process.

Each token has a label and a type, so a variable "count" in a programme would have the label corresponding to its name ("count") and the type "variable name". The tokeniser is also responsible for ignoring comments in the programme - these are words and phrases inserted purely for the benefit of any human reading the programme, and they have no function.

### Syntax Analysis

Syntax means "grammar" and the syntax analyser in a compiler checks that the right tokens appear in the right order to make grammatically correct instructions. For instance, in C++, the instruction xyz++; is syntactically correct, but the instruction +;xyz+is not - the order of the tokens is wrong.

### Semantic Analysis

The word "semantics" refers to *meaning*, and the semantic analyser checks the meaning of the programme. This refers to aspects such as whether the variables have been declared, e.g. xyz++; may be syntactically correct, but if the variable xyz has not been declared, then it is semantically incorrect!

The semantic analyser checks not only variable declarations and scope, but whether the programme has entered or left loops, or subroutines, whether classes are accessed correctly etc.

## ADVANTAGES

Choosing the right C compiler for your embedded-system projects may be a bigger challenge than you expect. The embedded-system-industry trend is moving from using assembly to using the higher level languages. Assembly language gives you more control over your code size and execution speeds. However, embedded C is easy to understand and portable from platform to platform.

Another benefit is that developing code in C generally improves your product time to market. These features are advantageous if you expect your firmware to have longevity or if your staff changes periodically. A variety of embedded-C compilers is available in the market today. Embedded-C compilers are available as shareware from controller- or processor-IC vendors; or from high-end, reputable software companies whose selling prices often reflect the sophistication of the software. Some compiler-software companies have great advertisements and competitive prices but inferior products. So, how do you choose your compiler software for now and for the future?

There are many issues to consider when choosing your compiler. The most important are ANSI compliance, size and speed optimizations, portability, and supporting tools.

Adherence to the ANSI standard for the C language is critical for about 80 to 85% of code. This feature facilitates portability from part to part, as well as from software platform to software platform. ANSI-compliant software also integrates easy-to-understand code into your library. This type of code—if it is well-written—will have a shelf life like a good red wine. Even if portability is not an issue, it is important to understand how the compiler differs from ANSI and whether those differences will impact your development.

If the compiler of interest is ANSI-compliant, you should then examine the software's machine-code-generation capability. You might ask whether the compiler output code is optimized for small code (because memory is precious in controllers or processors) or whether the application executes in a timely or time-accurate manner. These features are somewhat mutually exclusive, but the compiler software should be able to optimize one or the other.

Portability between platforms is critical in larger companies that have a diverse range of products. However, it can also be convenient in smaller companies that may want the flexibility to quickly change controllers during development. Portability allows you to change quickly from one controller to another during application development. It also makes your code libraries more valuable over time.

If you want to easily complete your programming projects, the compiler cannot stand on its own. Every compiler needs an integrated suite of other tools. This tool suite should have, at a minimum, an integrated development environment that comes complete with a simulator and a hardware-debugging interface. Sometimes, you can mix and match these tools from other vendors, but use the vendor for your compiler as a first source. It can be difficult and frustrating to mix and then match tools from various vendors.

Some other characteristics that make up a good compiler are the availability of code libraries and library support. This concept does not fit into organizations with the NIH (not-invented-here) philosophy. An NIH organization deserves everything it gets (or doesn't get). Libraries with code that implements useful functions help expedite your projects to completion. Many times, these libraries have gone through evaluations and debugging to ensure their value.

Some of the final details in your compiler evaluation have to do with customer service. You need to ask whether your compiler company supports your questions and helps with its software bugs. You will find this information in the company's application-notes library, discussion forums, and software-release history. Although frequent releases can be a sign of responsiveness, they can also be an indication of serious stability concerns. The ideal compiler vendor has more support than you'll ever need.

In the past, most firmware designers would write embedded-firmware programmes in assembly language. The embedded-C compiler transforms your source code into machine code. The C compiler you use determines the size as well as the execution time of your code. Many ways exist for determining these factors, so running your own test programmes is also important. Don't depend on the results from a compiler-software company that runs its own tests. Many times, these companies can consciously or unconsciously skew the results.

# 13

# Computer and Marginal Costing

## MARGINAL AND ABSORPTION COSTING

### CHARACTERISTICS

Marginal costing is also termed as variable costing, a technique of costing which includes only variable manufacturing costs, in the form of direct materials, direct labour, and variable manufacturing overheads while determining the cost per unit of a product. Where as Absorption costing, is a costing technique that includes all maufacturing costs, in the form of direct materials, direct labour, and both variable and fixed manufacturing overheads, while determining the cost per unit of a product. It is also referred to as the full- cost technique.

In the costing of product/service, a marginal costing technique considers the behavioural characteristics of costs (segregations of costs into fixed and variable elements), because per unit variable cost is fixed and total costs are variable in nature, where as total fixed costs are fixed and per unit fixed cost is variable in nature and furthermore variable costs are controllable in nature, while total fixed costs are un-controllable in nature. Marginal costing is useful for short-term planning, control and decision-making, particularly in a business where multi-products are produced. In marginal costing technique, the contribution is calculated after deducting variable costs from sales value with reference to each product or service, in order to calculate the total contribution from all products/services which are made towards the total fixed costs incurred by the business. As the fixed costs are treated as period costs, are deducted from total contribution to arrive at net profit. In the context of costing of a product/ service, an absorption costing considers a share of all costs incurred by a business to each of its products/services. In absorption costing technique; costs are classified according to their functions. The gross profit is calculated after deducting production costs from sales and from gross profit, costs incurred in relation to other business functions are deducted to arrive at the net profit.

Absorption costing gives better information for pricing products as it includes both variable and fixed costs. Marginal costing may lead to lower prices being offered if the firm is operating below capacity. Customers may still expect these lower prices as demand/capacity increases.

## Profit Statements

The net profit shown by marginal costing and absorption costing techniques may not be the same due to the different treatment of fixed manufacturing overheads. Marginal costing technique treats fixed manufacturing overheads as period costs, where as in absorption costing technique these are absorbed into the cost of goods produced and are only charged against profit in the period in which those goods are sold. In absorption costing income statement, adjustment pertaining to under or over-absorption of overheads is also made to arrive at the profit.

## TERMS

### Product and Period Costs

- *Product costs*: The costs of manufacturing the products;
- *Period costs*: These are the costs other than product costs that are charged to, debited to, or written off to the income statement each period.

*A Case Example on Marginal and Absorption Costing*:

**Table. Data for a Quarter for a Manufacturing Company**

| **Level of Activity** | **60%** | **100%** |
|---|---|---|
| Sales and Production(Units) | 36,000 | 60,000 |
| | Rs. ('000) | Rs. ('000) |
| Sales | 432 | 720 |
| Production costs: (Variable and fixed) | 366 | 510 |
| Sales, distribution and administration costs (Variable and fixed) | 126 | 150 |

The normal level of activity for the current year is 60,000 units, and fixed costs are incurred evenly throughout the year. There were no stocks of the product at the start of the quarter, in which 16,500 units were made and 13,500 units were sold. Actual fixed costs were the same as budgeted. Then, various calculations regarding Absorption vs. Marginal costing can be worked out as under:

| | **Production Costs (Rs.)** | **Sales etc costs (Rs.)** |
|---|---|---|
| Total costs of 60,000 units (fixed plus variable) | 5,10,000 | 1,50,000 |
| Total costs of 36,000 units (fixed plus variable) | 3,66,000 | 1,26,000 |
| Difference = variable costs of 24,000 units | 1,44,000 | 24,000 |
| Variable costs per unit | Rs.6 | Re.1 |
| | Production Costs (Rs.) | Sales etc. Costs (Rs.) |
| Total costs of 60,000 units | 5,10,000 | 1,50,00<br>0 |
| Variable costs of 60,000 units | 3,60,000 | 60,000 |
| Fixed costs | 1,50,000 | 90,000 |

The rate of absorption of fixed production overheads will therefore be:

Rs.1,50,000 ÷ 60,000 = Rs. 2.50 per unit.

- The fixed production overhead absorbed by the products would be 16,500 units produced × Rs. 2.50 = Rs. 41,250
- Budgeted annual fixed production overhead = Rs.1,50,000

| | Rs. |
|---|---|
| Actual quarterly fixed production overhead = budgeted quarterly fixed production overhead (1,50,000 ÷ 4) | 37,500 |
| Production overhead absorbed into production [see (i) above] | 41,250 |
| Over -absorption of fixed production overhead | 3,750 |

- Profit statement for the quarter, using Absorption Costing

| | Rs. | Rs. | Rs. |
|---|---|---|---|
| Sales (13,500× Rs.12) | | | 1,62,000 |
| Costs of production (no opening stocks) | | | |
| Value of stocks produced (16,500 × Rs. 8.50) | | 1,40,250 | |
| Less value of closing stock | | | |
| (3,000 units × full production cost of Rs. 8.50) | | (25,500) | |
| | | 1,14,750 | |
| Sales etc costs | | | |
| Variable (13,500 × Re. 1) | 13,500 | | |
| Fixed (1/4 of Rs. 90,000) | 22,500 | | |
| | | 36,000 | |
| Total cost of sales | | 1,50,750 | |
| Less over-absorbed production overhead | | 3,750 | |
| | | | 1,47,000 |
| Profit | | | 15,000 |

– Profit statement for the quarter using Marginal Costing

| | Rs. | Rs. |
|---|---|---|
| Sales (13,500×Rs.12) | | 1,62,000 |
| Variable costs of production (16,500 × Rs. 6) | 99,000 | |
| Less value of closing stocks (3,000 × Rs. 6) | 18,000 | |
| Variable production cost of sales | 81,000 | |
| Variable sales etc. costs (13,500 × Re.1) | 13,500 | |
| Total variable cost of sales (13,500 × Rs. 7) | | 94,500 |
| Contribution (13,500 × Rs. 5) | | 67,500 |
| Fixed Costs: Production | 37,500 | |
| Sales etc. | 22,500 | |
| | | 60,000 |
| Profit | | 7,500 |

## ABSORPTION AND MARGINAL COSTING SYSTEMS

A popular topic for examination at Foundation Level has been the preparation of profit statements in both absorption and marginal costing formats, and the reconciliation of the profits reported by the two systems.

*Example*: A company sells a single product at a price of £14 per unit. Variable manufacturing costs of the product are £6.40 per unit. Fixed manufacturing overheads, which are absorbed into the cost of production at a unit rate (based on normal activity of 20,000 units per period), are £92,000 per period. Any over-absorbed or under-absorbed fixed manufacturing overhead balances are transferred to the profit and loss account at the end of each period, in order to establish the manufacturing profit.

*Sales and production (in units) for two periods are as follows:*

| | Period 1 | Period 2 |
|---|---|---|
| Sales | 15,000 | 21,600 |
| Production | 18,000 | 21,000 |

*Required*:

- Prepare a trading statement to identify the manufacturing profit for Period 2 using the existing absorption costing method.
- Determine the manufacturing profit that would be reported in Period 2 if marginal costing was used.
- Explain, with supporting calculations, why the manufacturing profit in.

## ABSORPTION COSTING PRINCIPLES

In product/service costing, an absorption costing system allocates or apportions a share of all costs incurred by a business to each of its products/services. In this way, it can be established whether, in the long run, each product/service makes a profit. This can only be a guide. Arbitrary assumptions have to be made about the apportionment of many of the costs which, given that some costs will tend to remain fixed during a period, will also be dependent on the level of activity. An absorption costing system traditionally classifies costs by function. Sales less production costs (of sales) measures the gross profit (manufacturing profit) earned. Gross profit less costs incurred in other business functions establishes the net profit (operating profit) earned.

Using an absorption costing system, the profit reported for a manufacturing business for a period will be influenced by the level of production as well as by the level of sales. This is because of the absorption of fixed manufacturing overheads into the value of work-in-progress and finished goods stocks. If stocks remain at the end of an accounting period, then the fixed manufacturing overhead costs included within the stock valuation will be transferred to the following period.

## ABSORPTION COSTING PROFIT STATEMENT

The first stage in the preparation of absorption costing profit statements is the measurement of the gross profit (manufacturing profit) earned. This requires the calculation of unit production costs, including the establishment of absorption rates for manufacturing overheads. Referring to the example being used for illustration in this article (see earlier), variable manufacturing costs per units are given in the question (at £6.40 per unit). Fixed manufacturing overheads of £92,000 per period are to be absorbed at a unit rate (based on normal production activity of 20,000 units per period). The fixed manufacturing overhead absorption rate is therefore £4.60 per unit (£92,000 ¸ 20,000 units) giving a total manufacturing cost of £11.00 per unit (£6.40 + £4.60).

The use of normal activity as the basis for overhead absorption is similar to the use of budgeted activity. It is to be expected that actual activity (and indeed actual expenditure also) will be different to normal/budget thus giving rise to overhead over or under absorption. It is important that this is highlighted in profit statements. The use of normal (or budgeted) activity and expenditure to establish the absorption rate not only helps to focus attention on overhead recovery but also has the effect of 'normalising' per unit product/service costs.

Referring again to the example, fixed manufacturing overheads will be over-absorbed in Period 2 because the actual production of 21,000 units exceeds the normal activity, the basis used to establish the absorption rate, by 1,000 units. The extent of the over-absorption (the balance remaining in the fixed manufacturing overhead account) is, therefore, £4,600 (1,000 units at £4.60 per unit). This amount will be transferred to the profit and loss account in order to establish the manufacturing profit. It will have a positive effect (i.e., it will be added to profit) because more manufacturing overhead has been absorbed into stock in the period than has been incurred (see the entries in the fixed manufacturing overhead account demonstrated later in examples).

The Examiner's Report for the June 2000 Paper 3 noted that the over-absorption of fixed manufacturing overhead caused problems for many candidates. It was frequently not identified. Where it was calculated, it was at times described as 'under-absorbed' or was at least treated as such in terms of its impact on the manufacturing profit. Other candidates wrongly calculated the over/under- absorption based upon the difference between sales and production quantities, rather than upon the difference between actual production and normal production. Preparation of the remainder of the trading statement (to identify the manufacturing profit for Period 2 using absorption costing) should be straightforward (see Example 2). The manufacturing cost of sales (the transfer out of the finished goods stock account) is simply the 21,600 units sold in the period (which at a selling price of £14.00 per unit yields total sales for the period of £302,400) multiplied by the unit manufacturing cost of £11.00.

*Example*:

| Period 2 Trading Statement: | £000 | |
|---|---|---|
| Sales | 302.4 | (21,600 units at £14.00 per unit) |
| Manufacturing cost of goods sold | 237.6 | (21,600 units at £11.00 per unit) |
| Manufacturing profit (before adjustment) | 64.8 | (21,600 units at £3.00 per unit) |
| Fixed manufacturing overhead over-absorbed | 4.6 | (1,000 units at £4.60 per unit) |
| Manufacturing profit (after adjustment) | 69.4 | |

The Examiner's Report noted that there were many examples (in the examination scripts marked) of candidates matching the cost of the goods produced in the period (not the manufacturing cost of the goods sold) with sales.

Many examination candidates also got into difficulty because they attempted to introduce stock into the profit statement. There is generally no requirement to do this (unless opening and closing stocks are valued at a different rate per unit) but such an approach should (but often did not) lead to the same profit result.

In this example, no details of stock are provided in the question, but it could be assumed, for example, that 3,000 units were in stock at the end of Period I (production of 18,000 units less sales of 15,000 units). Finished goods stock at the end of Period 2 would then be 2,400 units due to the excess of sales over production of 600 units in that period.

*Example*:

| A trading statement including stock would be. | | |
|---|---|---|
| **Period 2 Trading Statement** | £000 | |
| Sales | 302.4 | |
| Manufacturing cost of goods sold: | | |
| Opening stock of finished goods | 33.0 | (3,000 units at £11.00 per unit) |
| Cost of goods produced | 231.0 | (21,000 units at £11.00 per unit) |
| Closing stock of finished goods | (26.4) | (2,400 units at £11.00 per unit) |
| | 237.6 | |
| Manufacturing profit (before adjustment) | 64.8 | |
| Fixed manufacturing overhead over-absorbed | 4.6 | |

In the adapted question used for illustration is no information provided about costs incurred in other business functions (selling, administration, distribution) and thus it is not possible to complete the profit statement. If information on other costs was available, the costs incurred in the period would simply be deducted from the adjusted manufacturing profit to arrive at net profit.

## MARGINAL COSTING PRINCIPLES

In product/service costing, a marginal costing system emphasises the behavioural, rather than the functional, characteristics of costs. The focus is on separating costs into variable elements (where the cost per unit remains the same with total cost varying in proportion to activity) and fixed elements (where the total cost remains the same in each period regardless of the level of activity).

Whilst this is not easily achieved with accuracy, and is an oversimplification of reality, marginal costing information can be very useful for short-term planning, control and decision-making, especially in a multi-product business. In a marginal costing system, sales less variable costs (regardless of function) measures the contribution that individual products/services make towards the total fixed costs incurred by the business. The fixed costs (regardless of function) are treated as period costs and, as such, are simply deducted from contribution in the period incurred to arrive at net profit.

## MARGINAL COSTING PROFIT STATEMENT

Referring back to Example 1, as there is no information regarding non-manufacturing costs, it may be assumed that sales less variable manufacturing costs measures contribution. NB. If any variable costs are incurred in non-manufacturing functions then they would also be deducted from sales in the measurement of contribution. The trading statement for Period 2, assuming that a marginal costing system was in place instead.

*Example*:

| **Period 2 Trading Statement:** | £000 | |
|---|---|---|
| Sales | 302.40 | |
| Variable cost of goods sold | 138.24 | (21,600 units at £6.40 per unit) |
| Contribution | 164.16 | (21,600 units at £7.60 per unit) |
| Fixed manufacturing overhead | 92.00 | |
| Manufacturing profit | 72.16 | |

Costing approach is more straightforward. The Examiner's Report noted that candidates generally had rather more success with the marginal costing statement in part (b) than with the absorption costing statement in part (a), although some confusion between the two was demonstrated.

In practice, the marginal costing profit statement would be completed by the further deduction of fixed costs incurred in other functions.

# COST VOLUME PROFIT ANALYSIS

## LEARNING OBJECTIVES

*After you have read and studied this chapter, you should be able to*:

- Discuss the assumptions underlying the conventional linear cost-volume-profit (CVP) model.

- Explain the implications of relaxing each of these assumptions in terms of the theoretical cost- volume-profit model.
- Explain the meaning of a series of graphic illustrations for both the linear and nonlinear CVP models including production functions, revenue functions and cost functions.
- Discuss the difference between performing a "what-if" analysis and converting from the linear model to the theoretical nonlinear model.
- Solve a variety of linear CVP problems for single product companies in either units or sales dollars.
- Define and use the margin of safety.
- Solve a variety of linear CVP problems for multiproduct companies in either units or sales dollars.
- Solve similar problems on a cash flow basis.
- Discuss the controversy concerning the compatibility of the contribution margin approach with activity based costing and the lean enterprise concepts of just in time and the theory of constraints.

## ANALYSIS OF CVP

Conceptually, conventional linear cost-volume-profit (CVP) analysis is a simplified, short term planning technique that evolved as a practical version of the theoretical model of the firm described in economics textbooks. From an accounting perspective it is compatible with the direct, or variable costing method of inventory valuation. To use the CVP model, a company must separate total costs into fixed and variable categories using one of the methods. Recall from our earlier discussions of these terms that variable costs are those costs that vary with changes in the level of activity. The only activities that are allowed to affect variable costs in traditional cost-volume-profit analysis are production output and sales. Remember that fixed costs are those costs that do not vary with changes in the activity level.

Conceptually, fixed costs are not constant. By definition, fixed simply means that these costs are not driven by short run changes in production or sales volume. Although explicit recognition of non production volume related cost drivers is a key concept in activity based costing, the idea is ignored in the conventional linear CVP model. Finally, it is important to recognize that the concept of fixed and variable costs is a short run concept. All costs tend to vary in the long run as the company adds to its' capacity to produce and distribute products and services. Therefore, the short run emphasis of CVP analysis tends to conflict with the long run emphasis of activity based costing and the lean enterprise concepts of JIT and TOC.

This creates another thought provoking controversial issue. The purpose of this chapter is to describe the assumptions and techniques of the conventional linear cost-volume-profit approach as well as the controversy concerning the compatibility of CVP analysis with ABC and the continuous improvement concepts. The chapter is divided into five main sections. The first section addresses the underlying assumptions of the conventional linear model and the implications of relaxing these assumptions. This section is mainly conceptual and is illustrated with a series of graphs. The second section illustrates the basic planning techniques for a single product company that provide the foundation for more realistic problems. The third section extends the basic analysis to multiproduct companies. Both sections two and three are more mechanical than conceptual and are mainly illustrated with a series of related equations. The fourth section is fairly short, but illustrates how to convert the analysis to a cash flow basis. The last section introduces the controversy associated with the CVP approach as it relates to the newer concepts of ABC, JIT and TOC. Since the CVP methodology is closely related to direct or variable costing, this chapter helps provide a better foundation for the more detailed comparison of direct and absorption costing presented in.

## ASSUMPTIONS OF CONVENTIONAL LINEAR CVP ANALYSIS

*Conventional linear cost volume profit analysis is based on five assumptions as follows:*

- Constant sales price.
- Constant variable cost per unit.
- Constant total fixed cost.
- Constant sales mix.
- Units sold equal units produced.

Note that these are the same assumptions that are applicable to the master budget, with the exception of number five. Now we will examine the implications of each assumption.

### Constant Sales Price

To assume that the sales price is constant implies that the company is facing a horizontal demand function as illustrated in Figure below. The implications of a horizontal demand function are that the company can sell any number of units at a constant sales price. Another way to describe this is to say that consumers are willing and able to buy any quantity the company offers for sale at a constant price. Average revenue (AR) is constant and equal to the sales price, (i.e., AR = PX÷X = P) as illustrated in Figure.

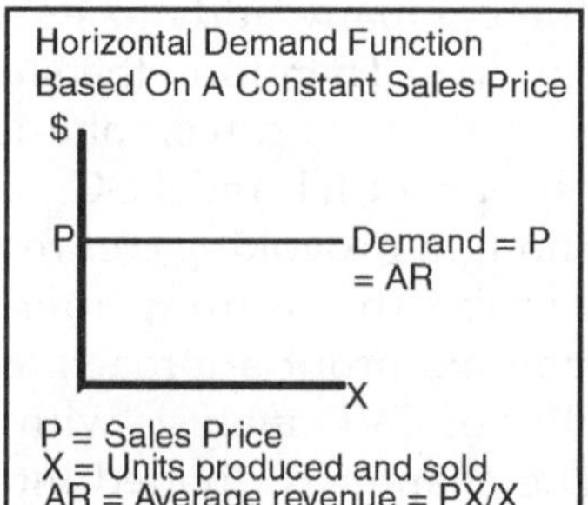

The slope of the total revenue function (see Figure 11-2) is equal to the sales price. When the company sells one additional unit, total revenue increases by an amount equal to the sales price of that unit. The fact that the sales price is constant causes the slope of the total revenue function to be constant which results in a linear total revenue function. Another way to describe this is to say that total revenue increases at a constant rate as additional units are sold.

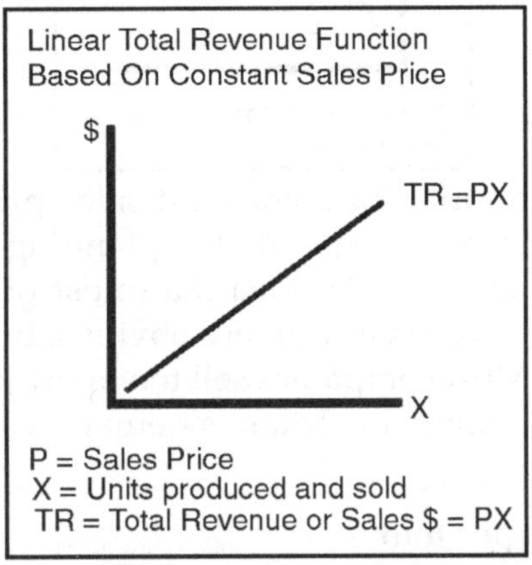


A more realistic down sloping demand function (see Figure below) illustrates what economists refer to as the law of demand. This law describes the fundamental idea that consumers are willing and able to buy more at a lower price than a higher price.

When the price is decreased from P1 to P2, the quantity purchased, or demanded, increases from X1 to X2. The total revenue function based on the law of demand is nonlinear as illustrated in Figure. Total revenue increases at a decreasing rate as additional units are sold. This is because the sale of additional units requires that the company reduce the sales price. Each price corresponds to a specific sales quantity. Thus, average revenue (AR) will be decreasing, rather than constant.

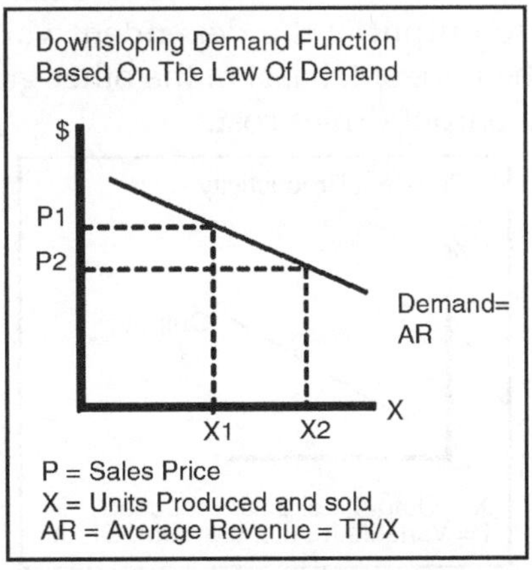

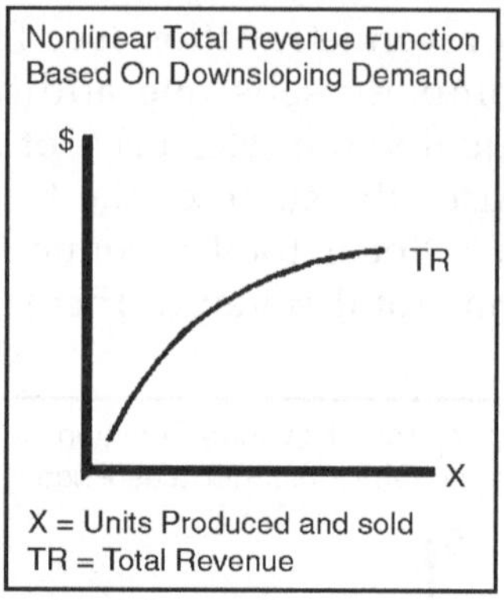


Although the assumption of a constant sales price is not realistic, it is defended as a practical way to expedite the planning process within a fairly narrow range of sales activity. The idea that most products are subject to a down sloping demand curve is intuitively obvious, but applying the concept is simply not practical. Most companies sell too many products in a constantly changing economic environment. Today's demand curve is very likely to be obsolete tomorrow.

### Constant Variable cost per unit

The second assumption of the conventional linear cost-volume-profit approach is that the variable cost per unit of output is constant. This includes two important underlying assumptions: a) input prices are assumed to be constant for all variable inputs such as direct material, direct labour, and the various types of indirect resources represented by variable factory overhead costs and variable selling and administrative expenses, and b) the firm experiences constant productivity, i.e., constant output per variable input.v Constant productivity is illustrated in Figure 11-5. When productivity is constant, each new unit of output requires an equal amount of input and thus each unit of output will cost the same amount. This causes both the production function to be linear (see Figure below) and the average variable cost function to be horizontal. Output (X) is placed on the vertical axis because output is the dependent variable, i.e., inputs drive outputs. Output is on the horizontal axis in the other graphs because cost is the dependent variable, i.e., output drives cost.

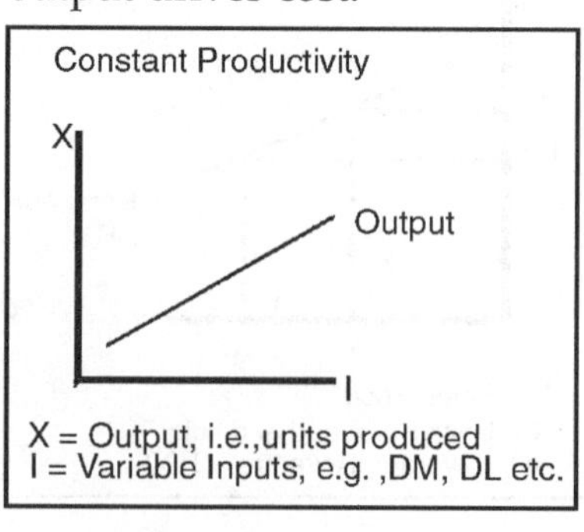

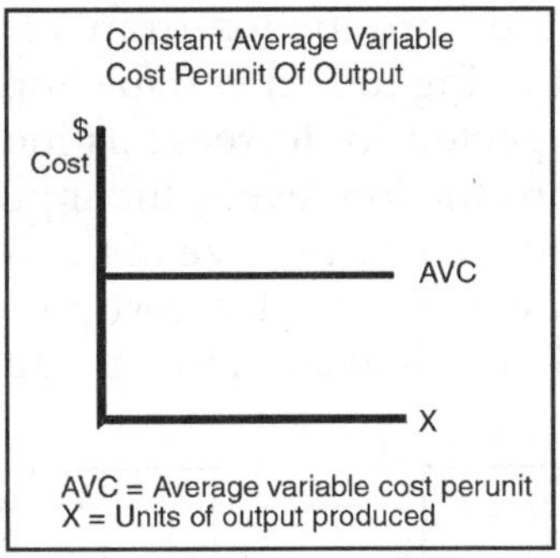


Although it is convenient to assume constant productivity for short run planning purposes, other types of production functions are more realistic when the whole range of production possibilities is considered. When a company begins to expand output from a low volume startup level to a medium volume level, productivity might be expected to increase due to the effects of increased specialization, experience and learning.

When productivity is increasing, output increases at an increasing rate (see Figures below). As variable inputs are added to production, each input generates more output than the previous input. When productivity is increasing, average variable cost per unit will be decreasing.

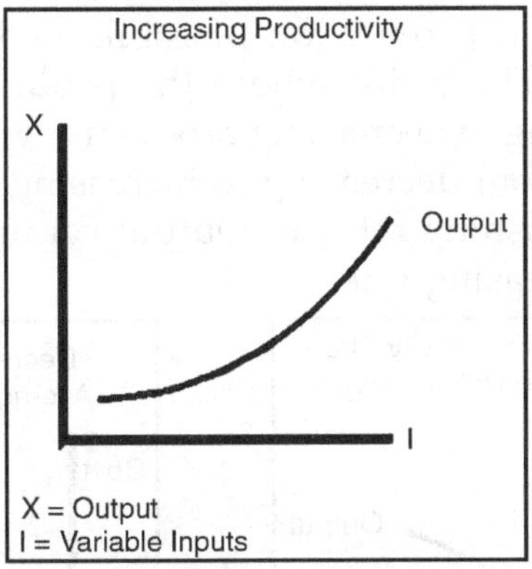


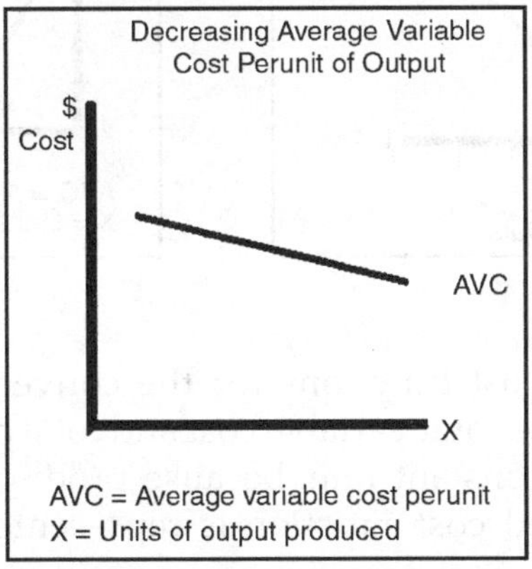

If the company increased production from a medium volume level to a high volume level by continuing to add variable inputs to a fixed size facility, productivity would be expected to decrease as indicated in Figures. This is because at high volume production levels, the inputs (labour, materials etc.) would become excessive relative to the size of the fixed facility. In the case of decreasing productivity, average variable cost per unit will be increasing as illustrated in Figures. Each unit will cost more because it requires more inputs to produce.

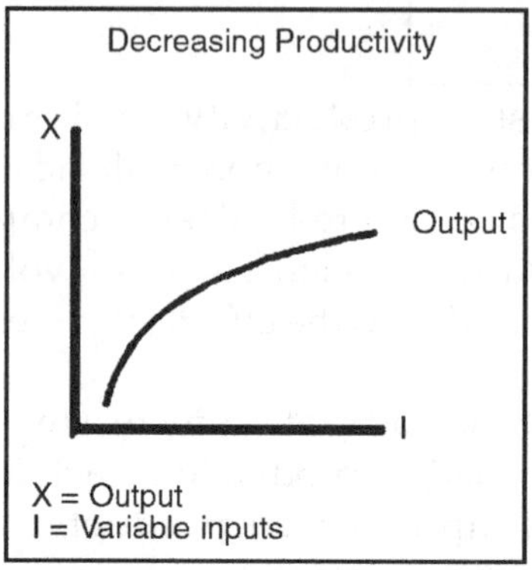


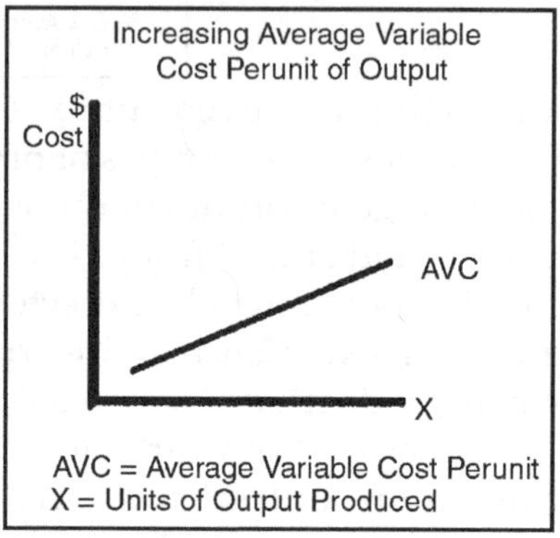


Theoretically, the production and average variable cost functions for the entire range of short run production possibilities will be similar to those illustrated in Figures. The point where the production function changes directions from increasing to decreasing productivity and the average variable cost function changes from decreasing to increasing cost per unit is referred to as the point of diminishing returns. Output continues to increase beyond this point, but at a decreasing rate.

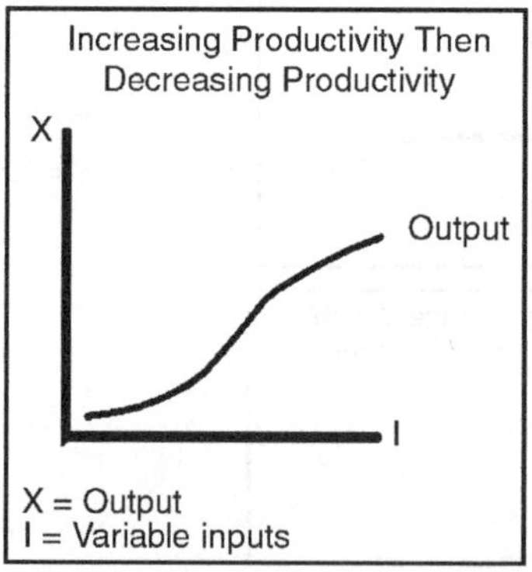


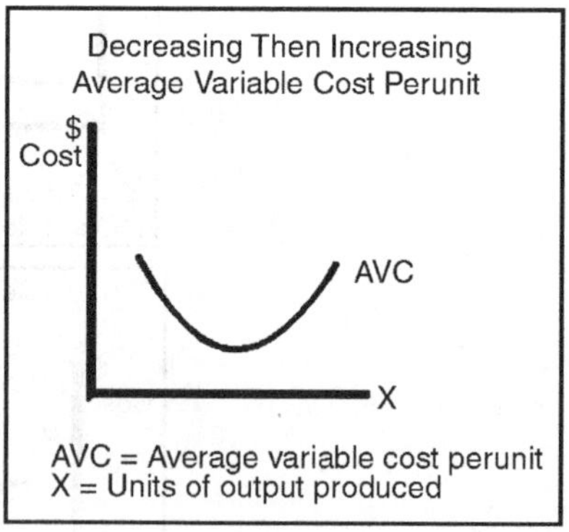


## Constant Fixed Costs

A family of total cost functions for the conventional linear model is presented in Figures. The total variable cost and total cost functions are linear, i.e., they increase at a constant rate, because productivity is assumed to be constant. The total fixed cost function is represented by a horizontal line because of assumption three which eliminates the possibility of a non-output related change in fixed costs during the planning period. No changes in the company's fixed factors of production can occur. The total cost and total variable cost functions are vertically parallel and separated by the amount of total fixed costs.

A comparable family of total cost functions for the theoretical economic model appears in Figures below. The total variable cost and total cost functions increase at a decreasing rate at first in response to increasing productivity. When the inputs are becoming more productive, additional outputs cost less per unit because they require less input.

However, when productivity begins to decrease, the total cost and total variable cost functions begin to increase at an increasing rate. In the case of decreasing productivity, the inputs are generating less output per input, thus the unit cost of additional outputs is increasing. The total cost functions are also parallel and separated vertically by the amount of total fixed costs.

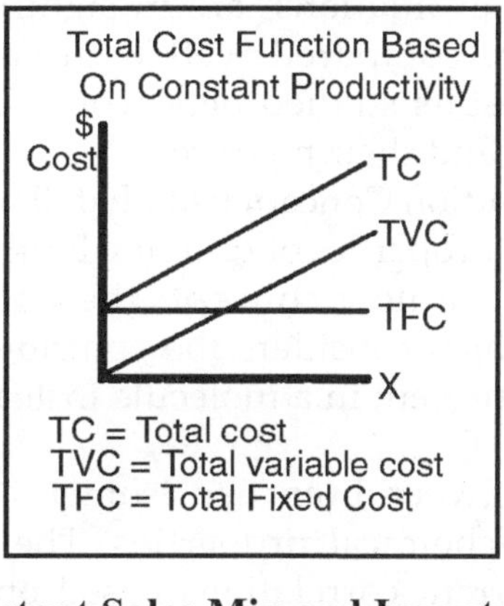


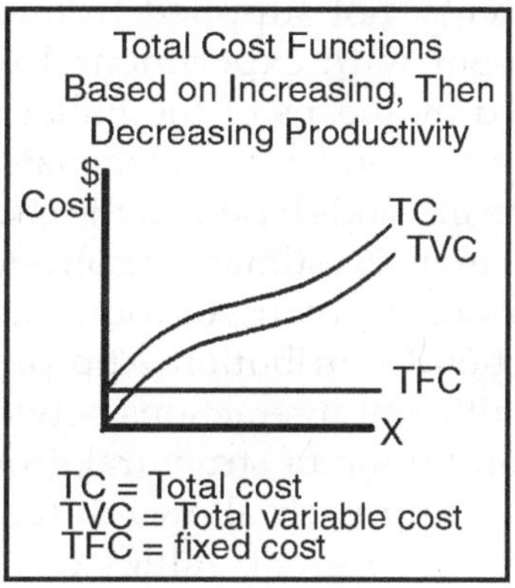


**Constant Sales Mix and Inventory Level**

The last two assumptions of the conventional linear cost-volume-profit model are more easily understood than the previous assumptions. The fourth assumption is that the sales mix will remain constant during the planning period for a multiproduct company. Sales mix proportions may be stated in terms of either units or dollars as explained in the illustrations below. The fifth and last assumption is that units produced are equal to units sold. This means that there will be no changes in beginning or ending inventory levels to complicate the analysis. This assumption along with the assumption concerning constant fixed cost will be relaxed in the following chapter where we will use the conventional linear CVP model to consider the differences between direct costing and full absorption costing.

## CONCEPT AND USES OF CONTRIBUTION CONCEPT

The concept of the group contribution using Kihara intermolecular potentials with a spherical core is extended to perfluorinated *n*-alkanes ($n$ = 1–

6). The effective Kihara parameters for groups ($CF_2$, $CF_3$, $CF_4$) are estimated by fitting second virial coefficient *B* and dilute gas viscosity ç together. The assumption of regarding $CF_4$ molecule as a single group is preferable to other two approaches based on the principle of group additivity: a combination of F–($CF_3$) and $CF_3$–(F) groups; a single C–$(F)_4$ group and four F–(C) groups.

Application of the model shows that second virial coefficients are represented with better results than those of the Tsonopoulos correlation, and are comparable to the correlation of Dymond's group and the Hohm correlation. Feasibility of the present method to calculate dilute gas viscosities is proved by comparison with the Lucas method, the Hohm correlation, the correlation of Yaws, and the Simsci Data Bank.

Mixture property calculations of the model are enhanced by including binary group interaction coefficients $k_{ij,gc}$, determined from second cross virial coefficient data, and are more reliable than other correlations for second cross virial coefficients and mixture viscosities. Prediction results of binary diffusion coefficients, not supplied to the parameter evaluations, are in significant agreement with experimental data and are compared well with values obtained by means of the Fuller method. Results studied here would be of use when extended to halogenated paraffins and their mixtures.

The methods based on the Group Contribution Concept usually fail when one attempts to estimate the physico-chemical properties of different branched isomers of a given compound. We present a new concept, the Group-Interaction Contribution Approach (GIC) which considers the contribution of the different interactions between groups present in a molecule instead of the contribution of structural groups.

This approach allows differentiation between branched isomers, thus leading to different values of the physico-chemical properties. The GIC Approach can be easily implemented in current correlations based on the group contribution concept. The estimates of enthalpy of formation, normal boiling temperature and critical temperature of a series of 51 saturated hydrocarbons showed clearly that the GIC concept leads to very good estimations for branched isomers.

Earlier this year, I spent an intense half-day closeted in a room with the top 70 executives at Intuit. Our aim was to come up with ways that people outside the company could volunteer their time, energy, and expertise to make life better for our customers.

Sound odd? Well, if you're not conducting an exercise like that at your organization, you risk missing the boat on a sea change that's transforming business. Every day, millions of people make all kinds of vountary contributionsto companies–from informed opinions to computing resources – that create tremendous value for those firms' customers and, consequently, for their shareholders. When I first encountered this idea, several years ago, it struck me as unfathomable: Volunteerism was for charities, not for red-blooded, profit-making firms. That was just my first surprise. I also began to see that user contributions are fueling some of the world's fastest-growing and most competitively advantaged organizations – in some cases revolutionizing the economics of entire industries by radically shrinking their cost structures. Think of eBay, which opened as an online store with no inventory, leaving it up to customers to fill its "shelves" with goods to sell. Or Wikipedia, which gutted the value proposition of 230-year old *Encyclopaedia Britannica* by offering a free encyclopedia written and updated frequently by unpaid amateurs.

In other cases, the contribution is not as obvious but just as central to the value proposition. Skype incursalmost no capital costs because its internet-based phone system is built on the unused processing capacity of its customers' personal computers. Google, too, is built on user contributions: Its search engine relies on thealgorithmic aggregation of links created by others between websites, and its ad placement system relies ondata from people's click behaviour.

OK, I'm not saying you can or should transform your company into a Google or a Skype whose business model is primarily based on user contributions.

But you should understand the power of the phenomenon and, as I have, learn from the growing number of companies in traditional industries – firms like Honda, Procter & Gamble, Best Buy, and Hyatt – that are tapping user contributions to improve products, better serve customers, generate new business, reduce costs, boost employee performance, and more. Contribution-driven results like those are achievable for pretty much any business.

The concept of user contribution isn't new. But the companies I've just mentioned – both the internet highfliers and the old-economy behemoths – have actively created something I call a *user contribution system*. That is, they've created methods for aggregating and leveraging people's contributions or behaviors in ways that are useful to other people. The *users* can be customers, employees, sales prospects – or even people with no previous connection to the company. Their *contributions* can be active (work, expertise, or information) or passive and even unknowing (behavioral data that is gathered automatically during a transaction or an activity). The *system* is the method, usually internet-based, by which contributions are aggregated and automatically converted into something useful to others.

Although the company retains control of the system and may choose to modify its design, the system converts inputs into useful outputs in real time with little or no intervention by the company. Such a system creates value for a business as a consequence of the value it delivers to users – personalized purchase recommendations, connections between buyers and sellers of hard-to-find items, new personal or business relationships, lower prices, membership in a community, entertainment, information of all kinds.

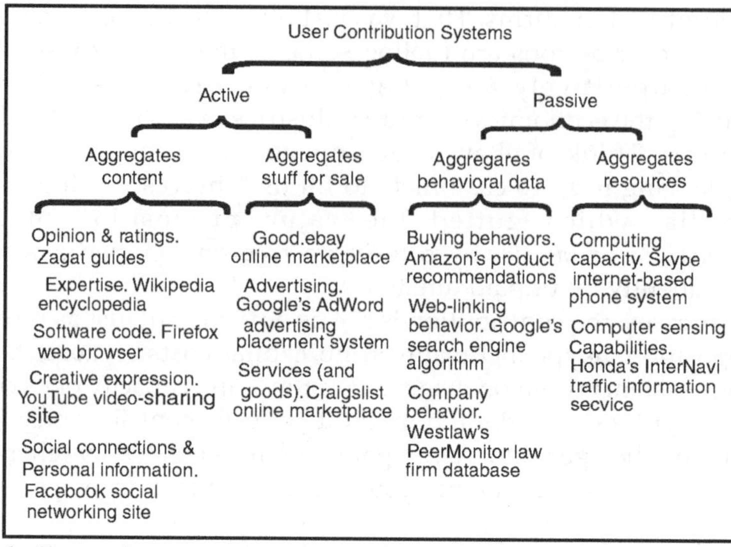


The challenge for executives is twofold. First, you must learn how to spot opportunities for creating value from user contributions. Second – and here's the difficult part – in acting on these opportunities, you must overcome natural organizational resistance to the idea of relinquishing significant control to people outside the company.

The advice I offer here is based on my personal experience at Intuit – the successes and failures, the moments of exhilaration and the times when I had to conquer my own fear of putting so much power in the hands of users.

## REVOLUTIONARY POTENTIAL

Though I didn't know it at the time, my interest in user contribution systems began in the early 1990s with a series of slim red books. The Zagat guides offered reviews with quantitative ratings based on sustained performance rather than on a single visit or two by one reviewer. And those recommendations originated not with paid experts but with regular diners like me. It was a decade, though, before I recognized the significance of the method to my own company. That "aha" came from watching the winners on the web.

The success of the leading internet firms has admittedly been touted ad nauseam by the media and business experts. Yet for better and for worse, the internet is a reflection of society and the preferences of hundreds of millions of people around the world. Like book best-seller lists, rankings of the most popular websites reflect what's winning the battle for people's attention.

The companies joining the list of most popular websites in recent years include Wikipedia, YouTube, Facebook, Craigslist, and MySpace. They have joined such older sites as Amazon, eBay, and Google. At first glance, these sites seem to have little in common, targeting unrelated areas of human endeavor: the cataloguing of information, video entertainment, social interaction, classified advertising, retail shopping, internet search. Some of the sites charge users; others are free. One's a nonprofit; another has one of the highest profit marginsamong public companies.

Despite their differences, all these winning sites rely on – or are themselves – user contribution systems. Much of their success flows from inherent characteristics of contribution systems that create advantages, detailed here, of a magnitude rarely known in traditional business.

## WHY CONTRIBUTORS CONTRIBUTE

Most contribution systems offer no financial compensation to contributors. In fact, payment can destroy participation by undermining a sense of collaboration and trust. Rather, they rely on motivations intrinsic to humanity – or involve contributions that require no motivation at all, because the user contributes without realizing it.

### Contributing

Some systems collect participants' resources or data as a by-product of things people are doing for other purposes. As shoppers buy from Amazon, they automatically contribute toits recommendation engine, which suggests products based on the ratings and purchase decisions of other customers.

### Practical Solutions

In some systems, participants contribute in order to get reasonably immediate rewards. For example, the site del.icio.usenables users to organize their bookmarks of websites. A byproduct of this activity is that, when aggregated, the bookmarks produce an index to the web that is valuable to others.

### Social Reward

Many systems provide the benefits of interaction with others: being part of a community with a common interest, generating business prospects, getting a date – the drivers behind social networks like Facebook and LinkedIn.

### Reputation

Contribution can be sparked by a desire for public recognition, like Amazon's badge for a "top 1,000 reviewer," or for the admiration of peers: Wikipedia articles carry no authorship credit, yet authors earn the respect of other contributors.

### Altruism

Why would a person write a glowing online review of a restaurant – when it may become harder to get a table if others act on the opinion? Some people want to help local diners or reward superb restaurant owners. Others simply want the truth to be heard.

**Cost Advantage**

What does Wikipedia pay the authors and editors of its articles? What does Facebook or MySpace pay those who painstakingly fill in and update the personal profiles that make the site so valuable? Nothing. These sites enjoy free "raw materials," as users perform gratis work that companies typically have to pay for. People contribute for various reasons, some of them self-serving but all of them sufficient to make formal payment unnecessary.

**Scalability Advantage**

Craigslist's free classified advertising sites feature more than 30 million new offerings every month, and eBay's virtual shelves feature 120 million items, many times more than any other store on the planet can offer. Such scale doesn't require broad or deep contribution: Only a small percentage of users may contribute (about one user in 1,000 for Wikipedia) and active contributions may require little effort (as with Flickr, the photo-sharing site).

**Competitive Advantage**

Some contribution systems give companies a structural advantage over rivals because of network effects. That is, the more people who contribute to the system, the more useful it becomes, creating an upward spiral in which increasingly more people choose to use and contribute to it. Network effectsonce drove the winner-take-all market-share gains of Microsoft's Windows; today, they propel the success of sites like Wikipedia and Facebook.

Contribution systems won't displace most traditional products or businesses: I'm not expecting Wiki-Milk to displace real milk or the dairy industry. Still, given the power of user contributions, too many business leaders are failing to look for opportunities to leverage these systems in their industries. I think that's partly because of the novelty of the phenomenon, but it's also because of beliefs rooted in the past. All too often, executives mistakenly view user contribution as:

## THREAT TO PROFIT BUSINESSES

But consider Schibsted, a 170-year-old Norwegian newspaper publisher that, instead of ignoring the online threat savaging much of the newspaper industry, started reinventing itself in the mid-1990s by embracing user contribution and becoming a leading European provider of online classified advertising.

**Only for Tech Companies**

But consider the Canadian grocery store chain Loblaws, which solicits online customer reviews and incorporates them in the marketing of new products.

### Unreliable and Error-ridden

But consider the study in Nature that found volunteer-written Wikipedia to be, in general, about as accurate as expert-written articles in Encyclopaedia Britannica's online edition.

### Lacking a Strong Business Case or Profit

But consider LinkedIn, whose social networking site for businesspeople now profits from numerous revenue streams: traditional ones, such as site advertising, upgrades to premium membership with more features, and paid job postings, along with more novel ones, such as tools that corporate HR departments can use to screen job candidates.

## CONTRIBUTION

Even without knowing your business, I'd be willing to bet that contribution systems can address one or more of the business challenges you face better than the methods you currently use. To spur your thinking, let's look at some of the different ways that traditional companies are employing user contribution systems in a wide variety of business activities and functions.

### Customer Service

Company-hosted online support forums, in which product users answer questions from other users free of charge, are commonplace among software and personal computer companies. I admit my initial surprise when I experienced firsthand how a user community can answer tough questions that even the manufacturer cannot. Now non-computer firms, such as AT&T, are beginning to follow this practice.

Troubleshooting is just one way to harness user contributions for service. Hyatt Hotels and Resorts has launched an online concierge service called Yatt'it that aggregates and lets users rate travel tips posted by Hyatt's customers and concierges. The aim is both to reduce the burden on concierges and to give travelers tailored, extensive city information in advance of their trip – and, if they've already arrived, without their having to wait in line.

Companies also use contribution systems to serve customers in ways that create a brand-new business. Westlaw, the legal research service, created a B2B contribution system that helps its customer base of law firms address important strategic issues. West PeerMonitor automatically aggregates anonymized financial and operating information from participating law firms.

The firms access the database to see how their performance compares with that of peers and how other markets compare with their own – data that may help a firm decide, for example, whether to expand geographically or whether a key practice area is operating efficiently. This customer service is valued so much that Westlaw charges handsomely for it.

## Marketing

The power of contribution systems is now being tapped by traditional marketing powerhouses, including two of the giants: Procter & Gamble and Unilever. Procter & Gamble has created a website, BeingGirl, aimed at teen and preteen girls – a difficult group to reach in the marketing of its feminine-hygiene products because young girls are often uncomfortable viewing TV ads on the topic in the company of friends or family. The site originally consisted solely of information from experts.

But in 2005, P&G borrowed the contribution concept from tech websites, adding forums where girls could interact with one another. Now users can share their questions and personal experiences and get support and advice from other girls. This creation of a community around an important topic promotes engagement with the site – and with the Always and Tampax brands that it discreetly promotes. P&G says that as a marketing tool BeingGirl is now four times as effective as comparably priced television advertising.

The website In the Motherhood, cosponsored by Sprint and by Unilever's Suave line of personal-care products, also offers a community forum where users can share stories and offer tips – in this case on the subject of being a mom. In addition, mothers can submit stories (3,000 of them so far) that serve as potential plotlines for an online comedy series.

The community votes on the submissions, and those selected by the users are produced by professional directors and actors and subsequently posted to the site. (Several dozen have been produced so far, and cumulative views have passed the 20 million mark — it has been picked up for television by ABC.) Unilever research finds that the site increases users' intent to purchase a Suave product and engenders a feeling in customers that the makers of Suave really understand their lives.

## Employee Support

Most company intranet sites are oneway streets, with management broadcasting the "company line" to employees. Best Buy, the U.S. retail chain, uses the opposite approach in a contribution system dubbed BlueShirt Nation. BlueShirt Nation allows employees to share and discuss their ideas and experiences: what works and what doesn't in carrying out a particular task or in interacting with customers, for example. The site, launched two years ago by two junior employees with no corporate IT support or funding, today has more than 20,000 registered employee users.

Best Buy has discovered that unfiltered information from colleagues can be more effective than memos from HR. For example, Blue Shirt Nation ran a contest in which employees submitted videos they had conceived and produced, with no company oversight, to spur employee adoption of 401(k) plans. The result of the buzz generated by the contest? A 30% increase in plan enrollment.

**Capital Resources**

Build a global telecommunications system with almost no capital equipment? Make free, high quality video calls anywhere in the world? Both once were unfathomable. But that's what Skype has done, thanks to a contribution system.

Founded by Swedes and engineered in Estonia, Skype is the marquee example of how a company can reduce the cost of capital equipment to almost nothing by having users contribute the capital goods.

Skype's free software utilizes idle computing power on users' PCs to manage the calls – as many as 12 million simultaneously – for its 300 million customers. Its costs are so low that the company, which was acquired by eBay in 2006, can deliver high-quality voice and video computer-to-computer calls between subscribers at no charge. And it's profitable: revenue comes from calls made by Skype users to mobile phones and landlines, as well as from services such as voice mail.

Traditional companies, too, get customers to contribute needed capital. In Japan, Honda captures real-time traffic data from GPS systems that Honda owners buy from the company. Speed and location reports from each vehicle contribute to a data stream that Honda aggregates with other traffic data to provide information on traffic jams and other conditions to Honda drivers who subscribe to the company's InterNavi service. Users benefit from enhanced traffic updates; the company can offer a superior subscription service without having to pay for the capital infrastructure.

And there's more: Honda drivers also contribute reviews of local businesses and points of interest that other drivers can read from their InterNavi-equipped Hondas – an automotive version of a Zagat guide. Honda's system thus combines three user contributions – capital equipment, data about user location and vehicle speed, and reviews.

**Design and Development**

User contribution can tackle creative challenges from the technical to the artistic. The emblematic example of contribution in R&D is open source software, such as the Linux operating system and the Mozilla Foundation'sFirefox web browser, which is created and regularly upgraded by communities of unpaid volunteer developers. (This low-cost model makes Mozilla one of the rare nonprofits that is highly "profitable.")

In the creative arts, Thread less, a company that manufactures T-shirts, relies on a community of volunteer designers and artists to submit designs and a community of customers to select those that will go into production. Both of the user groups, as well as the company, benefit. The designers get free exposure for their work and a chance at monetary compensation: They receive $2,500 plus a percentage of sales if their design is chosen by Threadless customers.

Note that the Threadless user contribution system is subtly different from customer innovation approaches likecrowdsourcing, which are used with success by Dell, Starbucks, and other companies. Crowdsourcing is not a user contribution system in the pure sense, because the company stands between the input and the output. For example, it sifts through people's ideas for new products and services, selects ones to pursue, and then invests the time and expense needed to develop them.

**Production**

In some cases, organizations can "delegate" some or all of the production process to users. Wikipedia delegates all of it. The producers of Fox Television's American Idol delegate part of the process. The show relies on users (through their votes for performers) to make decisions traditionally reserved for television producers; it relies on amateur performers to offer entertainment usually provided by high-priced stars.

The contributing singers benefit from a shot at stardom. Viewers, who contribute their opinions, benefit from compelling entertainment (if the show's high ratings are any indication) and a strong sense of engagement because their votes determine the show's content. Fox and its producers benefit from lower costs and fromadvertising revenue driven by the show's tremendous popularity – which results, in part, from the drama generated by the show's user-contributed surprises.

## INTUIT AND USER CONTRIBUTION SYSTEMS

As a member of the boards of eBay and Amazon in the late 1990s, I was exposed to user contribution through the work of Jeff Bezos, Pierre Omidyar, and Meg Whitman. But the concept seemed rare and specialized, so I missed seeing its broader application and value. (I once told Jeff Bezos I thought his plan to supplement professional book reviews on Amazon with reviews written by anyone who felt like it was crazy:

**Early Success**

At our annual off-site in 2005, I put this question to the company's top 300 executives: How might we leverage user contribution at Intuit, both to enhance existing businesses and to create new ones? Two executives in our Plano, Texas, division began to think about how to solve a common problem faced by professional tax preparers – getting answers to obscure questions.

The result was a quickly cobbled-together wiki/forum site where tax preparers could contribute both questions and answers for the benefit of other tax preparers. Just 33 days after the executive off-site, TaxAlmanac was launched. Today, it has 170,000 pages, drawing on the collective expertise of thousands of tax professionals, and is used by 400,000 unique visitors – about equal to the number of tax preparers in the country. Tax preparers benefit from expertise that's free. Intuit benefits when visitors then buy our tax prep software – customer acquisition at almost zero cost. However, despite my evangelizing, the idea of contribution systems wasn't taking off elsewhere within the organization. TaxAlmanac was a small island in a sea of indifference.

**A Major Setback**

I then resurrected an idea that had been proposed several years before by an Intuit engineer: a website with user-generated reviews of local businesses to help folks find a good plumber, car dealer, or restaurant, linked to our Quicken financial software products. It seemed like a sure bet, so we put a big team on it, we launched Zipingo. But the site failed to attract a critical mass of users, and we shuttered it in August 2007.

What went wrong? We made mistakes that stemmed from the difference between traditional products and contribution systems. User contribution is first of all about the users and their content. We failed to nurture and encourage early contributors, and we got distracted creating our own content – ancillary information like business addresses for the listings. Zipingo's failure hurt. I stopped pushing big team efforts to develop new contribution systems at Intuit. But even as I pulled back, small contribution-system projects started sprouting up

**Gaining Traction**

One of our engineering leaders conceived the idea of embedding a Q&A community into a product itself – that is, creating a user forum on every page of TurboTax, with questions and answers relevant to the topic of the particular page. Many were wary of the idea, and some were even hostile. I encouraged the group's efforts, but in an echo of my own skepticism about Amazon's user reviews years earlier, I wondered silently whether people striving to finish their own taxes would stop to answer some stranger's questions.

Working with the support of his division manager, the engineer's team of three built the system and tested it in the least popular version of TurboTax Online in January 2007. Just five weeks into the initial test, one-third of the questions posed already had answers. Crucially, our internal tax experts were pleased by the quality of the answers, which seemed to be self-correcting as other users refined them. TurboTax Live Community, as it's called, was the kind of clear success I'd been seeking. Live Community systems have spread to our other divisions and are inspiring more contribution experiments.

Yet wariness persists. This year, when the TurboTax marketing team decided to solicit and post all user reviews, unedited, on a prominent link from the product's home page, I blanched and took a deep breath. Again a surprise: The vast bulk of reviews are so positive that it looks as if we've posted only the good ones (which, I hasten to add, is not the case). Once again, we're learning from that most reliable of sources – our customers.

## COMPANY WITH UCS

User contribution seems messy and scary; giving customers a public podium to comment freely about your products and company seems to violate the management canon "Don't hold me accountable for what I don't control." Naturally, adopting these methods is easier when competitors have beaten you to the punch and shown you where user contribution works in your industry. But what if you want to lead your rivals? Here's my advice for senior managers trying to create contribution systems in their companies.

### Use Personal Experience to Move Mind-set

I've found that heads and hearts don't change until people participate in contribution systems themselves. To overcome wariness in inexperienced executives, ask enthusiasts to share stories of their personal experience with user contribution systems. To build awareness, have people count the user contribution systems found on an Amazon page and classify them by type. (If you look hard, you'll find 23 separate systems on a single Amazon product page.) Ask inexperienced executives to find and use contribution systems of personal interest to them – that helps develop a visceral feeling for how they work. Get sub-teams of leaders to brainstorm about contribution systems that might solve customer or employee problems and then ask them to sketch out prototypes they can present to a larger group.

### Nurture Small Experiments

Encourage unofficial and "guerrilla" experiments. Challenge employees to create contribution systems that they are passionate about, without requiring them to get clearance from management. Experiment with small batches of employees or customers. (At Intuit, we tried one experiment on the TurboTax version that has the smallest sales volume, accounting for less than 1% of customers for that product.) Most of the experiments will fail; tell the organization in advance that this is OK. Communicate the value of the lessons learned from those failed experiments so that other teams benefit.

### Ideas and Leadership

Expect ideas for contribution systems to emerge from those who use them the most. Often, these will be your youngest employees. Seek them out. Make them your mentors. Ask them to take the lead in creating ways for your company and customers to benefit from user contributions. Have them develop prototypes and show them directly to you; then help them act on some of the ideas that emerge.

### Set Boundaries

I'm not advocating that you blow up your current business and completely reinvent it around a contribution system. Experiment at the edges of your business. Give experimenters a defined sandbox – spacious, perhaps, but defined – rather than an endless expanse of beach. Within those limits, though, make sure they aren't distracted by experts and that their experiments aren't smothered by larger initiatives with broader mandates.

**Protect Experiments**

Ceding some control of business processes to outsiders, even in a sandbox, will be scary for your organization. Leaders in certain functional areas – marketers and lawyers, for example – will feel especially anxious. (I can identify, having had to swallow hard a few times over things we were about to try at Intuit.) To counter the instinct to preserve control and the status quo, name a godfather or godmother with big-time clout to protect experiments and break through barriers when initiatives meet organizational resistance. (Three people, two division general managers and I, played this role in our early experiments at Intuit.)

**Customer Base**

Some new contribution systems face a chicken-or-egg problem – that is, they're empty and useless until folks begin contributing to them, but few visitors will be attracted to something that is empty and useless. Your company probably has advantages that start-ups can only dream of: existing customers, traffic to your website, accumulated behavioral data, and, sometimes, media that will find your experiments newsworthy.

**Let users "vote," Early and Often**

Customers are better than executives at picking winners in this arena, so get experiments into the hands of real customers as quickly as possible. Minimize or eliminate time lost to market research, lengthy analysis, PowerPoint presentations, or frequent reviews by management.(We've borrowed an idea from Google by creating a public webpage – intuitlabs.com – that displays our current experiments and gives experimenters a fast, direct path to customers, bypassing normal product-launch procedures.)

**Seek Organizational**

The guerrilla experiments are designed to get around organizational resistance. Ultimately, you want innovation in user contribution to become embedded in the organization's normal processes, but you'll most likely struggle to shift mindset until you can point to a successful experiment or two. The meeting earlier this year of Intuit's top executives to spur action on user contribution systems would have been a wasted effort two years ago. Then, we had only begun to experiment. But with several successful initiatives now in operation, Intuit's newly promoted CEO, Brad Smith, and I felt the time was right to move the idea into the mainstream and talk about why user contribution is a focus of our evolving company strategy. I can't say everyone at that meeting bought into the concept. Some undoubtedly saw it as a distraction from their day jobs. Still, there was real energy in the room that day. In the middle of the meeting, I stopped to ask whether folks had questions. Rather than answer them myself, I wrote the questions on the board and asked the entire group to tackle them. As I watched, people provided answers, better than the ones I would have given. (In fact, some of them became content for this article.) As we moved to take a break, I reminded our executives that we all had just experienced user contribution in action.

# Index